Understanding Deleuze

Other titles in the series

CULTURAL STUDIES

Series editors: Rachel Fensham
and Terry Threadgold

Understanding Deleuze

Claire Colebrook

ALLEN&UNWIN

First published in 2002 by
Allen & Unwin
83 Alexander Street
Crows Nest NSW 2065
Australia
Phone: (61 2) 8425 0100
Fax: (61 2) 9906 2218
Email: info@allenandunwin.com
Web: www.allenandunwin.com

National Library of Australia
Cataloguing-in-Publication entry:

Colebrook, Claire.
Understanding Deleuze.

Bibliography.
Includes index.
ISBN 1 86508 797 1.

1. Deleuze, Gilles. S. Philosophers – France. 3.
Philosophy. I. Fensham, Rachel. II. Threadgold, Terry.
III. Title. (Series : Cultural studies (St. Leonards,
N.S.W.)).

194

Set in 10.5/13 pt Palatino by Midland Typesetters
Printed by SRM Production Services, SBN, BHD, Malaysia

10 9 8 7 6 5 4 3 2 1

Foreword

Introducing Deleuze to anyone, whether academic, student, scientist or artist, is tricky. They are either going to feel exhilarated by the new vocabulary and challenge to their current frameworks for thinking or exhausted by them. One of my favourite texts for doing this is Deleuze's short essay on 'Mediators' which consists of a series of notes and digressions on a range of different topics, including Cinema, New Caledonia, Literature, Couples, Style, Aids and Global Strategy (Deleuze 1992). I mention this work because it gives an indication of the breadth of Deleuze's thought as a project within Cultural Studies.

In Cultural Studies, we are faced with thinking about the problems of specific political contexts, aesthetics and cultural production, social relations, viral forces and identities beyond the bounds of the narrowly human subject of western capitalism. And we need to work with the most rigorous intellectual engagement available and possible. Among the many characterising features of Cultural Studies are its interdisciplinarity and a poststructuralist vocabulary that has emerged from its critique of, and struggle to disassociate itself from, traditional disciplinary formations. While Foucault, Lacan and Derrida have been the intellectual forces of late twentieth-century poststructuralism, in many ways the twenty-first century is likely to become more Deleuzean. It is already, molecular, nomadic and cinematic in ways that could not be predicted with old habits of thought. And it is Deleuze who speaks to a political and social context that requires us to make new forms of connection between one configuration of ideas and power and another.

Indeed, abstract thinking of universals, such as truth, justice, freedom, right, cannot answer the questions required of critical or creative thinking in the movement of our times. For this reason, there has been a rise of interest in Deleuze across a range of fields extending from philosophy (Elizabeth Grosz, Michael Hardt) to psychoanalysis (Phillip Goodchild, Eugene Holland); cinema (David Rodowick, Dorothea Olkowski, Gregory Flaxman); feminist theory (Rosi Braidotti, Tamsin Lorraine, Camilla Griggers); politics (Paul Patton, Brian Massumi); literature (Ian Buchanan, John Marks) as well as a range of more speculative investigations (Emanuel de Landa). The objective of this book in a Cultural Studies series is to introduce Deleuze not as a specialist theorist but as 'a practical philosopher' (Colebrook 2002, p. xii).

In *Understanding Deleuze*, Claire Colebrook shows us why Deleuze is so important in political and ethical terms for changing our thinking. As she writes: 'at the heart of all Deleuze's thought is his insistence that our relation to the world is dynamic, not just because our ideas about the world change, nor because the world is a thing that goes through change. Life itself is constant change and creation' (p. 51). We need therefore a philosophy that works with change rather than in opposition to it. *Understanding Deleuze* offers a fresh perspective on why a philosophy of flux matters for feminism, indigenous rights, ecological struggles and other contemporary cultural movements without attempting to define how Deleuze's philosophy might be put to work.

Colebrook begins by historicising the progression of Deleuze's ideas as a movement away from structuralism, and the negative dialectic, in the post-1968 context towards theorising relations between art, science and philosophy as an affirmative strategy of positive difference. A genealogy of the conceptual force of difference for an alternative mode of cultural analysis underpins her text and its reference points are scholarly and detailed. In fact, Colebrook provides a systematic discussion of connected ideas such as difference, immanence, synthesis, desire, perception, style, the virtual and the fold that recur across Deleuze's oeuvre. (A preliminary glossary provides a lively introduction to other key terms that are then usefully re-employed in the text.)

In her eminently lucid style, Colebrook moves easily from elaboration of a concept such as synthesis to a crisp discussion of Andy Warhol's soup cans. Indeed, her various examples are particularly suited to an international readership. Cinema, along with literature a plane of immanent cultural production for Deleuze and for the twentieth century, is utilised as one of the sites in which the notion of 'virtual' differences make possible new kinds of 'actuals'.

Understanding Deleuze is in itself a bold piece of work. That this work has emerged from a younger feminist scholar writing in a postcolonial context (both Australia and Scotland) is perhaps not surprising. Australian Cultural Studies and publishing is characterised by a willingness to get its hands dirty and to respond to new challenges. Colebrook's primer on Deleuze should provide just the right kind of freshness to appeal to a range of readers: advanced undergraduates, graduates and, more generally, people interested in culture, cyberstudies, film, politics and psychoanalysis. *Understanding Deleuze* extends to the reader Deleuze's own invitation to think differently about Cultural Studies.

Rachel Fensham
Monash University, Australia

Reference
Deleuze, Gilles (1992), 'Mediators' in J. Crary and S. Kwinter (eds), Incorporations, Zone Books, New York, pp. 281–93

Contents

Acknowledgements

I would like to thank the following people for reading and commenting upon this manuscript: Alan Nicholson, Sue Loukomitis, Lubica Ucnik, Lenka Ucnik and Lee Spinks. I am particularly grateful to Rachel Fensham and Elizabeth Weiss, who offered intelligent and supportive criticism in the final stages of writing this book, and gave me the opportunity to undertake the project in the first place. As always, I owe a great debt to Ian Buchanan, who is more than just a fellow Deleuzean.

The impact of Deleuze

We often think of philosophy as a purely academic exercise, a foray into abstract concepts and abstruse arguments. But there is a tradition of philosophy that rejects such a demarcation. Gilles Deleuze (1925–95) saw himself as part of a tradition of philosophy which challenged and disrupted life, such that new concepts and ideas would result in new possibilities for action and practice. One of the key figures in this tradition of what we might term 'practical philosophy' was Karl Marx, who insisted that the very idea of a separate realm of ideas, 'theory' or the intellect was symptomatic of a specific mode of life. We only divorce 'theory' from the world and practice when our ideas have begun to mask, rather than enhance, life. It is only when we have lost touch with the world that our minds seem to operate in an 'ideal' sphere of their own. For this reason, Marx insisted that a truly successful philosophy would not add just one more idea of interpretation to the world; it would change our very relation to the world. Marx's thought was revolutionary in the sense that despite the fact that many of the revolutions carried out in his name were not faithful to the spirit of Marxism, his ideas nevertheless seem to demand that we think and act differently. If our ideas are tied to life and action, then can we always ask of any idea: what type of life does it serve?

Once we accept the Marxist idea that we create and transform our world through our political and social existence, then we can

xi

no longer appeal to timeless and immutable values. Our practical world of life and action is lived through the ideas we form and the ideas that form us. Through theory, we are capable of questioning and changing our relation to the world and each other. Philosophy and theory are not merely related to life and practice; they are aspects of life. Gilles Deleuze also referred to a specifically revolutionary potential in thought: something is revolutionary not because it has this or that political content or 'message' but because it destroys the seeming naturalness or inevitability of what we take to be unchangeable. If we undertake a revolution in the name of 'man', we are actually operating in a reactionary manner: allowing ourselves to be guided by some seemingly timeless and unquestionable value (Deleuze & Guattari 1983, p. 105). If, however, we act for the sake of some end that remains open, provisional and fluid—such as the identity of a people that is not already given—then the event is truly revolutionary. A political disruption in the name of a 'queer' minority, for example, would not appeal to an already formed concept, identity and value; it would demand that we rethink and reconceptualise just what we take political identity to be. The force of Deleuze's philosophy lay in demonstrating just how reactionary many of our fundamental concepts are, such that most of the time we fail to really think, instead, simply wallowing in the inertia of common sense. By contrast, if we philosophise—if we create difficult, unmanageable and disruptive concepts—then we will question, provoke and challenge our lives.

Despite the difficulty and seemingly abstract nature of Deleuze's work he is, by his own account, a practical philosopher. He believes in, and carries out, the creation of concepts; but he does so for one reason only: the enhancement of life. The more difficult and challenging our concepts are, the more they allow us to change and expand our lives. A theory or philosophy which merely gave us an accurate picture of the world would present itself as a supplement to life; but a philosophy which challenged the form and structure of our thinking would be an event of life. Along with Marx, Deleuze regarded thinkers as diverse as Freud, Nietzsche and Spinoza as contributing to a tradition of practical thinking—thinking that does not passively mirror or represent the world, but allows new events and possibilities and thereby creates a world.

Perhaps the most important figure in this practical tradition in the twentieth century was the French thinker Michel Foucault, who was Deleuze's contemporary and the subject of his later work, *Foucault* (1988). Marx had transformed the relation between theory and practice by arguing that our ideas or theories—the concepts we use to make sense of the world—are not innocent, that the way we think about or represent the world is inextricably tied up with how we act and what we desire. Marx, for example, invented the concept of 'ideology'. (The word may have been used before Marx, but it was Marx who gave it its radical sense.) Ideology describes the way we live our world through ideas and concepts. The concept of 'woman', for example, is ideological. I act, desire and believe in a certain way because I have (or think of myself through) this concept. This does not mean that the concept is false, for ideology is not error. Ideology describes the way our relations and beliefs—and therefore what we do—are structured beforehand by forces that transcend any individual agent. I did not invent or decide upon the concept of 'woman', but it is nevertheless integral and constitutive of my being. Furthermore, the way I live this concept is political; it ties me into certain relations with others, and leads me to assume certain rights, duties and obligations. An ideological understanding of politics does not assume that we are all individual agents who then negotiate power relations; ideology constitutes us as individuals with quite specific positions of power. We might say, then, that Marx tied theory, or ideas, to practice and life through an understanding of power. Our concepts and beliefs do not just represent our world; they produce relations and forces of power, including class relations, sexual relations and racial relations. The concept of 'woman' can produce positive and negative power relations: it might disempower me in relation to 'man', but it might empower me if I think of the 'rights of women' or the 'women's movement'.

Foucault produced a concept of power that transformed the already radical Marxist tradition of the relation between ideas and life. Marxist notions of ideology focus on how our ideas, concepts, theories or languages produce power relations. Foucault argued that such an understanding was still far too negative: it is as though we have life on the one hand, and then ideology or power relations on the other; as though power structures and determines life from 'above'. Against this, Foucault formed a new notion of power as positive. Here, there is not life outside power. Contrast this with ideology. I can think of the notion of woman as ideological if we imagine that I am a human, an individual or a being, who then imagines myself as a woman—as though the concept of woman were imposed, and as though I might free myself from ideology, power or stereotypes. For Foucault, it is not as though there are first beings and then relations of power. What something *is* is produced through power, or the forces of life. I can consider myself to be human or an individual only because there are concepts such as 'woman'.

Foucault's most famous idea was his criticism of the 'repressive hypothesis'—we think that we have a being and sexuality that is then covered over or repressed by social norms and cultural expectations. But the contrary is the case—we do not have a humanity or sexuality that lies behind ideology or repression; we only think of what precedes or underlies ideology, concepts and relations after the productive effect of those relations. Our real or underlying sexuality is an effect of power, not something repressed by power. It is only in going to the psychoanalyst and investigating my sexuality that I have a sexuality at all (Foucault 1981). This means that relations of power—such as the relation between patient and analyst, or criminal and prosecutor, or human body and social scientist—produce positions of power. It is not as though there are masters and slaves, and then concepts and theories which justify and mask those relations. Mastery and slavery are both instances of power, produced through each other.

For Foucault, both theories and actions are modes of power. To refer to a body as 'white', 'male' or 'homosexual' is to produce a power relation; but to scar, punish or clothe that body is also a power relation. Foucault therefore created a whole new way of thinking about the relation between theory and practice. Our theories do not just mask, justify or sustain power relations;

our theories produce, and are produced by, power relations; relations among bodies, among words and among words and bodies. If Marx thought of power negatively—as ideology, which can conceal or distort the real relations of life—Foucault thought of power positively, as the very force of life that produces distinct terms. Deleuze took this tradition one step further by creating the concept of 'desire'. If we think of life as desire, we no longer have any single foundation or ground which thought ought to obey. Deleuze set himself the task of thinking desire positively: not a desire that someone has for something she wants or lacks; but a desire that is just a productive and creative energy, a desire of flux, force and difference, a revolutionary desire that we need to *think* in ways that will disrupt common sense and everyday life.

In the English-speaking world, Deleuze was known first of all through the translation of *Anti-Oedipus*, which he co-authored with Félix Guattari in 1972, but which was not translated into English until 1977. Although Deleuze had written a great deal of more conventional philosophical work from the 1950s onwards, it was the concept of desire in *Anti-Oedipus* that marked a transformation in the relation between thought and action. Like Foucault, Deleuze and Guattari insisted on an immanent and positive philosophy. Ideas, theories and concepts are not added on to life in order to picture or represent life; theory is not something other than, or a negation of, life. Life becomes in a diverse number of ways, and one of those ways is becoming through thought (through words, concepts, ideas and theories). Like Foucault's concept of power, Deleuze and Guattari's concept of desire allows us to think of the events and relations of life as productive. The key difference with desire is that it refers to the different ways in which life becomes or produces relations. It is not as though there are bodies or things that are then ordered through power relations. Nor is there a general system of relations, such as language or culture, which produces different beings. What something *is* is its flow of desire, and such forces produce diverging and multiple relations. My body is 'female', for example, through its desire for other bodies; one produces one's sexuality through desire. (Desire is not based on lack or what we do not have; desire is productive.) A female body is produced through certain desiring relations, but other relations would produce a different body. The same body can be 'female', 'lesbian', 'mother', 'human', 'citizen' and so on. These are not terms imposed on a body; a body becomes what it is only through these relations. And even the relation of being human is a relation of desire; I become human in perceiving other bodies as 'like me', in desiring or imagining some common ground. The important point for Deleuze is that desire is not something that we need to repress or tame in order to enter society. Desire is always productive; indeed, it produces the very idea of society.

In *Anti-Oedipus* Deleuze and Guattari insist that their concept of desire is 'anti-oedipal'. Oedipal desire, as defined by Freud, is negative and repressive; we feel we have to renounce our primitive, chaotic and essential desires in order to enter society. We have to abandon our childhood bonding with our mothers and identify with our fathers. Oedipal desire, Deleuze and Guattari argue, is part of a long tradition of repressive and *transcendent* thinking. We enslave life to some overriding (or transcendent) value—such as the value of the good social individual who has abandoned their desires to be just like the 'common man'. Anti-oedipal desire, by contrast, is positive and *immanent*. Desire is not something we repress to become civilised. Societies, cultures, images of the individual, and 'man' are all effects and productions of desire. Ideas do not come from outside to order and repress life; they are part of (or immanent to) life. Life is desire. When a plant takes in light and moisture it becomes a plant through its relation to these other forces; this is one flow of desire. When a human body connects with another body it becomes a child in relation to a parent, or it becomes a mother in relation to a child; this is another flow of desire. When bodies connect and become tribes, societies or nations, they also produce new relations and flows of desire. Identities and images are not, therefore, abstract notions added on to life and desire; they are events within the flow of desire.

Through this concept of desire, Deleuze and Guattari presented a challenge to the relation between theory and life. How might we think differently in order to avoid the notion that 'we' have a fixed identity or being that we then engage with through ideas? Would it be possible to think without assuming some pre-given (or transcendent) model? If we accept that life is desire—a flow of forces that produces relations—then we can no longer rely on a single relation or being to provide a foundation for thinking. We can no longer think of humanity, language or culture as the ground of life, for human life and thinking would be one flow of desire among others. *Anti-Oedipus* was a highly influential work, both in its original French and in English translation. But it was a key part of a much larger project. *Anti-Oedipus* aimed to free desire from fixed images of desire, to imagine a desire that is not tied to some pre-given human norm (such as the oedipal picture of the child in relation to its parents). The rest of Deleuze's work, in very different ways, sought to free life from fixed and rigid models, such as the image of the rational subject, the image of 'man', or even the ideas of thinking as information and communication. Philosophy, for Deleuze, was not about creating correct pictures or theories of life, but transforming life. Philosophy is not something we apply to life. By thinking differently we create ourselves anew, no longer accepting already created and accepted values and assumptions. We destroy common sense and who we *are* in order to *become*.

A guide to key Deleuzean terms

Gilles Deleuze began his career as a philosopher in the highly competitive and rigorous intellectual environment of Paris in the 1950s. In the 1970s he joined forces with the French psychoanalyst Félix Guattari and branched out into far less conventional modes of philosophical writing (including references to mathematics, biology, geology, sociology, physics, literature and music). More than any other thinker of this time, Deleuze's work is not so much a series of self-contained arguments as it is the formation of a whole new way of thinking and writing. For this reason he created an array of new terms and borrowed specialist terms from previous philosophers. Like that of Benedict de Spinoza (1632–77), Deleuze's terminology does not consist of simple, self-sufficient and definable key terms. Spinoza's philosophy formed a set of interweaving axioms and propositions, a style of philosophy that supposedly mirrored a world that is not an object outside us to be judged, but a dynamic plane of forces within which we are located (Deleuze 1992). Philosophy, for both Deleuze and Spinoza, cannot have a distinct foundation or beginning, for the life it studies has always already begun and the philosopher, scientist or artist who writes about life is also part of the flux of life. A philosophy or form of writing that aims to affirm the mobility of life must itself be mobile, creating all sorts of connections and following new pathways. For this reason there is an almost circular quality to Deleuze's work: once you understand one term you can understand them all; but you also seem to need to understand all the terms to even begin to understand one.

Deleuze argued that concepts were complicated in just this way: creating 'new connections for thinking', opening up whole new 'planes of thought' (Deleuze 1994, p. 139). Deleuze and Guattari also argued for 'rhizomatic' styles of thinking in which there would be not a fixed centre or order so much as a multiplicity of expanding and overlapping connections (Deleuze & Guattari 1987, pp. 3–26). In order to read Deleuze you have to accept that finding your way around his work is never going to be a question of adding one proposition to another. Rather, you need a sense of the whole in order to fully understand any single section; but the whole also seems to transform with the interpretation of each new section. For this reason I have put this glossary of terms at the beginning rather than the end of this book, even though the understanding of any term will only begin to be possible after some overall acquaintance with Deleuze's work. These terms and definitions, and this book as a whole, are a guide to approaching Deleuze. It will only be possible for readers to really understand the beginning of this book once they have reached the end, but this is an essential feature of Deleuze's intent—which is to challenge the easy acceptance and recognition of the ways in which we think. Thinking, for Deleuze, is not a self-sufficient act of judgement set over or against life; thinking is part of the dynamic flux of life. Great thinking, whether it takes the form of art, science or philosophy, does not settle with a fixed system or foundation. We create concepts not in order to label life and tidy up our ideas but to transform life and complicate our ideas.

Affect In its most general sense, 'affect' is what happens to us when we feel an event: fear, depression, laughter, terror or boredom are all possible 'affects' of art. Affect is not the meaning of an experience but the response it prompts. Deleuze refines this notion to argue that art is the creation of 'affects' and 'percepts' (Deleuze and Guattari 1994). Whereas affections and perceptions are located in perceivers—we can say that I have a 'perception' of red or that I 'feel' fear—Deleuze argues that art creates affects and percepts that are not located in a point of view. (Imagine a painting that just *is* terrifying or depressing; we may not be depressed or terrified when we view it but it presents the 'affect' of depression or terror. Imagine a novel that describes a certain light; we may not see the light but we are presented with what it would be to perceive such light, or what such a perception is regardless of who perceives; this is a percept.)

Assemblage   All life is a process of connection and interaction. Any body or thing is the outcome of a process of connections. A human body is an assemblage of genetic material, ideas, powers of acting and a relation to other bodies. A tribe is an assemblage of bodies. Deleuze and Guattari refer to 'machinic' assemblages, rather than organisms or mechanisms, in order to get away from the idea that wholes pre-exist connections (Deleuze & Guattari 1987, p. 73). There is no finality, end or order that would govern the assemblage as a whole; the law of any assemblage is created from its connections. (So the political State, for example, does not create social order and individual identities; the State is the effect of the assembling of bodies. There is no evolutionary idea or goal of the human which governs the genetic production of human bodies; the human is the effect of a series of assemblages: genetic, social and historical.)

Becoming-woman   This term is tied to 'becoming-animal', 'becoming-intense' and 'becoming-imperceptible' (Deleuze & Guattari 1987, pp. 232–309).

The problem with western thought is that it begins in *being*, which it then imagines as going through becoming or movement. Furthermore, it has tended to privilege man as the grounding being; it is man who is the stable knower or subject who views a world of change and becoming. Deleuze, however, insists that all life is a plane of becoming, and that the perception of fixed beings—such as man—is an effect of becoming. In order to really think and encounter life we need to no longer see life in fixed and immobile terms. This means that thinking itself has to become mobile and to free itself from the fixed foundations of man as the subject. Becoming other than man requires becoming-woman or becoming-animal. And if perception tends to view the world in terms of fixed and extended objects, we also need to become imperceptible or become intense (no longer fixed and located wholes within life, but open to the intensity of life).

Body without organs   We perceive and live the world as though it were composed of organised bodies. Our notion of man, for example, privileges certain organs: the brain that thinks, the eye that judges and the phallus that holds social power. But we also necessarily presuppose some disorganised 'life' or 'ground' from which different bodies emerge. The body without organs is the life we imagine as underlying our forms of organisation, so the body without organs varies historically. In capitalism, for example, we imagine that there is some basic flow of capital which we then exchange and manage in order to produce ourselves as social and political individuals. Prior to capitalism, societies imagined that it was the earth that formed the basic substance or substrate of life, such that primitive tribes imagined their distinct orders as distinctions of the whole or totality of the earth. The body without organs is the undifferentiated that we imagine underlies the differentiated or organised bodies of life.

Concept   For Deleuze, a concept is not a generalisation or a label that we use to name the world. Concepts are creations that testify to the positive power of thinking as an event of life. We create concepts in order to transform life. For example, at a material level the eye may watch one event following another, but the concept of 'cause' creates an immaterial event. We can now anticipate or expect events that are not given, or we can imagine what might happen, only because we have created a concept (of cause) that extends beyond the actual world we perceive to what we might expect or imagine. The creation of concepts is the peculiar art of philosophy, which allows us to think what is not given to material perception. We perceive a thing or being, but a philosopher can form a concept of being and ask what being is in general. What is it to exist? In such a case the philosopher would create through the concept of being—a virtual whole, for the philosopher imagines all of being, not just what is given and present.

Desire and **Desiring machines**   The idea of life as literally a machine (Deleuze & Guattari 1983) allows us to begin with functions and connections before we imagine any produced orders, purposes, wholes or ends. A desiring machine is therefore the outcome of any series of connections: the mouth that connects with a breast, the wasp that connects with an orchid, an eye that perceives a flock of birds, or a child's body that connects with a trainset. Thinking desire in this way gets us over desire as a fundamental lack. For Deleuze and Guattari, desire is not driven by bodies having become separated or cut off from life. They oppose the notion of the death-drive whereby all life wishes to overcome the loss and trauma of birth and return to a state of quiescence. Desire is connection, not the overcoming of loss or separation; we desire, not because we lack or need, but because life is a process of striving and self-enhancement. Desire is a process of increasing expansion, connection and creation. Desire is 'machinic' precisely because it does not originate from closed organisms or selves; it is the productive process of life that produces organisms and selves.

Deterritorialisation   Life creates and furthers itself by forming connections or territories. Light connects with plants to allow photosynthesis. Everything, from bodies to societies, is a form of territorialisation, or the connection of forces to produce distinct wholes. But alongside every territorialisation there is also the power of *de*territorialisation. The light that connects with the plant to allow it to grow also allows for the plant to become other than itself: too much sun will kill the plant, or perhaps transform it into something else (such as sun-dried leaves becoming tobacco or sun-drenched grapes becoming sultanas). The very connective forces that allow any form of life to become what it *is* (territorialise) can also allow it to become what it *is not* (deterritorialise). The human bodies that assemble to form a tribe or collective (territorialisation) can produce a whole that then allows them to be governed by a chieftain or despot (deterritorialisation, where the power for assembling has produced a collective disempowerment). There can also be *re*territorialisation. The tribe can take the deterritorialised term (such as the ruler or despot) and return it to the collective: we are all leaders, or we all govern ourselves (as in modern individualism). Territorialisation can occur at all levels of life. Genes connect or territorialise to produce species, but these same connections also allow for mutations (deterritorialisation). Such mutation can also be used, or turned back, to reinforce the territory that was initially the outcome of random mutation: say in gene therapy or genetic modification, where the motor for change and deterritorialisation (genetics) is used to arrest change and mutation (reterritorialisation). Deleuze and Guattari also write of *absolute deterritorialisation*, which would be a liberation from all connection and organisation. Such a process can only be thought or imagined, rather than achieved, for any perception of life is already an ordering or territorialisation; we can think absolute deterritorialisation as an extreme possibility.

Differenciation/Differentiation The world we perceive is made up of differenciated things, distinct terms or objects. But in order for us to perceive a differenciated world there must also be a power of differentiation. We have distinct or differenciated species only because of the differentiation of genetic creation (Deleuze 1994, pp. 206–7). We have the differenciated terms of a language only because there is the power of language to create different sounds and senses. We have the spectrum of different colours only because we have the differentiation of white light.

Genealogy/Geology Deleuze picks up the concept of genealogy from the late nineteenth-century thinker Friedrich Nietzsche (1844–1900). Nietzsche challenged the usual notion of history whereby we read back the end of a development into the beginning. Genealogy looks at the chaotic, multiple and chance emergence of the present. Instead of seeing all history as leading up to the moral individual, Nietzsche's *On the Genealogy of Morals* argued that our current ideals of morality and inhumanity grew from arbitrary and inhuman causes (Nietzsche 1967, p. 67). 'Punishment', for example, begins as 'festive cruelty', the sheer force and enjoyment of inflicting suffering to affirm one's power. But we subsequently come to imagine a law and morality that would justify and organise this pleasure of asserting force; in doing so we 'invent' man and morality. A genealogy does not accept the current reason or understanding of the present; it looks to the past in order to unhinge the present, to show that there is no justification for the present. Deleuze and Guattari's two major works, *Anti-Oedipus* and *A Thousand Plateaus*, are genealogies of capitalism and humanism; they both attempt to show how 'man' and 'capital' emerge from the play of forces and interacting bodies. Deleuze and Guattari also explicitly wrote a *geology* of morals (Deleuze & Guattari 1987, pp. 39–74). This extended the idea that there is not *a* history or single line of development, but overlaid strata or plateaus: the history of inhuman and inorganic life, as well as differing histories within the human.

Immanence   This is one of the key terms (and aims) of Deleuze's philosophy. The key error of western thought has been transcendence. We begin from some term which is set against or outside life, such as the foundation of God, subjectivity or matter. We think life *and* the thought which judges or represents life. Transcendence is just that which we imagine lies outside (outside thought or outside perception). Immanence, however, has no outside and nothing other than itself. Instead of thinking a God who then creates a transcendent world, or a subject who then knows a transcendent world, Deleuze argues for the immanence of life. The power of creation does not lie outside the world like some separate and judging God; life itself is a process of creative power. Thought is not set over against the world such that it represents the world; thought is a part of the flux of the world. To think is not to represent life but to transform and act upon life.

Lines of flight   Any form of life, such as a body, a social group, an organism or even a concept is made up of connections. Genes collect to form bodies; bodies collect to form tribes. The concept of 'human', for example, connects rationality, a type of body (white, male), the power to speak and so on. But any connection also enables a line of flight; there can always be a genetic mutation. The definition of the human as rational can also allow for a dispute over just what constitutes the human: is it rational to stockpile nuclear weapons? So any definition, territory or body can open up to a line of flight that would transform it into something else.

Minoritarian/Majoritarian   Deleuze and Guattari use the terms 'minor' and 'minoritarian' not to describe groups in terms of their numbers but in terms of the mode of their formation. Women, for example, are a minority. This is not because there are fewer women, but because the standard term is that of 'man'. Furthermore, a majority has a fixed standard. There is an image or ideal of the human or man which then governs who can or cannot be admitted; we exclude those who are deemed 'inhuman'. But minoritarian groups have no grounding standard; the identity of the group is mobilised with each new member. The women's movement, for example, has constantly questioned whether there *is* any thing such as 'woman'. A minor literature, also, does not appeal to a standard but creates and transforms any notion of the standard. If I seek to write a film script that is just like the popular and financially successful *Star Wars* (appealing to the spirit and tradition of American science fiction), then this is a *major* work. But if I aim to produce a film that critics may not even recognise as a film, or that will demand a redefinition of cinema, then I produce a *minor* work. For Deleuze and Guattari all great literature is minor literature, refusing any already given standard of recognition or success. Similarly, all effective politics is a becoming-minoritarian, not appealing to who we are but to what we might become.

Monad   This is a term that Deleuze takes from the German philosopher Gottfried Wilhelm Leibniz (1646–1716). We perceive our world as a set of related terms: the molecules that make up a plant or the bodies that make up a society. But each perceived set of relations is made up of monads, which are the self-sufficient substances prior to all relations. Each monad perceives the whole of the world from its own point of view, creating its own perceived relations. There are, therefore, as many worlds as there are monads. The whole of life is just the sum of all the infinite perceptions or worlds opened up by each monad. For Deleuze, the importance of this idea lies in the two key ideas. First, if the whole of life is made up of monads, then the whole of life is nothing more than a plane of perceptions. (The plant is a perception of heat, light and moisture.) There is no common or God's-eye viewpoint that would allow for a world, only the worlds of all the human, inhuman, organic and inorganic monads. Second, we perceive our world in terms of the relations from our point of view—we perceive light always in relation to our visual organs—but such relations are not intrinsic. There is the power of light itself, and not just the relation we have to it. True thinking, for Deleuze, aims to grasp all the inhuman perceptions and forces beyond the order of our point of view.

Multiplicity   At its simplest, a multiplicity is a collection or connection of parts. Deleuze uses the term in a number of ways but one of the most significant is his distinction between an intensive and extensive multiplicity, which also relies on the distinction between intensive and extensive difference. Extensive difference can be thought of as beginning from the extension of spatially distinct and bounded points. If we could look at all the members of a family represented on a family tree, each one of them being a 'Smith', this would be something like an extensive multiplicity. A multiplicity of this type is always a multiplicity of some distinct, generalised and bounded body. (Such multiplicities can be thought of as collections of things, bodies, numbers, qualities or species.) Alternatively, we could look at the microscopic genetic, social and historical mutations and gradations that cross these bodies, so that a genetic trait might connect two bodies, differentiate another two, alter in a third. Intensive difference cannot be mapped into clear and distinct points; it also becomes different as it expresses itself through time. It is closer to the dynamism, becoming and temporal fluidity of true difference than the spatialised, structured and organised difference of extension. An intensive multiplicity is not a multiplicity of an identifiable measure; it is a substantive multiplicity. What it *is* is an effect of its connections (or becoming-multiple).

Nomadology   Most of western thought has tended to operate from a fixed or grounded position: either the position of man or the subject of humanity. Even beyond the human realm, life works through fixed perceptions to produce a perceiver and perceived, an inside and an outside. The aim of nomadology is to free thought from a fixed point of view or position of judgement. Nomadology allows thought to wander, to move beyond any recognised ground or home, to create new territories.

Oedipal   Freud's theory of the Oedipus complex formed the heart of psychoanalytic method. Here, the entry into life and humanity occurs when the child abandons the mother, whose body is first desired because she meets the biological needs of life, but is subsequently fantasised as answering to all desire. The child can only deflect desire away from the mother with the threat of castration. It is the father, as symbol of social power, who represents the punishing law that prohibits the mother; the child must renounce the mother and identify with the social and phallic (or non-maternal) power of the father. For Deleuze and Guattari, this oedipal structure is the culmination of a western political tradition of lack. We imagine that we enter society and law—the domain of the father or phallus—because we renounced a prohibited and impossible object (the mother). Our desire is oedipal if it is imagined as being a signifier or substitute of a lost object; we are oedipal subjects if we imagine ourselves as self-punishing or self-prohibiting for the sake of some universal law or guilt.

Rhizome/Rhizomatics   Deleuze and Guattari explain these terms by first distinguishing between the 'rhizomatic' and the 'arborescent' (Deleuze & Guattari 1987). Traditional thought and writing has a centre or subject from which it then expresses its ideas. Languages, for example, are seen to share a basic structure or grammar which is then expressed differently in French, German or Hindi. This style of thought and writing is arborescent (tree-like), producing a distinct order and direction. Rhizomatics, by contrast, makes random, proliferating and de-centred connections. In the case of languages we would abandon the idea of an underlying structure or grammar and acknowledge that there are just different systems and styles of speaking, that the attempt to find a 'tree' or 'root' to all these differences is an invention after the fact. A rhizomatic method, therefore, does not begin from a distinction or hierarchy between ground and consequent, cause and effect, subject and expression; any point can form a beginning or point of connection for any other. (This is typical of Deleuze and Guattari's own method. They do not use philosophy to interpret biology or biology to explain philosophy; they allow the two styles of thinking to mesh, transform and overlay each other.) Further, they insist that what looks like a binary or opposition in their thought—such as the distinction between rhizome and tree—is not an opposition but a way of creating a pluralism. You begin with the distinction between rhizomatic and arborescent only to see that all distinctions and hierarchies are active creations, which are in turn capable of further distinctions and articulations.

Schizoanalysis   For Deleuze and Guattari most of western thought has been built on a paranoid structure. They even refer to the 'paranoid social machine' (Deleuze & Guattari 1983). Paranoia is connected with projection and perceiving (hearing) persecuting voices outside oneself. Typically we hear the voice of law, society, conscience or the father (or even, in capitalism, the laws of the market). Paranoia is interpretive: we always ask what things mean, attempting to find the law, ground or authority behind signs. Traditional psychoanalysis merely intensifies this tendency by interpreting all our dreams and desires as messages from our guilty conscience. Against this, Deleuze and Guattari celebrate the 'schizo' and 'schizoanalysis'. Instead of returning all our images and desires to one concealed ground (such as the law, God, the subject or 'me'), schizoanalysis disconnects and pulverises images to look at molecular intensities. The law, for example, will be made up of a certain magisterial tone of voice, an elevated expression, a male body, a uniform of judge's robes and so on. Schizoanalysis—unlike psychoanalysis—does not look at psyches or interpret desires to discover the psyche that speaks. Schizoanalysis looks at how the image of the psyche, ego or person has been assembled from the privilege and investment in certain body parts: the brain that thinks, the eye that judges, the self-contained and reasoning body or the judging mouth.

Transcendence/Transcendental Deleuze inherits this distinction from the German philosophical tradition, especially Immanual Kant (1724–1804) and Edmund Husserl (1859–1938), both of whom, like Deleuze, regarded themselves as transcendental philosophers. Transcendence, or the transcendent, is what we experience as outside of consciousness or experience. We experience the real world as transcendent, as other than us or as external. A transcendental philosophy or method asks how transcendence is possible. For example, I can only have a real or outside world if I make some distinction between what appears to me (perceptions and appearances) and a world that appears (the perceived or appearing thing). Both Kant and Husserl argued that before there could be the transcendent or the real world 'outside me', there had to be some concept of 'me' (or the subject) from which the real world was distinguished. Deleuze also argues that we should not simply accept transcendence or the outside world (reality) as our starting point, that we need to ask how something like a distinction between inside and outside (or subject and object) emerges. The error of western thought has been to begin from some already existing thing, some transcendence, some given point of reality (such as matter, the subject, God or being). Deleuze insists that we need to understand how the experience of the world as a real and external world is possible: this is a transcendental approach.

Transcendental empiricism Deleuze's method is transcendental because it refuses to begin with any already given (or transcendent) thing, such as matter, reality, man, consciousness or 'the world'. But it is a transcendental empiricism because it insists on beginning with 'the experienced' or 'given' as such. (Empiricism is a commitment to experience as the starting point of inquiry, rather than ideas or concepts.) The empiricism is transcendental because when Deleuze begins with experience he does not begin with human experience; for Deleuze experience includes the perceptions of plants, animals, microbes and all sorts of machines.

Virtual difference   Difference should not be thought of as that which relates already distinct points or substances. Difference begins as the production of intensities from virtual tendencies. Take human life and animal life: they have their origin in a flow of genetic material that has the tendency to actualise itself in various species. Deleuze and Guattari refer to this as the 'intense germinal influx' which then needs to be actualised into extended bodies (Deleuze & Guattari 1983, p. 162). Some tendencies will not be actualised; there are all sorts of genetic misfirings, unpursued paths and potentialities that are not actualised. Western thought, however, has always privileged a politics of the actual over the potential, and does this by stressing human life as already expressed and constituted. We base politics on man or the State, rather than considering the powers that produce the State. Only if we consider those virtual or unfulfilled potentialities can we transform the present into a truly new future. A politics of potentiality or the virtual powers of life looks to all those non-actualised tendencies in order to question what we might become (Hardt & Negri 1994). We would look away from the image of the State as an active expression of who we are to micropolitical forces: what are the chance events that have produced this particular image of human life? And what about all those expressions of life that do not actualise themselves as the essence of man? Deleuze considered certain literary expressions of malevolence, evil and stupidity as truly disruptive of our everyday common sense. Throughout literature, philosophy, and life in general, there are all sorts of expressions that have not been recognised as essentially human. Why should we take the current image of the rational political agent as an expression of what human life *is*? If we look at all the bizarre, aberrant and different expressions of human life we begin to intuit the virtual powers that are capable of transforming life beyond what it actually *is* to what it might *become*.

Introduction

Thinking through philosophy, art and science

We often think of culture and cultural value as socially constructed. We no longer believe in timeless values or essences. We value Shakespeare because of the beliefs of our culture and institutions, but we can easily imagine societies where *Hamlet* either makes no sense or does not seem particularly worthy. It seems futile to imagine some 'essence' of art; art is just what universities or critics canonise or consecrate. It seems equally futile to imagine any other sorts of essences. We live our world through meanings and representations. What we understand by the words 'femininity' or 'good' would be quite different in another epoch or culture. Today, we tend to think that systems of signs or representation produce our world as meaningful or socially coded—such that it makes no sense to inquire how such codes or systems of representation emerged.

It was against this background of representation that Deleuze launched his philosophy of difference. (Deleuze wrote most of his work following the movement in French thought known as structuralism, which we will look at in more detail later on. The main point to note here is that Deleuze challenged the dominant belief that we know and experience our world through imposed structures of representation.) To begin with, Deleuze insisted that our meanings or representations were not just arbitrary or culturally relative; we can, and should, intuit the forces of desire that produce representations. Doing so, Deleuze argued, will take us out of our dogmas of common sense and into entirely new ways of thinking. So, while there may not be timeless and static 'essences,' in the sense of meanings lying behind our representations, there are nevertheless essential powers or forces which make any act of thought or representation possible. Second, Deleuze recognised the importance of other essential powers: alongside philosophy we can also think scientifically and artistically. There may be no common feature or essence to all the art works that we have, but we can and should look at the essential force that makes all the different instances of art possible. We will not have an essence of art but we will realise something about the very power of thinking, its ability or potential to produce artistic events or events of art.

The challenge of Deleuze's thought is that it charts its way between two dominant paradigms. Like many thinkers of his time, Deleuze insisted that there was no ultimate ground or foundation; whatever values we have are created rather than given. He also reacted against the other extreme, whereby all our values are merely representations or constructions. His alternative was this: we can select and assess our values, not by giving them some ultimate meaning or foundation but by looking at what they do. Ask, he insisted, not what a text means but how it works. As a philosophy this lands us squarely in the terrain of art and culture. Art, Deleuze argued, is not just a set of representations; it is through art that we can see the force and creation of representations, how they work to produce connections and 'styles' of thinking. Art, especially literature, is in some ways a 'symptomatology', a way of diagnosing the language and styles which orient our thinking (Deleuze 1997, p. 177). Art can show us the force or productive power of our values.

The problem

Despite the fact that Deleuze produced a large amount of his philosophy before 1968, he is usually regarded as one of the post-

1968 thinkers (along with Michel Foucault, Jacques Derrida and others) who are also referred to as post-structuralists (Sturrock 1979; Descombes 1980). 1968 was a key political-intellectual landmark due to the revolt of students, not workers, against intellectual authorities in the government and universities. Deleuze and his contemporaries needed to re-think political revolt as tied to ideas and philosophical institutions. Deleuze spent a lot of his time co-authoring works with the French psychoanalyst Félix Guattari, thus a large part of his work was never 'pure' philosophy. Nor was it clear just where Deleuze's 'own' work stood in relation to either Guattari's work or that of the many artists and philosophers he wrote about. The difficulty of discerning Deleuze himself is typical of a lot of the writing around 1968, for this was a time when the autonomy of authorship was under serious attack (Barthes 1982; Foucault 1984). Far from writing being the expression of a unique vision or belief, Deleuze and those around him felt that it ought to be an open and almost involuntary response to the events of one's time. Deleuze himself described May 1968 as 'a becoming breaking through into history' (Deleuze 1995, p. 153). The standard notions of politics and writing, based on the rational human subject, were challenged by events that went beyond party politics and historical movements.

Most of the recent work on Deleuze has stressed the ways in which his interventions in philosophy have enabled an entirely new way of approaching modern political problems: problems such as feminism, which contest the traditional image of the subject (Buchanan & Colebrook 2000); issues of land rights and national identity, which challenge the norms of western reason (Patton 2000); and questions regarding the relation between art and politics—given that contemporary art (especially cinema) seems to have abandoned the role of moral legislation (Rodowick 1997). The post-1968 nature of Deleuze's thinking lies in its rejection of a politics that explains the relations among rational individuals in favour of a micropolitics that explains the construction of individuals from pre-personal forces. The 'problem' of 1968, the breakthrough into history, was a series of political events that displayed a power that did not emanate from organised groups or constituted historical agents.

According to Deleuze, in order to begin to read and respond to any event, we need to see its underlying 'problem' (Deleuze 1988, p. 15; 1991, p. 33). If we want to understand a development in evolution, such as the formation of the eye, then we need to refer back to an organism's problem in responding to light: 'an organism is nothing if not the solution to a problem, as are each of its differenciated organs, such as the eye which solves a light "problem"' (Deleuze 1994, p. 211). If we want to understand a novelist or film-maker we need to look beyond the story or narrative to the problem which the work and style 'answers'. Franz Kafka's production of a minor literature, for example, responds to the problem of writing in German as a Czech national (Deleuze & Guattari 1986). If we want to understand post-structuralism, and Deleuze's specific place in post-structuralism, we can begin with the historical problem of 1968 and the philosophical problem of structuralism. History, Deleuze argued, is usually seen as a mapped out order of dates within a single 'plane' of human life: 'All history does is to translate a co-existence of becomings into a succession' (Deleuze & Guattari 1987, p. 430). A history of events and problems, by contrast, looks at how certain disruptions create new understandings of life, the human, time and space (Deleuze & Guattari 1987, pp. 292–3). (Deleuze also refers to a 'geology', which looks at different planes of life, alongside 'genealogy', which traces the time lines of different life forms.)

If we use Deleuze's own terminology and say that 1968 is less a date than an event or problem, then we start to look at history not as a sequence of ordered events but as a number of diverging series of questions. No historical (or biological) event has a single cause; it is a response to overlapping, different and divergent series. This is what defines a problem: a multiplicity of highly different factors prompts the creation of a response. For Deleuze a 'problem' is not a simple question that needs to find an answer; a problem is something that disrupts life and thinking, producing movements and responses. Even molecular life proceeds by way of problems; all evolution and social–historical movement needs to be understood by way of the problem which is its motor. At the heart of all Deleuze's thinking is an insistence that understanding and thinking demand that we go beyond the seeming order and sameness of things to the chaotic and active becoming which is the very pulse of life. The challenge is to see life as a problem, as a constant proliferation of questions producing ever more complex series of further problems.

Deleuze's work begins from, but goes well beyond, two problems: the methodological problem of structuralism and the historical–political problem of 1968. Structuralism began as a way of understanding life in terms of its differential relations: how the being or identity of any thing is created in its difference from other things. The political problem of May 1968 was whether there could be an active political theory, a way of defining power and revolution that did not rely on already given moral oppositions, such as the opposition between (evil) capitalism and (innocent) workers.

The problem of structuralism, to which Deleuze's post-structuralism is a response, is the question of the emergence or genesis of all those structures which we use to explain life (such as language, culture, meaning or representation). We think, experience and speak through language, but how can we think the origin of language? In different ways, post-structuralists argued that the origin of structures is unrepresentable. Representation already relies on a given structure; we represent life through language, so we cannot represent the pre-linguistic origin of language. For structuralism, then, we always remain within structure, within a system of representation that we can never step outside. To really respond to the problem of structuralism we need to expand or overturn the forms of representation, we need to think the forces that produce systems of representation. For Deleuze this meant that we can only really think or respond to problems if we do not accept the current terminology and orthodoxy of our concepts.

This philosophical motivation can also be seen as a political response to the events of the late 1960s. It was after the events of 1968 that most post-structuralist thinkers realised that politics also needed to go beyond the usual notions of representation; there was a need to understand politics *not* as the competing claims of classes or groups. We need to see how such classes and identities are formed. We need to go to the pre-representational level to understand how the current political terrain emerged. How is it that we think of politics as the competitive relation between economically based and motivated individuals and classes? Class politics became problematic in the late 1960s for a number of reasons. To begin with, there had been economic revolutions—most notably in Russia and China—where the supposedly new communist State forms were just as oppressive, if not more so, than the previous tyrannies of the marketplace. This suggested that more than an overturning of the economy was required; change may have to begin from the very ways in which we think about human life.

Existentialism, phenomenology, humanism: From actual to virtual

The problem of 1968, according to the usual account, goes something like this: for most of France after the Second World War the dominant forms of thought were existentialism and phenomenology, both of which were underpinned by Marxism. Existentialism, as articulated by Jean-Paul Sartre (1905–80), argued that we needed to overturn the idea that there are ultimate and unchanging essences, such as human nature; rather, human beings are nothing other than processes of decision; at each moment of our lives we are 'radically free'. There are no rules, meanings or essences other than those that we produce through our existence (Sartre 1973). It is not that freedom is something we have or do not have, as though freedom were a quality or an attribute. There is no self or 'we' other than what is produced through our free existence. Every action, every way in which we think of the world is ultimately unfounded. Any references to human nature, God, biology or determinism are decisions we make about ourselves. Unlike natural beings, which do not decide and define themselves, human beings are self-defining (Sartre 1957).

Phenomenology, a movement related to existentialism, also argued that the human world was only possible because human life produces or constitutes the world as a meaningful project; there is no 'world' outside the human project of sense and meaning (Husserl 1970). We have a world only because we have language, but we have language only because we have projects and intentions. Language arises from the specific needs of life—to communicate, be with others, form projects and give our world order. For both existentialism and phenomenology, then, human life is essentially creative, because it lacks any natural foundation; human beings are historical and world-forming. For this reason, existentialism and phenomenology were highly compatible with a new form of Marxism that would respond to the failures of a strictly economic Marxism. The orthodox Marxist position maintained that if there were an economic revolution—if the people rather than the market controlled production—then all our ideological illusions would be swept away. We would no longer be subject to the capitalist illusion that the market is free and fair and that we are all equal in the marketplace; our ideas would be liberated once we were freed from the ruthlessness of the market and exploitation. Phenomenology and existentialism put human meaning before material or economic forces; if we want to change our world we need to change the way we think. We need to transform the very structure of our ideas.

The Marxism that was tied to phenomenology and existentialism insisted that political revolution could only begin when human life recognised that all those processes which seemed to be natural and unchanging—such as the conditions of labour, exploitation and economic determinism—were actually decisions of human existence that could be changed (Sartre 1976). The events of 1968 were a turning point in the development of this notion of the primacy of human freedom and its commitment to a Marxist revolution, with many French intellectuals beginning to push for a revolution in thought (May 1994). Such a revolution would not provide us with an illumination of human freedom and man's proper destiny; rather, it would challenge the notions of unified history, human freedom and the Marxist emphasis on lifting ideology to reveal our 'true' interests. Furthermore, because questions were now being raised about the value or existence of an authentic and universal human freedom that was simply there to be recognised, writers such as Deleuze started emphasising seemingly non-rational modes of thought, such as madness, radical art and the avant-garde. A divide was opening up between conventional Marxism and politics—based on class groups, economic criteria and representation—and a post-structuralist politics based on chance disruptions, non-identity and a far more radical sense of freedom.

Human freedom became *the* problem. If human beings are free, does this mean that there is some ultimate 'man' who can be liberated from the forces of production; or does radical freedom mean that there is no longer any human essence to which politics can appeal? All this came to a head in the student sit-ins and disruptions of 1968. There were protests throughout Europe in the late 1960s which were random, unthought out, and motivated not by the economically defined class of workers so much as by students and intellectuals. In the aftermath of these disruptions it was realised that politics was no longer the affair of economic classes and large or 'molar' groupings. Local disruptions at the level of knowledge, ideas and identity could transform the political terrain. Deleuze and others opened the politics of the virtual: it was no longer accepted that actual material reality, such as the economy, produced ideas. Many insisted that the virtual (images, desires, concepts) was directly productive of social reality. This overturned the simple idea of ideology, the idea that images and beliefs were produced by the governing classes to deceive us about our real social conditions. We have to do away with the idea that there is some ultimate political reality or actuality which lies behind all our images. Images are not just surface effects of some underlying economic cause; images and the virtual have their own autonomous power. This is where structuralism and post-1968 politics intersected. We need to see our languages and systems of representation not just as masks or signs of the actual, but as fully real powers in their own right. The way we think, speak, desire and see the world is itself political; it produces relations, effects, and organises our bodies.

Post-1968 philosophy and political theory is usually seen to be a response to this problem: can there be a politics that does not rely on some ultimate notion of shared human recognition? If there really is no shared human nature or essence, and if history really is decision and freedom, how can we justify any political movement? Most importantly, is there a way of thinking politics that does not rely ultimately on economic groups or classes? Can there be an inhuman politics that interrogates the ways in which the image of man as a political subject is produced from the very forces of life and desire? This would mean—and this was the general project of post-1968 philosophy in France—that we need to recognise the positive force of non-economic events. Art, culture, images and 'affects' produce, and do not just represent, the distinct forces and terms of cultural and political life. This means that politics is not about the relations between and among humans. For Deleuze, politics begins with the production of distinct human agents from forces and flows of life. And this raises the problem which Deleuze will articulate in different ways in nearly all that he writes: can thinking grasp the forces or differences that precede and produce it? Or, to use Deleuze's own terminology, can there be a micropolitics? This would consider the ways in which our image of the 'human' is formed from events that lie outside human decision. Ian Buchanan has referred to this as 'metacommentary', and in doing so has placed Deleuze within the tradition of a far more radical Marxism. The task of thought is to perceive the forces that produce the political and cultural terrain, and not just to accept the already given terms of that terrain (Buchanan 2000).

Feminists have also seen the work of Deleuze as helpful in thinking beyond the closed questions of humanism. Often, movements like feminism are divided over the question of whether to include women within humanity, arguing that we are all equal, or to argue for women's essential difference. The feminisms that followed existentialism and phenomenology, such as the work of Simone de Beauvoir (1908–86), argued that women were 'Other': always defined in opposition to, or as negations of man (Beauvoir 1969). Deleuze-inspired feminists have challenged this negative account by insisting that the images of both men and women are the result of prehuman and micropolitical productions; both are produced through a multiplicity of relations and connections, with neither grounding or preceding the other. One of the famous phrases from *A Thousand Plateaus*, 'a thousand tiny sexes', has been taken up by writers like Elizabeth Grosz, who sees the unified human body as the effect of processes of desire and becoming (Grosz 1994a). Against existentialism and phenomenology, Deleuze argued that whatever image we have of ourselves, we are affected by forces that lie beyond our active decision. Freedom needs to be redefined, not as the isolated decision of self-present human agents, but as the power to affirm all those powers beyond ourselves which only an expanded perception can approach.

Inhuman difference

From his earliest work in philosophy to his engagements with politics, art and culture, Deleuze insisted on the prehuman problem. What are the forces, differences, processes or (to use his term) 'syntheses' which produce recognisable entities such as human beings or political classes? In terms of structuralism we might phrase the problem this way: what are the forces of difference that produce the structures of language, culture and politics that allow us to live an ordered and meaningful world? In political terms, what are the forces and powers that have produced the various political terrains of history, including capitalism and the image of the free human agent?

If we accept that this is Deleuze's problem, then we can see why he (like so many French theorists of his generation) is so difficult to read. If thinking and human life have no fixed essence, and if thinking is the effect of forces that are not decided by thought itself, then we need to produce a style of writing that constantly produces problems. Instead of just accepting the questions and terms within which a culture already operates, we need to look at (and transform) the assumptions, propositions, distinctions or differences upon which any system of thought relies. But this does not just mean looking at language in the narrow sense, for a language only expresses more profound differential forces. The way in which our language divides up our world is a sign of far more subtle differences. To take an example: it is now common to use 'they' or 'he/she' or 'humanity' instead of the generic 'he' or 'man'. The idea behind this change is that we should no longer think of man as the standard, with woman as secondary or irrelevant. Changing our language, it is assumed, will overcome this prejudice in our thinking. For Deleuze, however, the problem lies far deeper. How did we come to think in terms of universal man? Changing one word in our lexicon will neither eliminate nor illuminate a far deeper commitment in our thinking. What we need to do is look at the forces, the history and the assumptions that produce the very concept or sense of man, regardless of the specific terms we use to refer to it. Admittedly, language is one way in which we know the structures and assumptions of our thinking. But we need to change the very terrain of our thinking: not just this or that word but the conceptual relations and sense that orient our thought. Some thinkers inspired by Deleuze have begun to write 'inhuman' histories of human life. Manuel de Landa's *A Thousand Years of Nonlinear History* (1997) looks at how geological movements such as alluvial flows and sedimentation can be used to read the formation of human cities, while his *War in the Age of Intelligent Machines* (1991), as the title implies, looks at how technological mutations can effect actions and interactions outside human intentions or bodies.

Language is just one structure among others and expresses more profound prehuman differences. The differentiated structures through which we live—such as language or culture—are organised or 'coded' forms of imperceptible differences. These differences are 'imperceptible' precisely because they have not been ordered, organised and represented in any systemic form. Think of the differences in sound that we do not hear in all the different articulations of a word, or the genetic differences that we do not perceive when we identify a group as belonging to the same species. These molecular differences are productive and positive. We do not have a language or species without these variations of sound or genetic mutation, but our perception or the way we live the world regards these differences as negative, as though they were deviations from the norm or form. For Deleuze, western thought has been committed to dogmas of representation which regard these productive differences negatively, as something that lies outside concepts and good thinking (Deleuze 1994). Against this, Deleuze ties philosophy and politics together by affirming the continual revolution in thinking enabled by these positive, imperceptible and productive differences. Deleuze, typically, refers to the totality or plane of these prehuman, prelinguistic and profound differences in a number of ways: as the abstract machine, as chaos, as the body without organs, as difference in itself, or as the virtual multiplicity. The reason he does not adopt a single or consistent terminology has to do with the nature of the problem. Any thought or image we might have of this profound plane of difference will always grasp only a part or expression of difference. We need to constantly overturn, question and disrupt our terminologies and our differences. True thinking does not operate from an 'image of thought', such as 'self-determining rational man'—it tries to take thought beyond any of its determined images (Deleuze 1994, p. 276).

This is why Deleuze objects to existentialism and phenomenology. He accepts that there is no ultimate meaning or stable essence upon which human life can base its decisions, but he does not then go on to argue that this makes human life self-deciding and self-determining. He does not accept the distinction between a human life that is free and responsible for its own becoming, and a nature which is merely 'in-itself' and determined. All life is constant becoming, including inorganic, organic and even virtual life. We need to do away with the idea that nature merely *is* while man *decides* his being. For one thing, we can see all nature as decision, as creatively responding to the forces that confront and cross it. Secondly, we need to rethink the notion of the human decision; for it is less the case that we decide who 'we' are than that forces 'decide' us. Our languages, our genes, our bodies, our desires, historical forces, social forces—all these things intersect and constantly mutate, in such a way that what we are cannot be traced back to a single point of origin or intent. Far from accepting the human point of view, and explaining the world from the position of human meaning, we need to see how the processes of meaning and human life are produced from what is essentially prehuman.

The project of difference

Deleuze is perhaps one of the most difficult and challenging thinkers of the twentieth century. Part of this is due to the very nature of his project. To begin with, Deleuze argued that all thinking ought to be creative and affirmative. This meant that philosophy was not about finding correct answers to already given problems, but about the creation of new concepts and problems, and that when a philosopher encounters other cultural phenomena, such as art, literature, cinema or science, he should not be concerned with disclosing some supposedly hidden truth or meaning; rather, he should respond actively and creatively. (But not just any response will do; thought does not impose its meanings onto the world. We only *think* when we allow the world to affect us, to grip us, or to do violence to our fixed and common-sense ways of perceiving.) Deleuze's method is directed against representation, the idea that there is a static or meaningless world that we then order or represent through culture. Signs are not uniquely human constructs that 'we' use to communicate. All life is a plane of interacting signs. We are confronted by a world of signs and codes: systems and series of biology, genetics, history, politics, art and fantasy. And each series of signs creates its own lines of difference: genetic differences, chemical differences, differences of sense, of sound, of colour and so on. And all these specific modes of difference are made possible by pure and positive difference: a 'differential power' that for Deleuze is life itself.

It is not that we have a simple and undifferentiated life that we then differentiate through signs, representations or languages. The signs of a culture are the effects of more profound differences. This means that we should not trace a sign back to some thing that it simply represents; we should instead try to grasp how signs and differences proliferate. Instead of finding a meaning behind events and texts, we need to ask how texts that appear as meaningful are created. For Deleuze, this leads us to the specific power of philosophy, which is not just an academic enterprise but a crucial event of life. Philosophy—as opposed to a common sense, which works with already given signs and conventions—is the creation of new signs or concepts, which will allow us to think the emergence of difference. Philosophers, therefore, should not give us definitions of what it is to be good or human; they should be creating concepts that lead us to question just what the human is. Art also has a distinct power—also opposed to common sense. While philosophers create concepts that help us to think of difference, art presents singular differences: the very being of colour, sound, tone or sensibility (Deleuze & Guattari 1994, p. 164). Neither art nor philosophy nor science, though, are forms of representation or interpretation. They don't re-present a world that lies passively outside our acts of thought. Philosophy is not interpretation; it is not discovering the essence of man in all the events of human life. Philosophy—like art and science—should *create* differences. Philosophy, for Deleuze, is not some meta-code that enables us to decode all other signs; philosophy is not the annulment of difference that would trace all signs back to some sense or meaning. Philosophy must create, conceptualise and affirm all those differences that allow texts and meanings to appear. You don't interpret a book or film by using philosophy; you allow the experience of literature or cinema to transform and renovate philosophy. Thinking is not translation: what does this film *mean*?—it is transformation: what does this film *do*? And this question—of the power or force of a theory, a film or a text—means that we need to look at all events of life not as things to be interpreted but as creations that need to be selected and assessed according to their power to act and intervene in life:

> For theory too is something which is made, no less than its object. For many people, philosophy is something which is not 'made', but is pre-existent, ready-made in a pre-fabricated sky. However, philosophical theory is itself a practice, just as much as its object. It is no more abstract than its object. It is a practice of concepts, and it must be judged in the light of the other practices with which it interferes … It is at the level of the interference of many practices that things happen, beings, images, concepts, all the kinds of events (Deleuze 1989, p. 280).

1

Beyond representation and structure

Stupidity and common sense

Deleuze, like many writers of the twentieth century, regarded western thought in general as being dominated by the dogmas of common sense and representation (Deleuze 1994). The very concept of thought as representation assumes that there is some objective, present, real and external world that is then re-presented by thought, as though thought were a passive picture or copy of the world. There would be an actual world (the real), and then its virtual and secondary copy. Deleuze wants to reverse and undermine this hierarchy. Both the actual and the virtual are real, and the virtual is not subordinate to the real. On the contrary, the virtual is the univocal plane of past, present and future; the totality of all that is, was and will be. It is therefore an open totality or whole, never fully given or completed. The virtual can then be actualised in specific forms.

The best model is perhaps evolution. Life is a constantly creative and transforming and thoroughly open plane, but only certain modes of life will be concretely actualised. DNA, for instance, holds a virtual becoming or information that may or may not be actualised depending on whether other becomings are actualised. Keith Ansell-Pearson (1999) has argued that Deleuze's philosophy and politics of the virtual can be best understood from a position of radical evolutionary theory. Against a supposedly Darwinian evolution that would see life as striving to maintain and select for the sake of species and organisms, Deleuze's uptake of evolution stresses the striving of creativity and difference itself. Evolution does not proceed in order to achieve the creation of species or beings; it is not governed by actual goals or already present organisms. Evolution is itself a virtual power: a capacity or potential for change and becoming which passes through organisms. (This would mean, for example, that sexual reproduction is not something 'we' do in order to continue our species; 'we' exist, and reproduce, for the sake of variation. Sexuality is something that passes through and beyond us, not an instinct 'we' have.) The aim of evolution is change and creation itself, not the creation of any actual being: 'The species, therefore, a notion which caused Darwin so much anxiety since an accurate definition proves so elusive, is a transcendental illusion in relation to the virtual-actual movement of life, which is always evolving in the direction of the production of individuation' (Ansell-Pearson 1999, p. 93). It is by confronting new developments in science that philosophy, thinking and the human can transform themselves. We will no longer take who we are (the actual) as the ground and measure of life; we will recognise life as a virtual power for becoming that can take us into an unforeseen future.

From the viewpoint of representation and common sense, the actual world provides a foundation or external model (transcendence), and thought ought to be a faithful copy or replication of the actual. If we were to accept this, then thought would be judged according to its accuracy or correctness or the degree to which it recognises some outside or external reality (transcendence). This would give us some notion of common sense (the correct way in which 'we' should think). For Deleuze, philosophy has been governed by just this dogmatic image of thought, the idea of a subject who passively and dutifully recognises and represents the world (Deleuze 1994). Philosophy, he argues, often begins from the most 'puerile' examples of recognition—such as 'this is a table'—but real thinking in all its difference, violence and inventiveness is not disclosed in everyday common sense but in the bizarre cases of stupidity, creativity and even malevolence.

If we begin with common sense, then we take the primary mode of experience to be the recognition of external objects or facts. We then see literature or art as a second-order representation. But by what right have we selected this form of representational thinking as foundational or exemplary? Representational thinking assumes that there is an ordered and differentiated world, which we then dutifully represent; it does not allow for thought itself to make a difference, and it does not see difference as a positive and creative power to differentiate. If thought were simply representation, then we could only imagine difference as the difference between the different beings that we recognise: 'the world of representation is characterised by its inability to conceive of difference in itself' (Deleuze 1994, p. 138).

Against representation, and its assumption that behind thought there is a standard thinker of good will and common sense, Deleuze suggests other instances of thinking which demonstrate quite different possibilities. Perhaps stupidity, rather than common sense, can show us that thought does not necessarily conform to models of correctness, and perhaps art is not another way of conveying information. Perhaps thinking is not the act of judgement, by a subject, of some world of facts. Thinking, Deleuze insists, is an event that happens *to* us. It is not something that is grounded on a decision; thinking is not the cataloguing of different external objects. Thinking invades us. Indeed, there is no 'us', no subject or individual, that precedes and controls the act of thought. There is thinking, and it is from events of thought that we assume that there was some subject, or common sense, that was their author. Thinking is differentiated by what is not its own:

> Thought is primarily trespass and violence, the enemy, and nothing presupposes philosophy: everything begins with misosophy. Do not count upon thought to ensure the relative necessity of what it thinks. Rather, count upon the contingency of an encounter with that which forces thought to raise up and educate the absolute necessity of an act of thought or a passion to think. The conditions of a true critique and a true creation are the same: the destruction of

an image of thought which presupposes itself and the genesis
of the act of thinking in thought itself.
   Something in the world forces us to think. This
something is an object not of recognition but of a
fundamental encounter (Deleuze 1994, p. 139).

As an example of the dogmas that have pervaded western
thought, Deleuze cites Plato's dialogues, although he argues that
all the philosophers he targets (including Descartes, Kant and
Hegel) have also provided positive insights that take thought
beyond recognition and common sense. Plato's dialogues (like
Descartes' *Meditations* or Kant's *Critique*) elevate a form of
thought that is the simple recognition of already differentiated
beings:

> Therein lies a costly double danger for philosophy. On the
> one hand, it is apparent that acts of recognition exist and
> occupy a large part of our daily life: this is a table, this is an
> apple, this is a piece of wax, Good morning Theaetetus.
> But who can believe that the destiny of thought is at stake in
> these acts, and that when we recognise, we are thinking?
> (Deleuze 1994, p. 135)

Plato's dialogues set up an opposition between those who are
correct and those who are mistaken. What philosophers do not
consider, however, are those who are stupid, evil or malevolent
(Deleuze 1994). If we all agree on the basic principles of logic or
mathematics, it is easy to point out where we go wrong or are
mistaken—and most philosophy is written in this way, as though
we all share a basic logic that can be corrected and freed from error.
But what if we don't recognise or refuse to recognise the basic
rules? Deleuze cites Dostoevsky's underground man, in *Notes from
Underground*, who is driven by the desire to contradict whatever
it is that is recognised as human, shared or self-evident (Deleuze
1994). But we can also think of examples of non-representative
thought taken from popular culture: the absurd delight we take
in characters from situation comedies who employ the most
bizarre forms of logic, or the infuriation we feel when we listen

4

to talkback radio and hear all sorts of illegitimate connections. Such experiences of thinking show just how illegitimate it is to assume a basic human rationality shared by us all. But even logic and mathematics, today, preclude us from recognising some general norm of thought. There are competing logics and radical disputes about the nature of mathematical theory. Once you accept a system of logic, then we all agree. But the person who works from a different system isn't incorrect or in error; she, like the illogical character in a comedy, is working within an entirely different way of making connections and conclusions. Real thinking, Deleuze insists, is not the manipulation of symbols within a system that we all recognise; it is asystemic, unrecognisable, perhaps 'inhuman'. Stupidity or malevolence differ from error; stupidity has not just made a mistake within the norms for good thinking. It does not have the same norms. It adopts an entirely different or perverse logic (Deleuze 1994).

For Deleuze stupidity and malevolence are important precisely because they disclose something about thought and difference. Philosophers have treated the world as though it were already meaningful, identifiable and logically ordered. They have regarded thinking as the passive repetition of the world's inherent meaning and logic. Stupid or malevolent thought, however, shows that thought does not naturally copy the world or inevitably provide one more example of common sense. There is a 'natural stupor' in thinking precisely because thought is not something fully owned or decided; thinking resides in an unthought element: 'Stupidity is neither the ground nor the individual, but rather this relation in which individuation brings the ground to the surface without being able to give it form' (Deleuze 1994, p. 152). How is it, Deleuze asks, that we have elevated a thought that is in agreement, correct, recognisable and obedient? He argues that this dogmatic image of thought is tied to a profound refusal of difference.

Indifferent difference

In the world of representation and common sense we imagine a world of presence and identities. A thing is simply what it is, and its difference from something else does not affect its being what it is. (I am female, and even if all males of the species were eliminated tomorrow I would still be female. I can only see myself as different from men after something or someone has been placed alongside my original identity.) Difference, on this model, is the relation between already identifiable things. At least until the eighteenth century this was the dominant conception of difference, and thought was understood to be the faithful representation of such differences. The world was a system of identifiable species that could be grouped into larger categories (or genera), and difference was merely the relations between these already distinct beings. Being was understood to be equivocal, distributed into various different types. Language and representation would then be a way of organising these different beings. Difference or language or relations would be secondary or subordinate to being and identity.

In the late eighteenth century the German philosopher G.W.F. Hegel (1770–1831) referred to this understanding of difference as 'indifferent difference' (Hegel 1977a, p. 102). He attacked the common-sense view of difference: difference, in the common-sense view, is indifferent; it has no effect on a being's identity. The difference between a chair and a table is no different from the difference between an animal and a plant. And chairs, tables, animals and plants are what they are, regardless of any relations they may bear to other things. Difference is simply the external relation between self-present beings; difference itself is indifferent.

From the nineteenth century to the present the theory that Hegel referred to as 'common-sense' or 'indifferent' difference has come under constant attack. The first philosopher to really insist on the primacy of difference was Hegel himself, who argued that there could be no being or identity without difference. Difference, for Hegel, was necessary, absolute and negative. Most twentieth-century thought, including key works in feminism, race theory and political theory, is indebted to Hegel, for whom what something *is* is defined through its other, its negation, or what it *is not*. We can only have a sense of being through non-being, of man and life through what is inhuman and beyond life, and of identity through difference. Post-structuralism, including the work of Deleuze, has often been read as an attempt to extend and criticise Hegel's insistence on the primacy of difference (Descombes 1980). Hegel argues that we can only think being, or 'what is' if we are other than being; if we negate or differentiate ourselves from being. If being were simply self-present and identical, then we would have no concept or idea of being. (Imagine matter or being that simply *is*. The minute that we call it 'matter' or 'being', or say that it *is*, we have already spoken about it, or related to it, and so it *is not* simply being or matter; we are in a relation to being, or different from being.) In order for being to *be*, it must be differentiated; there must also be a concept that says that being *is*. So there must be a difference between being in itself and the thought or concept of being. Being must be negated by difference. We need to have a language, thought or concept, which is *not being*, in order for *being* to be known. According to Hegel, there is no getting outside this negating power of difference. If we want to think or refer to what lies outside the difference of language or concepts, we can only do so from concepts. The pre-linguistic is only known as different from, or not, linguistic. This means that the identity of any thing is an effect of difference. It is not that there is a world of beings that we then perceive as being different from each other—a being is what it is only through its difference from another thing. The contemporary feminist Judith Butler has used this argument to challenge sexual identity—I can only think of my 'real' sexuality as different from performed stereotypes (Butler 1993). Slavoj Zizek has used Hegel to read cultural and national identity—I can only think of my 'nation' or 'community' in relation to an other who is threatening that community (Zizek 1991). Indeed, we only have a 'world' by thinking what is different from thought, what *is not* me. And we only have a sense of 'I' or self, in being other than, or different from, the world.

Hegel therefore set dialectical thinking against representational thinking (Hegel 1977b). Fredric Jameson has placed Deleuze in this dialectical tradition, a tradition that does not accept what a thing *is* but questions how any thing we experience comes into being (or becomes) through what it *is not*

(Jameson 1997). Representational thinking simply accepts already differentiated terms. On a representational account, men are men, women are women, and from these identities we can then think about all the specific differences between them. On a dialectical account, by contrast, men are only conceptualised as men through their differentiation from women (and vice versa). It is not that there are two sexes that then relate; there is a relation, negation or opposition from which we can conceptualise male and female. Men are non-childbearing, without breasts, slimmer-hipped; they are men in not being women. And feminists have long argued, albeit critically, that women have been defined in relation to men as irrational, without penises, physically weaker.

For Hegel, one could not have the being or identity of a thing without its concept, but the concept is always other than the simple immediacy of a thing. It differentiates the thing from other things; being is mediated through the concepts we have of it. We can only think what a thing *is* through difference, or what it *is not*. Even the word 'being' is a concept, and we could not think what 'is' without such a concept. Concepts allow the very thought of being, and concepts operate through differentiation. So, far from difference being secondary, indifferent or the mere external relation between beings, difference is what enables being. Difference, Hegel insisted, was absolute; any time we try to think of what lies outside the differentiating power of concepts, we can only do so through concepts, in relation to concepts (or as something being different from our concepts). We only know a being from what it *is not*. It is because thought *is not* being, or is other than being, that we can know being or have a relation to it. Nothing can be thought without difference. The thought of the pre-conceptual absolute is still only thinkable as *pre*-conceptual. And thus for Hegel it is not that there is a world that is present that is then *re*-presented in concepts—it is only through the difference of concepts that we have the thought of the present world at all. Experience is mediated, differentiated and ordered through concepts. Deleuze referred to Hegel's philosophy as one of 'infinite representation' (Deleuze 1994, p. 42), for it placed the representation of the world as the very being of the world. The world or being, for Hegel, does not exist outside the differentiating process of representation, and 'man' is just the vehicle for the representation of the world.

Structural difference

In Deleuze's own time structuralism was the dominant theory of difference. Structuralism began early in the twentieth century as a way of studying meaning in general. In addition to the structuralist linguistics of Ferdinand de Saussure (1857–1913), there was also structuralist anthropology (Claude Lévi-Strauss, 1908–), structuralist studies of popular culture (Roland Barthes, 1915–80), structuralist Marxism (Louis Althusser, 1918–90) and many structuralist analysts of literature. Deleuze is often included in the general movement of post-structuralism and his theory of difference is both indebted to and highly critical of structuralism.

Structuralism in general regarded itself as a scientific study of human meaning; it was able to do so because it defined itself against the vagueness of historical analysis. Rather than beginning from some being that goes through history, structuralists argued that any being could only be known through a system of difference. You cannot have a history of something until you have some system or structure that differentiates and marks out that something: so, before the study of any language, culture or text we would have to think of how that language or culture is differentiated. Instead of understanding an artwork, say, as having evolved from previous forms and genres, you would have to study the culture or system of meaning which allowed that object to be differentiated as art. System or structure must precede history or 'genesis'. Hegel had argued that difference was primary, but he thought that difference was historical: that being was differentiated or conceptualised through time (and that human life could understand and comprehend the construction of its identity by reflecting on its own history). Hegel argued that human life first has to think of some world as other than itself (negation). We then realise that such a world is known only through the ideas we have of it (so the negation is produced through ideas, or idealism). But if this is so, and all we have are ideas, and ideas give us the difference between ourselves and the world, then we arrive at the differentiating power of the absolute idea (absolute idealism or absolute difference). At the end of history, Hegel argued, we would recognise difference itself; difference would no longer be outside thinking. We do not use difference to think; and difference is not something that thought comes across. Thinking is difference, and what is other than thought—the real—is an effect of difference.

The structuralists contested this notion that we could recognise difference, doing so through an anti-historical (and anti-humanist) approach to meaning and language. In order to think of any thing at all, it must have been differentiated by the system of language. For the structuralists it is not thought that differentiates the world, it is a system of language. Before we can think or conceptualise there must be a system of differentiated marks—such as the letters of a language—which allow difference to be organised. Thought is not autonomous but has to be located within a system of sounds, marks or 'signifiers' in order for there to be ordered concepts or meanings. Structuralists thus argued that meaning could only be explained by structures or systems of difference, such as languages. Their method was therefore synchronic (or atemporal). Before you can look at how any thing goes through time or history you have to have identified that thing, and you can only do so within an entire system of markings or signifiers. This system is atemporal; we can only think of time because there is a static system, for time relies on meaning and progression, but meaning is always produced through some atemporal system, such as language. (We can only write about a historical transition from one point in time to another if there is a system, such as a language, which could tie those two points together.) The structuralists set their synchronic method against diachronic or historical approaches.

If I wanted to study a language historically, or diachronically, I would look at the way words evolved from previous languages (Latin or Greek origins), and I would look at the way meanings shifted through time. I might take the word 'monster', which today refers to Frankenstein-like or alien figures, and show how it was once associated with spiritual omens, and how it originally derived from the Latin verb *monstrare* (to show). And this might tell me that the word 'monster' carries the meaning of being significant or revelatory. Such an historical (or diachronic) analysis presupposes that there is something like a meaningful human history, which is then expressed in languages. We try to understand who we are and how we speak by examining our origins and development. This is also referred to as a genetic account or an emphasis on genesis. A structuralist account, by contrast, examines any term *within* the present system; it abandons any idea of finding the origin of meaning. For the structuralists we are always within a system of meaning, and can never step outside that system to understand its origin or genesis. What we mean by 'monster' would be explained by looking at how our current language and culture differentiates the monstrous from the normal, the abnormal, the hideous and the deformed. We could show what a word means, not by interpreting the past, but by looking at how each language structure divides up its world.

Structuralists argued that the historical forms of interpretive studies were unscientific and far too humanist. Like Hegel, they insisted that there was no experience that was not already differentiated by concepts. But they wanted to go beyond Hegel by rejecting his idealism. Hegel believed that the mediation, negation or differentiation of the world was produced by concepts or the activity of mind or 'spirit'. Structuralists argued that the systems that differentiate the world are not ideal but material. We can only have a system of concepts or meanings because there are material structures, like the sounds or script of a language. Before there are meanings we have to have what are essentially arbitrary, meaningless and contingent systems of difference. This was why the structuralists studied face-painting, fashion, myth, totems and other systems that were not linguistic in the narrow sense. They insisted that their studies were scientific precisely because they did not presuppose human consciousness or its historical development; they studied static systems of signs. Their analysis was synchronic, not diachronic. We cannot have a genetic account precisely because looking at a thing's genesis presupposes that there is some original being that then goes through time or history. Structuralists argued that there were not some beings or identities that then differentiate themselves through time from some point of genesis, there are only things or origins because of the systems of structural difference. Any origin or genesis could only be grasped or thought through and within structure. We only know origins or the genesis of a system through the system itself. If I want to understand how a word can have a meaning, I do not trace it back to its origins. I look at its differential relation to all the other words in a language. A language works by differentiating the world.

Beyond Hegel and structuralism: Genesis and structure

Deleuze's own philosophy of difference, like Hegel's idealism and structuralism, is directed against common sense. Deleuze also felt that difference was primary, but he demonstrated it by combining the demand for genesis (the origin of difference as it occurs through time) and structure (that this origin is never an identifiable thing but itself already differentiated). Deleuze thought that great philosophy, art and thinking were attempts to confront the 'genetic element', but this genesis or power of difference and creation could not be traced back to either a system (language or structure) or a being (consciousness or origin). Rather, difference is groundless, anarchic, constantly creating and never the same as itself. We cannot say that 'it' differs, so thinking difference brings us up against the very limits of speaking (or our tendency to use nouns and conventional sentences): 'Difference must be shown *differing*' (Deleuze 1994, p. 56).

A common-sense view is that we have meanings, concepts or experience and we use language to convey that sense to another person. Structuralism reverses this order; we only have meanings and experience because we have a system of differences through which we order and recognise the world. Anyone who speaks more than one language will know that there are certain differences that are possible in one language, but not another. German has two words for experience, *Erlebnis* and *Ehrfahrung*: one refers to the experience of an object, the other to the flow of experience or lived experience. We can get some sense of this difference if we start to qualify our terms, but the difference has to be carefully refined; it is not a self-evident aspect of our language. The meaning (the signified) is produced or structured by the two words or signifiers. So we could argue that the way we think and carve up our world depends upon the distinctions of our specific language. In English (unlike German), we do not have two signifiers for 'experience' so we do not have two meanings. For the structuralists there is no meaning outside the system of signifiers. The differences of a language produce meanings, produce consciousness or produce our world. These language differences are in themselves meaningless: the sounds of our language are so much noise, script is so much material marking. But sound and script make sense because they are systematised, repeated and exchanged. We know what a word means not because we grasp some mental event of the speaker, but because we also use, exchange and repeat the same system. When we 'translate' from one language to another, we move from one set of differences into another.

The key challenge of Deleuze's thought lies in its acceptance of the problem of both genesis and structure. On the one hand, against Hegel, we have to recognise the positivity of difference. There is no origin (such as consciousness) that must negate the world in order to think the world, for consciousness itself must already be differentiated. Difference is therefore not grounded on anything other than itself. It is only through difference that we can think of any origin, including consciousness. On the other hand, Deleuze will not accept that there just 'is' a structure of differences. He insists on thinking the genesis or emergence of difference: how is it that we have a system of differentiated signs, such as a language? How did we come to think of ourselves as differentiated from the world, as subjects? Deleuze insists that we have to confront this problem by thinking difference positively. Only positive difference can explain the emergence of any differentiated thing, whether that be the system of differences of a language or the differentiated human individual. Thinking difference positively is no easy task, however, for it is the very nature of thought, as common sense, to accept a world of already given identities and to subordinate difference to the relations among those identities. Positive difference must therefore destroy the pacifying and stabilising intellect of common sense; it must allow thought to move beyond a logic of fixed terms. For Deleuze, positive difference is not so much a theory or proposition as it is an eternal challenge. We tend to perceive the world as already differentiated; we do not, for example, perceive the differential genetic powers that produce organisms. At any time that we try to think of the difference that produces distinct terms, we tend to label it, identify it and subordinate it once again to common sense and representation.

The next chapter will chart Deleuze's resistance to the negativity of difference, but will also look at why such negativity is a constant tendency for thinking.

2

The politics of life and positive difference

Negative difference

According to structuralism, the world in itself is neither meaningful nor identifiable. We do not have a world of present meanings that we then re-present—rather, the world is made meaningful or differentiated through structures. Like Hegel, the main example used by structuralism was that of human language, and one of the foremost structuralists was the linguist Ferdinand de Saussure, who made the famous remark that 'in language there are only differences without positive terms' (de Saussure 1960, p. 120). Deleuze, however, insisted that difference was positive, so we need to understand what negative difference means.

To say that difference is negative refers to a number of features. First, we know that difference negates; it is because one sign is defined against another that it makes sense. We have a different sense of what blue is and what green is because we have two words, and a structure that divides one from the other. We have a sense of what an adolescent is and what a child is because we have two signifiers or words, but we can easily imagine a culture that made no such distinction or differentiation. Thus these terms are not positive because in themselves they mean nothing; they can only have meaning when placed within a system of other terms. Most importantly, the negativity of difference means that difference is not something that exists or is experienceable; we cannot say that difference *is*. I can point to a chair or a table, but I cannot point to the difference between a chair and a table. Indeed I can only have something that *is* once I have a system of differences that identify or recognise it. No experience is self-present or positive (it always relies on what it *is not* or what is not present). When I experience this as 'blue' I am already identifying it according to a recognisable, repeatable and differentiated sign. Before there are any beings or identities there are relations of difference, and a relation is not something that we experience; it is what makes experience possible.

Negative difference and psychoanalysis

This primacy of language, or the Symbolic order, was also expressed in psychoanalytic terms (it was the critique of negative difference in psychoanalysis that motivated Deleuze and Guattari's *Anti-Oedipus*). It is only possible for me to think of myself as a subject or 'I' if I have a system of signs within which I can speak and refer to myself. Anything that I might want to say must be articulated within a system that is not my own. Indeed, I only have a sense of my self *because* I speak; and yet my speech is always articulated through some sort of system or structure that is not, and cannot be, unique to me. (The structure of a language or the Symbolic is never presented to me; I am installed within it and subjected to its order. It remains absent and Other.) The French psychoanalyst Jacques Lacan (1901–81) argued that the speaking subject was possible only through an alien (or Other) order of speech (Lacan 1977). Anything we might demand must be subjected to a system of signs or a Symbolic order. When I speak it is not 'I' who am speaking; rather language speaks through me. 'I' am an effect of the system of signifiers, rather than its author. For Lacan—and this was important for Deleuze and Guattari's critique—desire was negative. If all my demands and wants must pass through the order of language, then what I can ask for or demand will only be representable through the social conventions of language. What I desire can only be imagined as other than any articulable demand. I will necessarily imagine a desire or fulfilment that lies forever out of reach: that inexpressible origin or presence that can never be grasped through the general system of signs within which we are all located. We are essentially alienated from our desire, for insofar as 'I' am, I am already within speech, system and order. And if speech is systemic and differential, or possible only because of a structure that is never fully present, then we are always dislocated from presence. We are necessarily within difference, and any presence that we might think of, or desire, is only thinkable through a difference or signifier. We desire presence, to have what *is*, but our desire must be articulated through a system that *is not*. Desire is negative because what is desired can only be imagined as other than the signifier. It is only because we have signifiers, or the signs of a language, that we can then imagine, mourn and desire what lies beyond our language. What we desire is imagined to be what is lost or negated when we submit to the structures of language, culture and meaning. According to Lacan, it is because humans speak that they are necessarily alienated from their desire. Indeed, desire—the imagination of a presence that lies beyond the differences of language—is an effect of language (Lacan 1977).

One of the main challenges to Deleuze's work today comes from those who still follow Hegel and Lacan by insisting on negativity. Even if we could conclude, as Deleuze insists, that life is full, productive and positive, Lacanians argue that we never think or live life this way. Insofar as I speak, I must submit myself to a law of language and I will necessarily desire what lies beyond that law; I will also require some symptom or object that seems to compensate for, or stand in the way of, my full enjoyment. Without the fantasy of one who is standing in the way of my desire I would have to accept that my desire is essentially unattainable, precisely because it is the negation of all thought and system. For Zizek, this explains the necessity of the cultural 'symptom' (Zizek 1992). If we did not imagine ourselves as having lost some original enjoyment, desire or presence we would have no self or identity at all. We need the fantasy of the migrant, the lost love or the trauma in order to imagine the origin or fullness of which we have been deprived. Without the trauma of subjection to some imagined law or other we would have no identity (Butler 1997). The challenge of Deleuze's work lies in not accepting the necessity of negativity: we can, he insists, think a desire that is positive in itself, and not just what lies beyond all law, systems and structures. To pursue this project of positive difference, we have to accept first that difference is not just imposed by language on the world; difference is not a single system or structure to which we, as speaking subjects, must 'submit'.

Language was not the only object of structuralist analysis, and the argument for the primacy of difference extended across all domains of culture and human life. Claude Lévi-Strauss was an anthropologist who argued that social structures could only be understood through systems of difference. He reversed the standard way in which we understand the formation of human societies, and it was this reversal that ultimately enabled an entirely new approach to political theory in structuralism and post-structuralism (Lévi-Strauss 1968). Deleuze and Guattari rely heavily on Lévi-Strauss precisely because—against psycho-analysis—he does not assume that individuals begin in nuclear families but sees them as defined through tribal and collective systems.

We tend to explain the emergence of social structures by looking at the ways in which individuals form groups. We argue that individuals form societies to express their collective interests, so the State could be understood as an expression of a general will. Or, we argue that individuals have to submit to the State or allow the State to curb their interests because individuals in a state of nature would be aggressive, destructive and self-seeking. Either way, we assume that social structures—such as the State—arise from individuals and human interests. Lévi-Strauss offered (at least) two objections to this type of understanding. First, individuals do not precede social structures; it is only through the structure of social relations that I can think of myself as an individual or 'human'. Second, these social structures of exchange produce human interest.

The signifier: Structuralism

Let us take the first point raised by Lévi-Strauss. The production of human interests is the specific focus of Deleuze and Guattari's own work on desire, where they argue that desires precede and organise interests and persons; desires begin pre-personally—say, as the desire for food by the mouth, which then becomes an interest between the persons of mother and child. Before considering desire in detail we can focus on the ways in which structuralism argues that systems of relations, rather than specific desires, produce individuals or distinct terms. For structuralism, human beings as individuals are produced through the differentiations of social systems. On the usual picture we would think that I understand myself as an individual because I have an identity—a sex, a nationality and so on. But Lévi-Strauss showed how such identities were produced through exchange. It is only through relations to others that I have an 'I' at all, and such relations to others occur through exchange—the exchange of goods, of women or symbols. This cultural system of exchange occurs with an imposition of a system of differences over an otherwise undifferentiated or 'unmediated' nature. Life becomes cultural when simple biological needs are deferred for higher ends; rather than immediate sexual gratification and reproduction, we relate to others through marriages or kinship structures. Biology is no longer immediate but is represented through a system of culture. For Lévi-Strauss this move away from biological life to culture occurred through the prohibition on incest and the exchange of women.

On a representational or common-sense model there are simply men and women who enter relations of marriage or kinship and then gather into societies. Structuralist anthropology reverses this relation. The identity of individuals, especially their sexual identity, is an effect of a system of exchange. (Indeed, much French thought after the Second World War insisted that the very being of human life was an effect of kinship or marriage systems, an effect of the differentiation of human life through exchange. Much of Deleuze and Guattari's *Anti-Oedipus* is an extension and critique of this explanation.) The structuralist argument goes something like this: in order to speak to you and recognise you as human, I have to have a general concept of recognition (some notion of 'man', 'subject' or 'individual'). The very basis of speech is that I take what you say as meaningful, as the expression of some subject which I can recognise. This was why Lacan insisted that the subject was an effect of speech, but that speech—to be meaningful—also required the effect of a subject. In order to speak I must recognise what you say as human language, but I also require language in order to have a concept of the human. So I need a signifier of a being who signifies. For Lacan, then, 'a signifier is that which represents the subject for another signifier' (Lacan 1977, p. 316). We have to relate to each other through some shared concept or signifier. But in order to get this process of a shared system going we must have not just a system of marks but the idea that these marks or sounds signify. There must be some signifier that signifies signification. What you say to me is not just noise; I have to have the concept of meaning in order to posit a sense behind what you say. Thus according to Lacan there has to be one signifier that gives me this concept of meaning; it is not just one word among others but the signifier that gets the whole system going. If signification is, in general, a sign that stands in for what is not present, then this signifier of all signifiers, or 'transcendental signifier', is the signifier of what is absent, not present. This signifier signifies that towards which all meaning and speaking is directed; it signifies a promised or deferred presence. In order to speak or have a symbolic system, Lacan argued, we have to imagine some presence outside that system to which all speech is referring. There is an 'Imaginary' or fantasy of lost presence which allows a system to function as a system of exchange, for we exchange signifiers in order to arrive at sense, meaning or presence (what is other than the system of signifiers).

All language or speech presupposes a relation between the given signifier (the word which we hear or read) and the signified, which is not given or is absent (the meaning). There must be a transcendental signifier that underpins this system; a signifier of presence towards which all speech and exchange is aimed. For Lacan this transcendental signifier is the phallic signifier, for

it is the phallus that is the first imagined absence. It is in perceiving the mother as not-having 'all' that the child turns to speech,
so speech must have the power of that which the mother lacks
(the phallus). Speech stands in for an imagined presence that is
now lost, but which we try to regain. All speech therefore has the
structure of desire, for our signifiers always strive to re-present
what is not, or is no longer, present. The very idea of the signifier is therefore one of lack and negative difference, of what *is not*.
Without the system of signifiers we would have no way of
thinking what is not present, and we would have no human and
shared world. (In *Anti-Oedipus* Deleuze and Guattari refer to the
'despotic' signifier, and show how the social form of the State
requires this quite specific notion of language as shared signification, standing-in for some lost presence.)

For structuralism, recognition between any two human
beings—any self and other—already requires some system or
culture to which they are both subordinate. In order for me to
speak to you, and for us to recognise each other as speaking
beings, there must be the system of signifiers *and* the notion that
the signifier stands in for, or represents—some meaning, presence
or subject. There is a 'third term' which allows any two subjects
to exist in relation to each other; this third term (such as language
or signification) is what structures, differentiates or orders human
exchange. Human relations are essentially mediated. The question is (or was for the structuralists) just how we move from
the meaningless, instinctual and undifferentiated realm of nature
to the meaningful system of culture. The answer lay in incest
prohibition and the exchange of women. First, human life has to
subordinate nature and need to some higher end. The animal has
a need that it immediately fulfils, but humans conceptualise,
order and regulate their needs. Most importantly, as Lacan
pointed out, human needs first have to be addressed to an other,
for we are born dependent on an other (maternal) being who must
answer our demands. Humans articulate their needs in language,
which means that they are no longer just needs, strictly speaking,
but become demands. Demands are articulated within a shared,
recognisable social form, such as language. In speaking of my
needs I therefore abandon my immediate relation to objects of

desire and allow my desire to be structured by language. I take part in a system of law.

This subjection to the law of language is possible only by renouncing the immediate object of natural fulfilment (the mother). Once I speak about, request or demand what I need, I have to situate myself in a system of signs. My desire is now meaningful, signified and structured through language. But this language is never adequate to the needs expressed in it. Indeed, we necessarily imagine some desire or presence above and beyond the specific words we use to express our desires. In order for language to work, or be meaningful, I have to imagine that these signs we exchange are more than mere noise or script, that they signify some sense. I have to posit a signified behind the signifiers, a meaning or sense behind the word, or a subject behind speech. I have to posit or imagine some object or value for which these signifiers are exchanged, some presence which is substituted by representation. If I am subjected to this system of lawful signs (the Symbolic), then I imagine that there was some renounced object that was lacking (but which the law promises). If speech or the symbolic order is the order of the signifier, exchange and recognition, then I imagine the pre-Symbolic as lacking recognition or signification. It is only by being other than maternal that signification opens up.

This is why the signifier is phallic (for Lacan) and despotic (for Deleuze and Guattari). The signifier is the negation of natural desire, and is what the maternal original object lacks. When marriage structures are formed, women are no longer the immediate objects of desire; women are exchanged and function as signifiers. What is desired is that subjects recognise each other as other than natural, as beings who speak, as beings who have renounced nature (the feminine/maternal) for culture (the phallic/symbolic). Law must be other than, or the negation of, immediate nature. We accede to law because nature lacks the order of signification, system and recognition. The phallus is the signifier in general, other than lack, or that which stands in for presence.

This means that language or culture must open up an opposition between those who recognise each other through an agreed system of exchange and the objects of exchange. (These objects are not valuable in themselves, but only valuable for producing relations between members of a culture or system.) The key argument from structuralist anthropology is that the first event of exchange or differentiation—the one that inaugurates culture—is the exchange of women. Human recognition, Lévi-Strauss argued, occurs with the prohibition of incest, or the demand that sexual relations be governed by kinship structures of exchange; sexual desire is regulated by law. We prohibit sexual desire with certain persons (mothers, sisters) and prescribe marriage with others (members of other tribes or clans). It is only with this original prohibition that desire is submitted to law and culture is opened. All language, meaning and recognition require this passage from the immediacy of nature to the mediation, negation and law of culture. Women become the tokens or signifiers of exchange in general; in exchanging women 'we' recognise ourselves as not merely natural, but as speaking, cultural or human beings. The very opposition between men and women is produced through social exchange and incest prohibition. The feminine is that which is renounced or negated to become human. This is why Lacan argues that 'woman does not exist', and why he defines the feminine as a function of lack (Lacan 1982). The logic of sexual difference begins with $-\varphi$ (minus *phi*, or that which lacks the phallus). We must imagine a lack at the heart of presence or the origin in order to account for the signifier as re-presentation, what presence or the origin lacks.

To a greater or lesser extent all structuralists insisted on the two outcomes that followed from this theory of the primacy of exchange. The first is the primacy of the signifier. All human life is human only in its location within systems of signifiers. Marriage does not fulfil a biological need; it is the outcome of one's subjection to a social system. The same applies to food, fashion and any recognisable practice of life. Any human act is already located within a system of meaning and is significant; it sends a message. The second is that all these activities are also necessarily culturally coded. We may have to eat, live in a house and wear clothing, and there may be some material or necessary constraints on the differences between what we choose. There is no meaning in itself that can be attached to a leather jacket, but this item of clothing signifies because it is located in a system of signs. It may serve the same function as a woollen sports jacket. It may even cost the same. But a leather jacket can signify masculinity or toughness, while a sports jacket can signify refinement. And if I want to not take part in the fashion system, by wearing punk, grunge or 'alternative' styles, this is still a social message, a signifier that says 'I am not taking part'. We cannot avoid meaning, precisely because these systems are trans-individual. We do not choose languages; we are situated within them.

Capitalism and Oedipus

Structuralist psychoanalysts such as Lacan insisted that subjection to the Symbolic order was essentially oedipal. Because we must submit to law or system, and articulate our desire through signifiers, we imagine some lost original object that was prohibited. This fantasised lost origin is the prohibited mother, and the law to which we submit is imagined as the law of the father. It is just this all-encompassing law of Oedipus and lack which Deleuze and Guattari target in *Anti-Oedipus.* They agree that modernity and capitalism do indeed function through the image of law, lack and the individual; but they argue that this is because we are not asking the question of difference properly. If we accept that difference and desire are negative, then desire will be defined by what we are not or what we do not have, and so there will necessarily be some lost object towards which desire tends. Similarly, if we accept that difference is the effect of some overarching system (such as the system of signifiers), then difference will be imagined as a law to which we are subjected, a law that deprives us of immediacy and presence. And this is where, according to Deleuze and Guattari, the theory of difference connects with capitalism and individualism. Capital quantifies all desire and production according to the general (and exchangeable) equivalence of money and labour. Individualism demands that we all recognise ourselves as human, as subjects, as selves: equal, exchangeable and unified. So capitalism and modernity are oedipal: they both work on the notion of a difference that is nothing more than the relations between equivalent units produced by subjection to a universal and inescapable law. And we can only have this idea of a uniform and imposed system of difference if, oedipally, we see difference as a law that prohibits, and saves us from, the undifferentiated, unmediated and absent origin. But, Deleuze and Guattari insist, desire and difference extend well beyond the 'imaginary' or myth of capitalism. We need to see difference as something other than an imposed system of differentiation or the negative prohibition of law (other than castration or the threat of the father and law). This will enable us to understand desire as productive and positive, and not just that which is excluded by submission to the system of signification.

Deleuze and Guattari regarded this theory of structuralist psychoanalysis, which ties the system of signification to the Oedipus complex, not as a recent invention but as the very truth of modern desire. We imagine that there is some origin, presence or lost maternal plenitude behind the system of signs within which we are installed. And we also imagine that if we have lost that originary fullness then there must have been some prohibiting law or father who robbed us of our enjoyment. The whole system is built on original guilt and loss. There has been, Deleuze and Guattari argue, from the opening of civilisation, an imagined centre to the system of signification. Originally it is the social and political figure of the king or despot who we imagine as the author or origin of law. In modernity and capitalism this social and political figure is given an oedipal interpretation; it is the father (or the imagined fantasised father in my unconscious) who imposes law. We imagine some lost (maternal) object for which we exchange signifiers, and for which we renounce our specific desires, in order to enter the (father's) order of speech and symbolisation.

Psychoanalysis, Deleuze and Guattari argue, has diagnosed modernity correctly. We have 'internalised' and fantasised our submission to a system of difference through the image of the punishing father, the prohibited mother and the phallus (or ultimate presence) that no one can possess but that we all strive for nevertheless. What Deleuze and Guattari want to do is politicise and historicise this oedipal explanation. How did we come to fantasise the system of difference as the punishing law of the father? How did we arrive at a 'familial' interpretation? Even more radically, how is it that we have come to see difference as an imposed system that differentiates a life that would otherwise be undifferentiated, meaningless or beyond any possible experience?

In their theory of desire, Deleuze and Guattari attack the notion that desire begins from lack. It is not that there is some (imagined) lost or lacking origin that we try to represent and retrieve through all our subsequent objects of desire. Psychoanalysis, they argue, has created the value of the phallus through its own explanation—that is, there must be some imagined object (the phallus) for which we abandon the maternal origin and submit to the system of exchange, law and signification. Deleuze and Guattari's theory of productive desire reverses the relation between desire and lack. (We will look at their account of desire later, in Chapter 6.) What needs to be grasped here is the structuralist theory of difference and its connection with lack, subjectivity and the idea of the signifier.

For structuralism the system of differences that enables us to know the world is necessarily experienced as Other. We submit to a general system of language. Difference is a system imposed on an otherwise undifferentiated and meaningless 'presence'. This system creates us as subjects, creates a world of objects and enables us to think of different beings. For structural psychoanalysis, it is this experience of language as a lawful order that produces a myth or fantasy of oedipal subjection: I imagine that there was some pure presence prior to differentiation (maternal plenitude); I imagine that 'I' abandoned this origin and submitted to this system for some end or law (the phallus, social recognition, or what can only be held by another and never presented in itself). However, 'I' am nothing outside this oedipal fantasy; 'I' am an effect of the speaking system. Subjectivity is an imagined presence behind signification that is necessarily lost, lacking, alienated and absent.

Positive difference

The structuralist and, more generally, modern argument for the primacy of difference is usually interpreted as a radical break in the history of ideas. The argument goes something like this: we used to think of a world of meaningful entities, each with their own essence and way of being, ruled by a God or nature that guaranteed the 'truth' and 'order' of this reality. In modernity, however, we realised that the world is only meaningful through the language or differences we impose on it. It is only through the human subject's acts of speech, knowledge or 'construction' that we have a world of different beings, a world of meanings, or a reality. This means that we shift from the idea of a world of identities that we then come to know and represent, to a system of differences that we impose on the world, such that knowledge and representation actually constitute the world. In the eighteenth century this system of differences was described by referring to the concepts or ideas that we impose on the world. In the twentieth century it was described as a structure of signifiers. The structuralists argued that we couldn't even have concepts without some material system (of sounds or marks) that enabled us to conceptualise.

Deleuze is in agreement with structuralism (and Hegel) that difference, rather than identity, is primary. But he differs from structuralism by arguing that difference is not an imposed system, nor is it a system. Difference is not a set of relations. Difference is neither the relation between one identical thing and another (as in common sense), nor is difference the general system that creates a world of objects (as in structuralism). For Deleuze, difference is itself different in each of its affirmations: sexual difference between bodies is different in each case (although we generalise and refer to men and women); genetic difference creates differently in each mutation (although we generalise and refer to species); visual differences are in each case different (although we generalise and refer to the colour spectrum). Life itself is difference, and this difference is in each case different.

Whereas structuralism is usually seen as a radical break with the western history of identity thinking—or the assumption of some ultimate presence or foundation—Deleuze argues that structuralism is really not such a breakthrough. Pre-modern thought had grounded the truth, being and identity of the world on God. All differences emanated from this undifferentiated origin. Each being had its own essence in some divine hierarchical whole (and difference was just the relation among self-identical essences). In modern thought, while difference is regarded as primary, it is still grounded in the subject. Differentiation, for the structuralists, was produced by human signifying systems. It is the speaking subject who differentiates the world into specific identities, and differentiation issues from a structure (such as language, culture, myth, marriage exchange systems and so on). The supposed radical shift from God to man, Deleuze argues, is no shift at all (Deleuze 1990). Even the supposed anti-humanism of structuralism—the fact that no single human authors the system that makes speech possible—is still a form of subjectivism. For difference still originates from some subject (or grounding origin), even if that subject is 'language' or 'culture' in general. Difference is still organised around some centre or structure.

Against this notion of difference as imposed and structured, Deleuze will argue that difference is positive and singular. Difference is positive, because there is not an undifferentiated life that then needs to be structured by difference. Life itself is differential. Think of the way any living being exists; it is in a state of constant becoming or differentiation. Second, difference is singular because each event of life differentiates itself differently. There are linguistic differences, but there are also genetic differences, sensible differences (such as those of colour, tone, timbre and texture), chemical differences, animal differences and imperceptible differences. In fact, the very essence of difference is its imperceptibility; a perceived difference has already been identified, reduced or 'contracted'. When we perceive the difference between red and blue we do so only because we do not perceive the difference of each vibration of light; our eye contracts complex data into a single shade or object of red or blue.

Curves and inflections

According to Deleuze the structuralist and common-sense location of difference within a system renders difference both negative and extensive. In the common-sense view difference is negative because it depends on being the relation between things that are in themselves self-present and identical. So difference is secondary. And Structuralist difference is also negative; it is the differentiation *within* some undifferentiated being—again making difference dependent on some structure which differentiates. Structural difference is given only through its effects, and the effect is that of the system—and thus difference is ultimately traced back to an identity (such as language, structure or culture) which we can never grasp in itself. For structuralism, there is supposedly some single medium or agent of difference, even if this is signification, culture or language in general. All difference has been reduced to one governing system or form of difference, and so what is primary is not difference at all, but some thing that differentiates. In the structuralist picture, difference is what divides, 'cuts up' or organises some supposedly pre-linguistic or pre-differential real. The 'real' is therefore out of reach, other, lost, lacking. Reality is now constructed or 'synthesised'.

Against this negative understanding of difference, Deleuze insists that difference is positive. It is not that there is some undifferentiated real that we then differentiate through language. There are real differences and becomings that are far greater (or smaller) than the differences we mark in language. We cannot enclose difference or synthesis within human or even organic life. Life itself is difference and synthesis. We cannot even say that each 'point' of life differentiates itself in its own way, because life is not a collection of different or distinct points. It is continuous difference, and between any two points that we might locate on this continuum of difference there is an infinity of further difference, each different in 'its' own way. Rather than understanding the world as a totality of equivalent points, each relating to each other across some unified space, Deleuze refers to curves and inflections (Deleuze 1993). So what we have is not a world which is then differentiated, but curves or inflections: a life of distinct and infinite variations or deviations, while no curve or event of difference and becoming is the same as any other. The 'atoms' or smallest units that make up life are not things but events of difference:

> Inflection is the ideal genetic element of the variable curve or fold. Inflection is the authentic atom, the elastic point ... Bernard Cache defines inflection—or the point of inflection— as an intrinsic singularity. Contrary to 'extrema' (extrinsic singularities, maximum and minimum), it does not refer to coordinates: it is neither high nor low, neither right nor left, neither regression nor progression ... Thus inflection is the pure Event of the line or of the point, the Virtual, ideality par excellence (Deleuze 1993, pp. 14–15).

We could imagine one point of life as apprehending or perceiving another, such that points preceded perception, relation and becoming (mind perceiving world, for example). Or, with Deleuze, we could regard life as a series of curves or inflections. A's relation to, or perception of, B would not be a straight line or direct picture, it would be inflected by the specific manner of what A *is.* And the same would apply to B's relation to A. Relations and differences would be neither uniform nor symmetrical—and this would be because the style or manner of difference would depend on each specific event of difference. (A and B are what they are only because they have their own forms of becoming, or their own tendencies for difference.)

It is only if we locate difference within the human mind or language that we then see what is outside mind or language as undifferentiated. (We tend to think of the absolute or infinite as what lies outside or beyond our knowledge of finite concepts, but Deleuze sees the infinite not as some great beyond, but as infinite difference within life itself: microscopic, imperceptible and inhuman differences.) The negative understanding of difference— difference as a system imposed on some undifferentiated real—is an illusion. It comes from elevating some image of God, man or the subject as the author and origin of all difference. The illusion posits some point outside difference that will then explain and produce difference. For Deleuze this is *the* illusion of thought: the illusion or subjection to transcendence. Instead of accepting one univocal plane of radical difference, where no form of difference can explain or be elevated above any other, we tend to see difference as the difference *of* some being; some transcendent or outside point is erected as the origin of difference.

Transcendence: The plane of transcendence

In *What is Philosophy?* Deleuze and Guattari refer to this illusion of thought as a 'plane of transcendence' (1994, p. 49). That is, we imagine some external or transcendent origin from which difference emerges; we think of some grounding substance that is then differentiated. The plane is transcendent because it is located outside difference; it explains or transcends difference. Against this, Deleuze and Guattari claim that the question and task of thought is the 'plane of immanence', all the different ways in which thought has (from within its own flux of experience) constructed an outside or 'transcendence': 'But if it is true that the plane of immanence is always single, being itself pure variation, then it is all the more necessary to explain why there are varied and distinct planes of immanence that, depending upon which infinite movements are retained and selected, succeed and contest each other in history' (1994, p. 39).

We need a transcendental theory to explain transcendence. A transcendental method does not begin from some thing—some transcendence—but looks at how any thing or transcendence is formed. We need to begin from a plane of immanence with no presumed distinction between an inside and an outside. Beginning from this plane of immanence we then need to see how it is that we think of the world as, say, the difference between mind and a transcendent world. The plane of immanence is the starting point for a transcendental method that does not accept that life takes the form of some already differentiated or transcendent thing. Now, if this plane of immanence is not to function as some ultimate explanatory point outside difference, it cannot be given some final substantive description. Even if we were to give immanence the most general name of all, such as 'being', we would also have to acknowledge that this being is eternally different. No concept or name can step outside the difference of life and name or fix life as such, for life always has the power to produce further events of difference, to go on speaking. Immanence is just this commitment to staying at the level of difference, refusing any external explanation of difference. In refusing transcendence, or some external principle, we also remain committed to the transcendental: there is no point or transcendence outside being or life. We take life as transcendental, as having no ground outside itself. There is, therefore, no being in general, no ultimate ground. Being is different in each of its expressions, and no expression can explain any other. Once we accept that there is no grand being that lies outside difference, and that all being expresses the same plane of immanent difference differently, then we arrive at the equation expressed in *A Thousand Plateaus*: 'PLURALISM = MONISM' (Deleuze & Guattari 1987, p. 20).

The commitment to one univocal being (or monism) precludes us from separating some distinct being as a centre or foundation; all beings are located on a single plane (pluralism). Only a dualism could give us a being that has some sort of foundation. We need two types of being in order to have a ground/foundation set against what is grounded. Only with dualism, or 'equivocity', could we subtract this foundation (such as God, consciousness or reason) from what it grounds. But if being is univocal and immanent then no point of difference can be privileged over any other: 'Univocal Being is at one and the same time nomadic distribution and crowned anarchy' (Deleuze 1994, p. 37). Deleuze's near contemporary, French philosopher Alain Badiou, has insisted on the primacy of the concept of univocity in Deleuze's work. For Badiou, the very challenge of Deleuze's thought lies in whether we can conceptualise a single being that is nothing more than its different expressions (Badiou 2000). If being is univocal this means that any thought or representation that we have of being is itself an event of being. All the images and concepts we have of being are not pictures, metaphors or representations of being; they are beings in their own right. There is not being plus representation. Univocal being demands that we think all that is as within being, as immanent to life. But this also means that we need to confront all the different ways in which this immanent plane of life becomes: not just through art, science and philosophy, but also in genetics, geology or microbiology. So, alongside immanence and univocity Deleuze's work also focuses on difference. For if there really is only one univocal plane of being, then no single differentiated being will be able to account for a life that is infinitely different:

> The essence of univocal being is to include individuating
> differences while these differences do not have the same
> essence and do not change the essence of being—just as
> white includes various intensities while remaining essentially
> the same white.
> ... Being is said in a single and same sense of everything of
> which it is said, but that of which it is said differs: it is said of
> difference itself ... It is not a matter of being which is
> distributed according to the requirements of representation,
> but of all things being divided up within being in the
> univocity of simple presence (the One–All). Such a difference
> is demonic rather than divine ... Univocal being is at one and
> the same time nomadic distribution and crowned anarchy
> (Deleuze 1984, pp. 36–7).

We cannot explain difference through consciousness, language, concepts or structure. When Deleuze and Guattari do use general terms, such as being, desire or life, to describe the plane of immanence, they also have to take great care to insist on the differential nature of these terms. That is, desire is not some substance that remains the same; it is becoming. Life is not a ground or foundation, not an inert matter or substance, which then needs to be given meaning or form; life is dynamic and open becoming.

The problem, Deleuze insists, is that becoming has always been thought of as the becoming of some prior agent, subject or substance. Indeed, this problem is inherent in our grammar and way of thinking. We attach verbs to nouns, and our propositions tend to ground actions, predicates and events on subjects. In order to think difference and becoming more radically—as positive and intensive—we need to think and write differently. This would mean moving beyond subject/predicate propositions to, for example, infinitives. Instead of thinking that there are beings that then have qualities and actions, we need to think of activity and quality from which thought then abstracts beings. Instead of thinking that there are pre-given objects—a tree which is green, a subject who thinks—the infinitive expresses the event: 'to green', 'to think': 'The infinitive—"to think," "to green," "to act," "to write," "to be"—does not admit of a division between what something is and what it does. There is the event itself and not some prior transcendence of which the event would be an act' (Deleuze 1990, p. 221).

Politics of perception: Univocity

Deleuze and Guattari's *Anti-Oedipus* and *A Thousand Plateaus* both examine difference in its social and political dimensions. What makes these two volumes of *Capitalism and Schizophrenia* so significant is that they directly politicise the analyses of perception and difference that Deleuze had undertaken in his earlier 'philosophical' texts. He had argued as early as 1968 that 'representation' traces differences and perceptions back to some grounding or 'metaphysical' subject (Deleuze 1994). Later, with Guattari, he shows the diverse political forms this reduction of difference will take. Both *Anti-Oedipus* and *A Thousand Plateaus* tie the productive nature of difference, with its formation of 'souls' or 'territories', to the formation of the State. It is only after we see perceptions as the perceptions of subjects that we can have something like the modern individual. We will look at this in the later chapter on desire, but it is important at this stage to see how Deleuze ties his philosophy of difference to desire and ethics. If we imagine difference as a system imposed on an otherwise formless being or matter, then we will always have subjected difference to some differentiating or organising power. Our thinking, our morality and our politics will have some tran-scendent point outside difference (such as 'man', 'language' or 'culture'). On the other hand, however, if there is just one univocal plane of difference, with no transcendent outside, then ethics and politics cannot adopt some separate position of judgement. The task of thinking and ethics will be one of *amor fati* ('love of what is'): not judging what is, but rather living up to the differences of life:

> Nothing more can be said, and no more has ever been said: to become worthy of what happens to us, and thus to will and release the event, to become the offspring of one's own events, and thereby to be reborn, to have one more birth, and to break with one's carnal birth—to become the offspring of one's events and not of one's actions, for the action is itself produced by the offspring of the event (Deleuze 1990, pp. 149–50).

Perception will no longer be a window onto some outside world; it will itself be an encounter or event of difference, an active or desiring becoming. Not a perception and then the object perceived, but interacting perceptions each producing itself and its other through the encounter. In a univocal plane of being we do not divide the world into perceivers and perceived; there are just perceptions from which relatively stable points are effected. Imagine if we could perceive all the differences that confront us: each ray of light, each sound wave. We would not have a 'world' so much as a vast and chaotic influx of data. We perceive 'things' by slowing difference down. Deleuze also uses the word 'contraction' to describe the ways in which one living being manages to form or experience its world from the flow of difference and becoming. In keeping with the attempt to not subdue difference by explaining its emergence from one single point, Deleuze uses different terminologies and different modes of difference: speed and slowness, territorialisation and deterritorialisation, contraction and contemplation. All these forms of difference are themselves different. But throughout there lies a challenge of 'becoming-imperceptible', of not remaining at the level of different beings or things but of confronting all those microscopic differences that our perception—for the purposes of life—has reduced to identity or sameness.

If movement is imperceptible by nature, it is so always in relation to a given threshold of perception, which is by nature relative and thus plays the role of a mediation on the plane that effects the distribution of thresholds and percepts and makes forms perceivable to perceiving subjects. It is the plane of organization and development, the plane of transcendence, that renders perceptible without itself being perceived, without being capable of being perceived. But on the *other* plane, the plane of immanence or consistency, the principle of composition itself must be perceived, cannot but be perceived at the same time as that which it composes or renders (Deleuze & Guattari 1987, p. 281).

More importantly, difference needs to be rendered positive by being de-subjectivised. There is not a subject who differs or perceives; there is difference from which subjects and substance are 'contracted'. Deleuze's arguments for forms of difference that exceed language and human life are both historical and geological. Historically, Deleuze and Guattari argue that there were forms of differentiation prior to language. Geologically, the extended human individual must be formed from flows of intensive difference, not just the formation of the body as a bounded organism but also the formation of the person or self from tribal wholes or territories. Before there are beings who speak, human life must go through a series of 'territorialisations'. (This is the terminology of *Anti-Oedipus* and *A Thousand Plateaus*.)

The intense germinal influx and territorialisation

Radically, imagine a pure flow of genetic material—what Deleuze and Guattari refer to as the 'intense germinal influx'—whereby there are just streams of 'human' life, not yet organised into individuals. Both animals and humans group themselves into 'territories', and in so doing create spatial differences on the earth. (Indeed, they create the 'earth'. Only after cutting space up into territories can we think of the earth as some general ground upon which territories are located.) The earth is not some undifferentiated mass; it is already differential. Molecules, particles and all forms of imperceptible differences become the general plane of the earth only with territorialisation. We only imagine the earth as some undifferentiated and inert mass that is there to be differentiated after the process of territorialisation. Systems of difference such as language, kinship, tribes and persons do not differentiate some pre-given mass; on the contrary, they reduce difference. In territorialisation we go from a flow of genetic differences to the organisation of those differences into a recognisable group of similar bodies. How do we think of a collection of human beings as belonging to the same tribe? How do we establish filiations or genealogies, such as the relations between fathers and sons? Only by first establishing orders of alliance. The collective gene pool with its dynamic, impersonal and virtual differences must be ordered into sameness: this tribe against that tribe. Only then can we have father/son relations within tribes (or lines of filiation).

So kinship systems or structures of exchange and relations rest upon creative differences that form specific territories. Tribes are formed through the reduction of a complex genetic flux that recognises only certain perceptible differences and the creation of some 'territory' or intensity that can assemble those differences (such as when a tribe might be marked out by a colour, animal, mythic symbol or body part).

This challenges the structuralist argument for negative difference, the idea that tribal relations impose a system of cultural difference on an otherwise undifferentiated human nature. Whereas the structuralist begins with a general concept of human life that is differentiated by social codes, for Deleuze, tribes and territorialisation reduce or 'code' an infinite proliferation of differences. More importantly, the structuralist begins with the family, such as the mother–child–father relation of filiation, and then explains how this supposedly natural relation enters into cultural alliance. For Deleuze only the relations of alliance—the social and political differences from one tribe to another—can produce the family (a group of individuals who recognise each other as the same).

Synthesis and the repression of difference

For Deleuze, the world is the outcome of taking an infinite and open array of difference and reducing it to manageable identities. Generally he describes this process as 'synthesis'. There is the synthesis of mind, whereby we connect a cause and an effect, and the synthesis of life, whereby molecules, body parts, bodies and sensations connect to form more complex assemblages. In *Anti-Oedipus* and *A Thousand Plateaus* Deleuze and Guattari write a history of the syntheses that lead up to the modern State and the individual. There are two key features to Deleuze's overall understanding of synthesis. First, there are prehuman syntheses, such as the imperceptible differences of life (forms) that are not organisms or subjects (Deleuze 1994). Second, this process of synthesis has a politics and a history culminating in capitalism (Deleuze & Guattari 1983). (This is explained in Chapter 5, on desire.) Synthesis is the becoming of life itself, the connection of creative differences into further lines of creation. Synthesis is productive and positive difference. It is not difference as the differentiation of, or relation between, beings; it refers to the connections of becomings (an animal connecting with a plant, a man connecting with an animal, a human body connecting with another body).

Deleuze makes difference positive by reversing the order of difference and the undifferentiated. Structuralists felt that language differentiated an amorphous and undifferentiated mass—we only perceive the difference between blue and grey, for example, or trees and shrubs, because our language gives us distinct words. Deleuze argues the contrary: language reduces difference. Only through the process of synthesis do we recognise radically differing perceptions as 'blue'. We do not differentiate life; life is a flow of difference that constantly challenges us, provokes us and confronts us. Indeed, there would be no 'us', no notion of the human or the subject, if the full positivity of difference could be felt. It is only because we do not perceive the totality of differences, only because our perception slows down and 'selects' difference, that we form ourselves as distinct zones or minds within difference. 'We', like all other souls, are the contractions and contemplations of difference, an oscillation between how much difference we take in (contemplation) and how much difference we reduce or do not perceive (contraction):

> It is simultaneously through contraction that we are habits, but through contemplation that we contract. We are contemplations, we are imaginations, we are generalities, claims and satisfactions ... We do not contemplate ourselves, but we exist only in contemplating—that is to say, in contracting that from which we come ... To contemplate is to draw something from. We must first contemplate something else—the water, or Diana, or the woods—in order to be filled with an image of ourselves ... Underneath the self which acts are little selves which contemplate and which render possible both the action and the active subject. We speak of our 'self' only by virtue of these thousands of little witnesses which contemplate within us: it is always a third party who says 'me' (Deleuze 1994, pp. 74–5).

The challenge of all thought, then, is to think these molecular differences from which 'we' emerge. But we also need to understand why the history of western thought has worked in the opposite direction, beginning with the unified subject rather than the 'genetic element' of difference itself. According to Deleuze and Guattari, the homogenisation, subordination and subjection of difference to identity have characterised the process of human history leading up to capitalism and psychoanalysis. We now imagine only one system of difference—the subjective signification of the world (or the social construction of reality)—and have an Oedipus complex to explain it. We imagine that we submitted to a system of difference, or language, in order to achieve recognition as human speaking subjects. In so doing, we supposedly gave up an original plenitude because of lack and the threat of castration; we chose to renounce the undifferentiated and obey the order of signifiers. We think of difference as human and cultural, imposed on an otherwise inert and undifferentiated nature.

Like psychoanalysis and the fantasy of the individual,

capitalism also reduces difference to the figure of 'man', erasing the ways in which difference emerges from pre-human and collective processes of territorialisation. In capitalism we locate difference within one system of exchange—the economy—with 'man' or the individual being the agent of a uniform exchangeable and quantifiable labour. Difference is again reduced to a system to which we submit and within which we are located. We often criticise capitalism from a humanist position, arguing that our true individuality has been alienated in the impersonal system of capital. For Deleuze and Guattari, though, the problem with capitalism is its 'humanity' and 'personality', for it relies on seeing all difference as reducible to the system of labour and exchange, to some general notion of the human worker. At the heart of capital is the unit of the oedipal individual, the self whose desires can ultimately be explained and translated through one single, quantifiable and exchangeable value. What is repressed is not our humanity and individuality; it is the idea of the human individual that represses chaotic, inhuman and dynamic difference: 'Man must constitute himself through the repression of the intense germinal influx, the great biocosmic memory that threatens to deluge every attempt at collectivity' (Deleuze & Guattari 1983, p. 190).

Man, they argue, does not repress his oedipal desire for his mother. Understanding desire in familial terms is repression itself: reducing the intensive flows of desire to images of persons. Both capitalism and psychoanalysis explain desire from the individual, but the individual is the outcome of a reduction and homogenisation of difference. The concept of the individual is itself repressive or reactionary, reactionary because it grounds all desires on some prior value of the self. This is why Deleuze and Guattari historicise the individual's emergence from desire, and in so doing hope to provide a political theory of difference, rather than one based on the emancipation of identities.

Sexual difference

As an example of how this positivity of difference might affect our understanding of the world we could look at one of the major issues of difference for our time: sexual difference. One of the first objections to Deleuze was that his emphasis on difference robbed us of the notion of the subject just as certain groups—such as women—were trying to claim their subjectivity (Braidotti 1991). Difference, as Braidotti points out, is crucial to the understanding of identity politics. First-wave or early feminism began its claims from an appeal to women's common identity and humanity. For first-wave feminists 'real' women are unique individuals who are constantly misrepresented by stereotypes or imposed images. By this reading we would criticise advertising, pornography and ideology by appealing to some notion of woman that precedes representation and needs to be emancipated; we would demand that women be able to speak for themselves, represent themselves authentically, in their true identity.

Of course, the problem with an account that locates identity outside the system of representation and difference is that women themselves often repeat and express the very patriarchal system that is supposedly imposed from above. Structuralist accounts of difference have been extremely influential in feminism and cultural studies for just this reason; they explain just how it is that 'we' seem to agree and go along with repressive images. In a structuralist account, I can only think of myself as female because of a system of signs. The idea that there is a real 'me' behind the stereotypes is an effect of the difference of signifiers. It is not that I am feminine and then have stereotypes imposed; femininity is the effect of signification (Butler 1993).

Not only feminism, but cultural studies in general, looks at the ways in which systems of representation produce identities. Race, class, sexuality and gender are effects of systems of signs; they are semiotically produced. Cultural studies, post-colonialism and feminism often work with a structuralist notion of ideology. Ideology is not a system of fictional or false beliefs imposed on pre-existing individuals. We become individuals through ideology, by recognising ourselves in society's dominant images. This means that we could look at texts for the ways in which they produce or differentiate genders, and we could insist that gender is nothing other than its representation, a representational system that individuates us as subjects. We might also see this as a 'top-down' model of difference. There is a system of difference, which then produces subjects, and any sense we have of the 'real' subject behind difference is an effect of the limits of representation.

Following on from this structuralist model, we might say that femininity is effected through the circulation of dominant images: thinness, passivity, irrationality, submissiveness and domesticity. Such images are given through systems of difference: films that oppose the good, submissive, loving woman to the domineering, emasculating and power-hungry female villain. This was how popular culture tended to read the phenomenon that surrounded the film *Fatal Attraction,* where a man is tormented by a childless, single, power-hungry career woman, and yet finds solace with his loving, domesticated wife. Popular culture has to re-produce these differences over and over again. Today, the differentiation between masculine and feminine might take a slightly different form; if the 1990s separated the bad woman of power from the good woman of the home, we can now see differences between good (contained) forms of power and power that impinges on masculinity. Perhaps women can be represented as successful and powerful—but need to be constrained by thinness or sexuality; this is how cultural critics have read the phenomena of thinness in *Ally McBeal* and the strong female characters in *Sex and the City.* We no longer oppose female passivity to male activity. We now have a valued female activity that is sexual and yet constrained by thinness, (mainly) heterosexual coupling and a suitable amount of corporate power. (This would typify the positive female characters of American situation comedies such as *Friends.*) This is contrasted with other images of a devalued female activity, overly sexual, overly powerful and disruptive of corporate and marital boundaries. (This extends from the 'nightmare' figures of women in the *Fatal Attraction* style of feature film to the metamorphosis of the classic 'bitch' figure in soaps, who is now frequently the overly sexual, predatory, promiscuous and ruthless corporate female.) On such a structuralist or representational account, signifiers produce values through oppositions. Femininity is produced through differentiating systems, and because of these differentiating systems social meanings are produced. There is nothing essential that precedes these systems. Difference is an ideological imposition and ideology creates the supposed 'real' upon which it is imposed.

To put it crudely, and in contrast with structuralism and the dominant methods of cultural studies, Deleuze offers a 'bottom-up' theory of difference which is directly opposed to any notion of ideology. Social codes do not differentiate otherwise meaningless human bodies. We begin with a multiplicity of differences—not just linguistic differences, but genetic, geographical and microscopic or imperceptible differences. We eventually have two sexes, not because difference is imposed but because it is reduced. From all the possible sexual and genetic variations we have coded bodies into the binary difference of male and female. We might begin with the idea of a 'thousand tiny sexes'—all the ways in which bodies are different—or even an 'intense germinal influx'—differences in the flow of genetic material that cuts across bodies or persons: 'For the two sexes imply a multiplicity of molecular combinations bringing into play not only the man in the woman and the woman in the man, but the relation of each to the animal, the plant, etc.: a thousand tiny sexes' (Deleuze & Guattari 1987, p. 213). More recent forms of cultural analysis have taken up this positive account of difference, including those who were initially critical of Deleuze. Rosi Braidotti has looked at cultural events that produce indefinable events of difference (Braidotti 1994). Transsexuality, for example, neither appeals to an essential biological identity nor accepts the self as a simple cultural construction. Rather, for the transsexual, it is the 'essence' of one's body and nature to desire becoming other than what one is.

Intensities

We will look further at sexual difference in the chapter on desire, but briefly here. For Deleuze, sexual difference far exceeds the distinction between men and women (Grosz 1994a). Even at the level of cultural representation we can look at sexual

43

difference in terms of intensities. Intensities are not signifiers or creations of a systemic opposition; for Deleuze, intensities are directly desired or perceived qualities which *then* allow us to form the distinct differences of a system. It is not, as the structuralists argued, a question of having or not-having the phallus, as though sexual difference were produced through this symbolic opposition. Following Deleuze, many prominent feminist theorists have argued that we can see sexual difference in multiple and positive terms: as the expression of bodies and body-parts and not as a meaning imposed upon bodies (Grosz 1994b). We can think of the ways in which certain qualities or intensities are 'invested'. Take perhaps one of the images of femininity of the last century, Marilyn Monroe. Her success as an image relied on intensities: the platinum blondeness, the sheen of her lips, the curves of her body, the timbre of her voice. She was not so much a person or image of 'woman', not so much a meaning or signifier, as a directly invested intensity. (What was desired was not what she symbolised or represented, but the very qualities of her image.) This is the way love and desire work: through a passion for affective qualities. Before Monroe can act as a signifier for 'femininity', which is supposedly imposed on us all, there must be an investment in forms of intensive difference. Before there is a signifier with meaning, desire works by connecting with partial objects—breast, whiteness, curved hip. A structuralist study, by contrast, analyses how difference is produced through opposition: for example, Monroe's softness, passivity and mystery would be contrasted with the male characters who govern the plot and action. Cultural studies, in its structuralist forms, tended to look for social meaning and oppositions. Here, Monroe represented 1950s woman, an ideal of a non-aggressive but potent female sexuality. Such signifiers of the feminine could only be understood through differential relations: the soft child-like timbre of Monroe contrasted with the abrasive hardness of Marlon Brando or James Dean. On such a view, difference was created through a system that organised difference from above in order to sustain a meaning—in this case, patriarchy or ideology. The material elements (blondeness/softness versus darkness/aggression) were deemed to be non-meaningful and apolitical in themselves but rendered meaningful through a political end, such as the elevation of men over women.

By contrast, Deleuze produces a politics of desire. Intensities may not be meaningful, but they are no less political; it is not the message that we consume in culture but the investment in intensities. Society is ordered not by the imposition of meanings but by the production of styles. Deleuze argues for a 'micropolitics'—how do specific qualities such as whiteness, softness, curvaceousness—signs of a desire that is singular and impersonal—come to be coded as signs of 'the feminine'? We have femininity not because we have imposed difference but because we have abstracted certain qualities and taken them as signifiers. The problem comes when desired intensities—such as the image of Monroe—are taken to be a signifier for woman in general; this is how the 'social machine', according to Deleuze, 'overcodes' desire. It reduces intensive difference—the investment in impersonal qualities such as blondeness, curvaceousness, vulnerability—to extensive difference—the investment in 'woman' or 'femininity'. We can look at Andy Warhol's repetition of Monroe's image in relation to this reduction of intensive difference. Warhol's art takes the signifiers of modern America—everything from Marilyn Monroe to Campbell's soup tins—and repeats them as intensities. Monroe becomes a certain shape of lips and hair. The soup tin becomes the design-label, its colours, lettering and logo. The repetition of the image precludes us from seeing its uniqueness or being; we are given imaging and appearance itself. So that it is not that we have identities such as femininity or American home-life that we then signify through images—there is no 'woman' or 'America' other than the proliferation of intensities. Identity occurs with the reduction of intensities to a signifier, when we imagine the intensity as the image of some thing—when we think our love of apple pie signifies our Americanness. The reverse is the case; identities are formed from desires, such as investments in colours, body-parts, tastes and styles. Desire is originally productive, connective and intensive, the investment in qualities that are neither masculine nor feminine but singular. Through repetition and coding these qualities are read as signifiers of some individual essence that precedes and governs the intensities.

Micropolitics

Deleuze offers a political reading that is micropolitical rather than ideological. We do not look at texts for the ways in which systems of meaning are imposed (masculine versus feminine, white versus black), rather we look at the production of intensities from which meanings will be abstracted. How, for example, has cinema celebrated the intensity and quality of whiteness? How, from Monroe to the present, have we taken all forms of intensities—of flesh, shape, colour, affect and so on—and reduced these to images of woman? According to Deleuze and Guattari, there is a history of desire that culminates in the reduction of 'a thousand tiny sexes' to the male/female binary. Such 'sexes' do not begin in the form of persons or distinct terms but as 'partial objects'. It is not that we have a power relation—the patriarchal elevation of men over women—and then a use of images to reinforce and convey the meaning or ideology of that relation. First, there is a meaningless, but no less political, investment in intensities and part objects (the anus, the phallus, the breast); not just the male body and the female body, and not just persons. The very pleasures of a society—what we eat, how we move, what we wear, the commodities we desire, the very desire for commodities as such—are politically coded. It is the desire for the image and affect itself, and not what it means, that is political.

Imagine a group of Catholic churchgoers on Good Friday gathered around a procession of the crucifix. The crown of thorns, the wood of the cross, the suffering body, the subdued lighting and the recording of Bach's cantata in the background unite the group through direct affect. We feel the pain, the suffering, the mourning, the melancholy and the elevation. This is a political event, but not because the procession is a way of imposing the meanings of Christianity on the crowd (although that may happen subsequently). The politics lie in the relation between image and perceivers, the desiring investment in affect. The event produces a group through an organisation and coding of intensities. (The coding occurs with the organisation of affect around a single body—this is the body of Christ; all these affects are passions of Christianity.) It is this politics of affect that has been so crucial for the cultural theorists who have been influenced by Deleuze. Brian Massumi, for example, has shown how the US president Ronald Reagan achieved political success not because he conveyed a coherent message but because his stammering voice and body presented an almost comforting retreat from meaning. It was his style and affective quality, the visual and aural experience of his body, that made viewing him compatible with nearly any political 'position' (Massumi 1996). In quite different ways, Paul Patton has also stressed the contribution of Deleuze to a theory of micropolitics. We no longer look at relations among already formed subjects within the law; we need to see the ways in which the becoming of law produces a political terrain and the subjects who occupy it. Patton looks at questions of native title and shows the ways in which land claims do not operate on pre-given borders between right and wrong, human and inhuman. The Australian Aboriginal claim for land, for example, showed how a political terrain could be opened to deterritorialisation, where we would be forced to confront new intensities, affects and possibilities, which are not just 'arguments' within our own logic and legal system (Patton 2000, pp. 126–7).

For Deleuze and Guattari, the history of politics is the history of the coding of affects and intensities. Primitive cultures experience intensities collectively: a common affect unites or assembles a group of bodies. While such collective intensities still survive in modernity (such as in the example of religion above), capitalism refers all intensities to a flow of capital. Intensities are 'decoded'; it no longer matters what is felt (passion for the body of Christ, hysteria for the elevated pop star). What is important is not any meaning or particular image so much as that all images can be decoded into the flow of capital. There is still a direct investment in intensities: the image of Monroe, the affects of Americanness that range from soup tins to flags and anthems. But all these intensities are organised to produce a 'territory' of identity. In capitalism there is a direct political investment in images that sustain social coding. What is most important is not the imposition of messages or meanings so much as the production of desires that pass directly into social organisation. It is not that, say, the Campbell's soup tin or the Coca-Cola logo are signs of some imposed value, such that they signify an 'America' or modernity that we have been led to believe. We desire the colours, the affects, the textures of images: this is a sexuality that passes across persons, and a desire that has nothing to do with belief. The unconscious and desire are neither meaningful nor believing; desire invests intensities. There are not groups that impose images for a message; the images themselves are the very 'machine' of social organisation.

Capitalism and coding

The difference between primitive and capitalist social machines is the difference between coding and decoding. The investment, say, in the crucifix is the investment in a specific intensity that defines and produces the collective; 'we' become a social body through the common feeling and perception of the elevated suffering body. (Thus the social is marked or coded in this collective organisation of pain and affect around the body of Christ.) In capitalism, by contrast, the investment in intensities is one of decoding: what is desired is not this or that specific thing, not the body and affect itself. Desire is not managed or coded according to a specific social object, such as the cross, the flag or the body of the king. The capitalist desire for money and commodities reduces specific intensities to being the sign for some general or 'axiomatic' value. We see all social objects as representative of one general value—money—that can act as a translator or decoder for any system. (So we could think of the value of religion today in terms of its capacity to produce obedient bodies for work or its explicit use as a commodity: the evangelist industry on television, religious tours to the Holy Land and so on.) The point is that in capitalism it does not matter what we believe or desire so long as the form of our desire can be channelled into the flow of a general value; we must be able to see all desired objects as signs of some underlying general quantity: all goods are reducible to capital, all sexual desires are reducible to a general human 'life'. Sexual investments are read or interpreted as signs of masculinity or femininity; behind all the body parts and gestures is the organising substance of the human. Behind all the images of commodities that we desire is the general equivalence of money. There is no longer an 'elevated' object that organises and codes intensive difference (such as the body of Christ). The code is immanent, or decoded: just the flow of capital, just the general and uniform sexuality of man.

In capitalism, difference is not organised around a transcendent object such as God or the king; difference is homogenised from within. All differences are differences of two uniform, equivalent flows: money and man. The intensity of difference is reduced to two extended terms: man and his other. The transcendence—or organising value—is now no longer explicitly imposed from above but appears as 'our' inner life; it is a transcendence in immanence. It seems that in capitalism and humanism we are no longer subjected to any specific (transcendent) values; it seems as though we no longer have organising or shared religions, ideologies or cultural beliefs. But this cynicism (or absence of belief) is the most insidious subjection of all, for now we appear to allow and affirm a free flow of differences— different sexes, styles, cultures and values—differences that are all grounded on the underlying identity of man who differs. Difference is now subjected to an axiom, an homogenous medium whereby all difference is a difference of degree: we can be multicultural, but deep down we are all human. We can believe in any politics, but at the end of the day we go to work and sell our labour. Capitalism, unlike other forms of social coding, does not need to work indirectly by constructing social objects that control difference; capitalism has mastered difference directly by managing it economically.

In order to produce an event within capitalism, therefore, we need to do more than point out its unfairness, its contradictions and its biases. We need to think difference differently. For if we no longer think of difference as the cultural or sexual difference of otherwise similar (human) beings—if we can think radical and positive difference—then we can deflect thought away from its path of common understanding and recognition. We might think differently. There is, therefore, a two-way project in Deleuze's writing. On the one hand, capitalism is the epitome of a tendency in western thought to reduce becoming to being. In capitalism, all the flows of desire, and all the intensities of life, become grounded on one single flow: the quantifiable medium of capital and exchange. On the other hand, capitalism also opens up new possibilities for thinking if we extend its power of decoding. If no single object or measure can organise the flows of desire then we might liberate desire (and thinking) from any fixed ground or axiom. It is this utopian potential for extending capitalism beyond itself that is stressed by Ian Buchanan (2000), Michael Hardt (1994) and Eugene Holland (1999). For Holland, particularly, the political task is to convert the flows and revolutionary force of desire into political action (Holland 1999, p. 108). This will be achieved by assessing not just anti-production, or the power of society to seize excess and use it to create power, but surplus production: the specifically capitalist tendency to enslave life just with the imperative to produce more and more, to keep desire in a coded flow of production (rather than enjoyment):

> Capitalism makes universal history possible, yet at the same time hinders its realization by recoding and reterritorializing for the sake of private surplus accumulation. Realizing universal history, according to Deleuze and Guattari, requires bringing both psychoanalysis and bourgeois political economy to the point of auto-critique, targeting asceticism and axiomatisation in theory, and eliminating them in practice (Holland 1999, p. 109).

Deleuze will therefore insist that we can only transform life if we transform the power to think, no longer thinking according to some already given logic or system. But we can only release this power of thought through an attention to the conditions of production that lie beyond the thinking subject; we need to recognise the life and desire that flow through thought. (This will require looking at thought's biological, political, historical and stylistic conditions.) In the next chapter we see how Deleuze challenges the conventional 'image of thought' with the aim of producing 'thought without an image'.

3

Style and immanence

Style and immanent becoming

Deleuze's insistence on the active, affirmative and constantly renewing nature of thought prompted him to use a variety of philosophers, artists and scientists in order to forge a complex vocabulary and method. His books are written in an idiosyncratic style. Indeed, Deleuze insisted that style was not just some ornament that we use to convey our thoughts. Style is productive of the very form of our thought. (If we believe that the world is a simple collection of facts then we will tend to write and speak in the style of subject/predicate propositions, as though the world were simply 'there' waiting for its re-presentation in this or that style.) But Deleuze insists that the world is not a simple, closed and inert presence that is then clothed in certain styles of representation. Speaking and writing, for example, are not forms of representation set outside life; to speak or write is to produce an event of life, to become or change with life. It is not that there is a world and then our representation of it. Acts of speaking, writing and thinking are events within life, producing the sense of the world, allowing life to change and become.

At the heart of all Deleuze's thought is his insistence that our relation to the world is dynamic, not just because our ideas about the world change, nor because the world is a thing that goes through change. Life itself is constant change and creation. We tend to think of change as the mobilisation of something immobile. Against this, Deleuze insists that we need to begin from a mobility, flux, becoming or change that has no underlying foundation, which he refers to as the 'plane of immanence'. Rather than think a world that has change within it (so that change would be immanent to some unchanging ground), Deleuze puts forward a theory of immanent becoming; becoming is not the becoming of some being. There *is* becoming, from which we perceive relatively stable points of being. It follows, then, that if there is not some world or being that then becomes, but just a life of complex and dynamic change, we will have to see writing and speaking as events within this plane of change. We would need to write with full awareness of the power of becoming; the world we write about is transformed and effected through writing. And our writing ought to be transformed by our perception of the world.

Brian Massumi was one of the first writers in English to take up the challenge of Deleuze's work. His *A User's Guide to Capitalism and Schizophrenia* (1992) is not a work about Deleuze and Guattari so much as an attempt to continue and extend their style. If, as Deleuze argued, we regard the world as a highly complex, open and dynamic plane of becoming, then we will have to write in more complex sentence forms, using allusions, quotations, neologisms, borrowed and invented images, and figures of speech. We should not think of the world as an object, simply there to be represented (or re-presented) by a separate subject. This is the error of transcendence, the idea that there is a world that simply transcends or lies outside thought waiting to be passively pictured or represented by a viewing subject. Against the notion of transcendence—or the idea that what lies outside thought is some static transcendent object—Deleuze argued for worlds, planes, surfaces or folds. Much of the writing that is now inspired by Deleuze's thought is—in contrast to this book—far from being explanatory or propositional in style.

There is not a mind (or minds) that then represents an outside world. We should not begin our thinking from the assumption of a simple difference between mind and world (or words and things). Each act of thought, perception, action or life creates a border between inside and outside. We often think of the inside or 'interiority' of minds that represent or picture an actual or 'outside' world. This would give us a simple binary between inside and outside, subjects and objects or the virtual (representations) and the actual (the world). But Deleuze argues that the distinction between inside and outside depends on specific events within one single plane of being. We can think of this plane as a virtual totality. From this virtual whole certain beings are actualised, and each event of actualisation creates an inside and an outside. We can begin to think of this imbrication of the actual and the virtual in terms of genetics and genetic creation. DNA, for example, is a virtual power; our genes hold information or a potential to become which is not yet actualised, and which may—depending upon what it encounters—take a number of forms. It is from this virtual potential to become that each actual life is effected. We can consider the virtual totality as the potential or power of life in general to become. We can only have an actual world, or worlds, when this virtual totality of potential difference produces a perceiver such as the human eye (or the diverse perceptual apparatuses of other organisms). The world, or the perception of some actual, outside and objective reality, is only possible when certain events of difference create a 'fold' between inside and outside.

The fold

Let us say that human life is actualised from the virtual potential in DNA, which is its real condition of possibility. In the case of the human, perceptions create an inside (the subject who represents the world virtually) and an outside (the actual external world). But we can observe other 'folds' between inside and outside, depending upon just how perception occurs. Even molecular changes are folds: a molecule becomes or changes by some perception or response to its environment. What this molecule *is* is an effect of a certain folding, an interaction of stimulus and response. Thus a thing's essence is not what it *is*, but its power to become or perceive: 'Essence is always difference' (Deleuze

2000, p. 75). Each evolving being within the plane of life does not just passively react to or perceive the world; its response, or the world it actualises or materialises, is inflected by the specific difference of each perception. A rock, an animal, a plant and a human body all 'perceive' a world, insofar as such beings are nothing other than an active response to environment or life. So we cannot say that there is an actual world that is then perceived or represented virtually, as though the distinction between the actual and virtual were a pre-given and rigid binary. There is no single distinct domain of perception (such as mind) set over against a separate domain of inert matter. Life is a series of divergent perceptions which actualise worlds.

Deleuze refers to this possibility for the creation of worlds as the 'fold' (Deleuze 1993). There is not a distinction between perceiver and perceived, virtual and actual, inside and outside, or subject and object. If there were, this would give us two types of being: subjects and objects, or representing beings and an outside or transcendent world. But Deleuze insists that there is an infinity of folds, creations of a distinction between inside and outside. There are not two types of being (inert matter and representing subjects). There is one virtual whole of being that is given or actualised through an infinity of perceptions, including the worlds and 'souls' of animals, plants, rocks and other machines. 'The plant contemplates by contracting the elements from which it originates—light, carbon, and the salts—and it fills itself with colors and odors that in each case qualify its variety, its composition: it is sensation in itself' (Deleuze & Guattari 1994, p. 212).

Along with new styles of writing Deleuze uses the idea of the fold to express a becoming that is not grounded on being. In order to privilege a being or identity which simply *is* and then becomes, we have to have a single point of view, a single world and a single line of time through which that world becomes. However, we could work against this by thinking a single plane or matter that is known from different curves or folds: the animal has a different outside world from the human, while inanimate matter does not really have an 'inner' or outer world at all. So we could think of a plane not of distinct beings located within a world but of differing perceptions, different folds or inflections that create different vectors of becoming. It is not that there is a world or being that then goes through difference and becoming. Rather, there is an open and eternal becoming (or becomings) from which certain worlds are formed. Deleuze does not use the word 'formed' in this way (Deleuze 1993). This is too close to a form/matter, or dualist, conception— as though there were a matter that was then formed or perceived. Rather, there are various styles or manners, each opening out onto an infinite plane of other styles. (The infinite is perceived differently from each point of its becoming, and so is never given once and for all in an encompassing or God's-eye point of view.) In his book on Leibniz, Deleuze (1993) refers to matter and manner, and this is also where he makes an explicit reference to 'the fold' and 'curvatures'. What Deleuze finds in Leibniz is a philosophy in the style of the baroque. Unlike classicism where there is an ordered or uniform system, baroque art and thought multiply the openings or foldings of matter. 'We begin with the world as if with a series of inflections or events: it is a *pure emission of singularities*' (Deleuze 1993, p. 60). We may perceive a distinction between body and soul, or actual and virtual, but this is not because there are two distinct beings. Rather, there is a matter that bears within itself the capacity to enfold or perceive what is not itself. Souls, minds or 'interiors' are produced by certain events within dynamic life: one becomes a mind or subject by perceiving. Matter, by contrast, is produced by being fixed—by not perceiving or becoming in relation to something else.

From one plane of life both souls and material bodies are produced. It is by enclosing, or folding matter in, that souls are effected, while non-enclosure gives matter: 'Pleats of matter in a condition of exteriority, folds in the soul in a condition of closure' (Deleuze 1993, p. 35). A soul is enclosure precisely because it does not just respond immediately to what is outside; it forms a 'theater' (Deleuze 1993). The soul is not just a transparent opening or window onto the world; it has its own world. Think of the way the mind does not just respond to stimulus (is not fully open to the world) but considers, images or thinks of its world. Matter, by contrast, does not represent or enfold its world; it has no memory or 'contraction' of the world into its own point of view.

Soul and matter are not two types of being; within being they differ according to folds. Matter is a 'pleat' rather than a fold; it still becomes and responds but does not perceive its own becoming. Deleuze uses this matter/manner distinction and the idea of the fold to overcome the dualism of matter and form, and the idea that form differentiates a formless matter. Matter itself folds and pleats or becomes through styles and manners. Manner is not a form imposed on matter, it is the very soul of matter: 'the soul is the expression of the world (actuality), but because the world is what the soul expresses (virtuality)' (Deleuze 1993, p. 5). But there are different levels of folding or becoming. We can think of mind as a fold of enclosure. In mind, the constant becoming of the world is slowed down to give a 'world'. The mind (or soul) selects and synthesises the flux of perceptions to produce things that are sustained through time: 'There are souls down below, sensitive, animal; and there even exists a lower level in the souls. The pleats of matter surround and envelop them' (Deleuze 1993, p. 4). The soul is the active becoming of matter, its manners or styles of folding: 'Matter is marbled, of two different styles' (Deleuze 1993, p. 4). And this means that there is a virtual soul, or a manner of becoming, that is actualised in matter (Deleuze 1993, p. 35). Form is not imposed difference, and there is no soul or world in general that is distinct from its manners, inflections or style:

> It is not only because the fold affects all materials that it thus
> becomes expressive matter, with different scales, speeds, and
> different vectors (mountains and waters, papers, fabrics,
> living tissues, the brain), but especially because it determines
> and materializes Form. It produces a form of expression, a
> *Gestaltung,* the genetic element or infinite line of inflection,
> the curve with a unique variable (Deleuze 1993, pp. 34–5).

Manner or folding is one way in which Deleuze refers to positive and active difference and the transition from the virtual whole to actual worlds. In *Anti-Oedipus* and *A Thousand Plateaus,* Deleuze and Guattari write of territorialisations, which describe the ways in which infinitely complex differential flows are actualised or come to appear as having a consistency or stability. They also refer to speeds and slownesses, where we can see colour if we do not perceive all the different rays of light but slow vision down, or where we can perceive cinematic action if we speed images up. The point is that our actual or perceived world comes about from virtual difference; there is a creation or flow of differences (the virtual), only some of which are perceived by 'us' (as actual). As in all of Deleuze's work, we begin from positive difference or the 'genetic element'; not some being, such as mind or matter, but the difference, becoming or genesis from which we discern identifiable beings.

Immanence and virtual difference

Everything in Deleuze's thought comes down to the crucial idea of *immanence*. (Immanence is a concept in the Deleuzean sense: a way of connecting new ideas and possibilities for thinking. Immanence is also necessarily connected with other Deleuzean concepts, concepts that open up the new style of thought.) Immanence begins with the commitment to the given. There is just one flow of life or one plane of being. This plane ought not to be thought of as some thing or being—some object towards which we bear a relation—but as a dynamic and open flow of becoming. This means that the whole of life or the totality is not given—the whole is virtual, not actual, for we cannot know the future in advance, nor can we determine the effects of the past. And this virtual whole is not a collection of beings, but potentials or possibilities for becoming. Even more importantly, this becoming is not uniform or homogenous; there is no overall goal or end towards which change is directed. Each flow of life affirms its distinct power to become; there is no evolutionary trend in general, only the striving or creative change of singularities. Change or becoming does not take place in order to reach an end or goal; life is change itself. Genetic mutations, for example, are expressions of the power of life to change; they are not changes for the sake of some form or being.

It is becoming which is the power of life, a becoming that has no end other than itself. Deleuze refers to distinct tendencies of becoming—the becoming of animals, the becoming of plants, the becoming of human bodies, and even the becoming of philosophy and art cannot be unified by some general form or goal of becoming. The flow of life or becoming is not a general progressive development. This is why Deleuze writes in the plural of flows, becomings, multiplicities, series and singularities. If we do need to think of the difference, flow or becoming from which beings are differentiated, then we need to avoid thinking of this difference or flow as yet one more being. The unity or One from which all life emerges is, Deleuze insists, not an identity but a difference that differs from itself: virtual difference or pure difference, a difference that is not yet actualised into any distinct and determined form, a pure power to differentiate. This means that life does not unfold itself in any single form or manner; there are multiplicities of folds and flows.

Multiplicity

The task of Deleuze's theory of becoming and transcendental empiricism is to overcome the illusion of transcendence, the idea that there is some ground or substance that then becomes or that is then perceived. We tend to imagine that behind the differences or interactions of forces there are distinct substances; we imagine that there is some 'plane of transcendence' that grounds our perception. We imagine our perceptions as copies or virtual images of an actual world. Deleuze insists, however, that 'the real', or life, is not an actual substance that is then perceived or pictured virtually; rather, we begin from the virtual: from powers or forces of difference and becoming from which the material world is actualised. Transcendence (as opposed to the transcendental) is, according to Deleuze, the dogma of western thought: transcendence posits a subject, substance or being from which becoming, relations, forces or difference are derived. It is true that we only know a world of relative differences—the difference between, say, one colour and another. But what lies behind the world of relations is not an actual substance (say, colourless objects or blank substance without qualities) but pure virtual difference. In the case of colours, it is the differentiating power of white light, or imperceptible differentiation, which gives us the differences we do see. What produces the relation between different things—perceived as extensive multiplicities, or sets of distinct terms—is a non-relative difference, a difference that is differentiating.

This can be explained through the idea of an intensive multiplicity. If I have an extended collection of red objects, I can add or subtract one or more things and still have a set of red objects. This is an extensive multiplicity. The difference in quantity does not change the nature of the set because I am measuring quantity by a standard unit (the general shade of red), so that more or fewer red things can be added or subtracted without the identity of the collection changing. It would always be a collection of red things. If, however, I have a multiplicity of dynamic forces, say the light that makes up a perception of red, and alter the amount or speed of light, then I no longer perceive the same colour. The difference in quantity alters just what this is a set or multiplicity *of*. An extensive multiplicity just collects more or less already differentiated things. An intensive multiplicity, on the other hand, changes with each addition or subtraction; more light gives us a different colour. This gives us two ways of thinking about identity. We can begin with an already distinct term and see extensive multiplicities as collections of this distinct quantity: we can imagine a nation as a collection of British persons. The grouping relies on already determined units, and being British is not affected by how many persons are included. Deleuze and Guattari referred to these types of political grouping as 'subjugated groups', where the identity of members precedes and is unaffected by the quantity or collection of members (Deleuze & Guattari 1983, p. 348). By contrast, an intensive multiplicity alters with each addition or subtraction; it is not a collection of units that remain the same. Deleuze refers to this as a substantive multiplicity; that is, what this multiplicity *is* is directly constituted by what it includes. There is no external measure, such as redness or Britishness, which gives the multiplicity its identity. The intensive multiplicity alters with each alteration of the forces that make it up. The addition or subtraction of light would not give us the same red. However, we might say that the addition and subtraction of bodies might not give us the same sense of Britishness, the same nation. Certainly, Britain is currently gripped by just such an anxiety of mutation; if we start including 'asylum seekers' as members of Britain then we may no longer have a standard of Britishness (English-speaking and white) which could govern the set. Instead of a group subjugated to some calculable unit—a subjugated group—we would have a set that constantly transformed the nature of its units (a subject group). The very idea of selfhood might change with the addition of new members. We could also think of this as a collective assemblage, where it is the assembling or connecting that produces the identity of the group, rather than there being identical things which then make up a homogeneous group.

Subject group/subjugated group

Deleuze and Guattari refer to 'subject groups' in contrast with 'subjugated groups' (Deleuze & Guattari 1983). Subjugated groups are governed by an identity of units, so that we can understand being British, for example, as a condition for entering the group. There is an identity that precedes and underlies the assemblage, group or multiplicity. For the most part, this is how we tend to understand nationalism: that there is something like a national character, birthright or quality which can be grouped into a 'nation'. Many appeals to nation invoke just such an identity above and beyond the collection or assemblage of members. The republican movement in Australia today, for example, frequently rejects the British monarchy on the basis that Australians have now formed their own identity and character. It is this character which supposedly allows Australians to call themselves 'Australian'.

In contrast to the subjugated group or the extensive multiplicity, where what a member *is* refers back to a distinct identity or substance, an intensive multiplicity or subject group transforms with each alteration of force; what a member *is* would also alter with each transformation. Minority groups, for example, are constantly in transformation: they are not governed by an image or identity. For Deleuze and Guattari, a minority is defined not by how many members are in the group but by the nature of the grouping. Although women make up the majority of the population they can be, but not always, thought of as a minority. This is because they do not recognise the dominant standard of 'man' or humanity. In theory, we all know what it is to be human; and there are criteria of humanity that allow for inclusion and exclusion, such as whether one is rational, moral or social. We could refer to those who weren't rational, moral or social as 'inhuman'. Humanity has a definite standard or measure by which it decides who can be included in its group, and we are all measured by this standard. Not fitting in amounts to being *in*human; there is no other category, no real difference. When the women's movement started it began as a grouping that refused the recognition of male reason while not yet having some other standard to which it could appeal. We can think of this as a subject group and an intensive multiplicity, where what it is to be a woman was open to question and formation, and varied with each new inclusion.

Accordingly, there would be two modes of nationalist political claims. Those that were 'majoritarian' would appeal to some finite and perceived unit—national character, birth or spirit—as the basis and reason for grouping together. Those that were 'minoritarian' would be an identity constantly transformed by the events of its grouping or assembling.

As an example, we can think of the contemporary campaign for rights by indigenous Australians. One way to understand this is as a subjugated group: Aboriginal peoples could claim that they, too, are just like the rest of 'us' and would demand to be accorded the rights and recognitions that are owed to all Australians. Aboriginal communities could be added to the Australian populace, given the right to vote, own land and be recognised. Or, we could think of this movement as a subject group: the demand for recognition frequently comes from a group that does not have a pre-given identity. The notion of a unified Aboriginal people demanding inclusion belies the diverse historical, cultural and geographical differences of Aboriginal cultures. The formation of '*the* Aboriginal people' occurred through the demand for power and did not precede it; Aboriginal identity was effected through the gathering or 'assemblage' of forces. But this also meant that it would not just be a question of expanding a group (of Australians) to include Aboriginality. What Australia *is* would have to change: it could no longer be tied to the model of the white, rational, property-owning individual of the nuclear family. Further, the very notion of group and inclusion would have to change. It would not be just a question of extending recognition—granting the new group rights, property and autonomy—for such modes of recognition are already those of the majority group. Even new modes of grouping would have to be thought: not just inclusion and recognition but intensive connections, such as the feeling for place which groups many indigenous bodies. The difference between majorities and minorities is not quantitative; it has to do with the mode of quantity. A majority defines itself through an identity to which the group then submits: a group that recognises itself as Australian, because there is some general notion of Australian-ness that can be shared and distributed. A majority is like an extensive multiplicity: a collection of already distinct units. A minority, by contrast, has no identity outside its specific collocation of forces; each addition or subtraction gives the group a new force. In the case of Aboriginal claims, for example, as more rights and autonomy were accorded to the minority group the very notions of rights and autonomy were opened up for question. (Patton has analysed this opening using the Deleuzean concept of 'line of flight': Patton 2000, p. 126). As Aboriginal peoples were included within the procedures of democracy, by being given the vote, they were also able to question the demo-cratic notion of the pre-social self who possesses rights that protect him from others. More communal notions of selfhood and definitions of the self through place and spirit challenged the western notion of the atomised political subject. As Aboriginal peoples were included within the economy by becoming owners of land, they also questioned the western understanding of land as something to be owned, as property (Malpas 1999). Each polit-ical event in the movement for indigenous rights allowed for greater expansion and complexity of the very identity of the indigenous group as well as the political whole that was being contested.

Becoming minoritarian

We can look at political contestation in two ways. Conventionally, we assume that there is some norm of human rights and citizenship which ought to be accorded to all, and which needs to be disengaged from prejudice, distortion and power. This would assume that the forces of politics were ultimately based on some underlying goal or principle. A majority always presents itself, not as a specific group or contingent assemblage, but as representative of man or humanity in general. Alternatively, we could assume nothing other than an arena of forces. Each political event questions just what we understand the political to be, and this is because each force creates new distinctions and difference. A minoritarian politics does not see itself as the expression of the people but as the creation of new peoples, a 'people to come'.

There are, therefore, direct political consequences of thinking of a world of forces and powers that produce distinction rather than differences and forces being referred back to already distinct substances. Life is the power or potential to produce relations, not a set of relations among already distinct substances. The task, then, is to think difference positively: not as the difference between distinct terms, but as a constant, ungrounded and unbounded process of differentiation. The world does not consist of distinct substances but of differentiating forces, each expressing substance in different ways. If we think of one immanent substance as constantly differentiating and expressing itself differently, then we have to abandon the idea of forces and powers being grounded on some representative normative unit or measure, such as 'man'. All societies, though, have tended to relate forces and differentiated terms back to some undifferentiated origin. Deleuze and Guattari refer to this political process as the production of a 'body without organs'. The forces of life produce distinct bodies or organisms, but we then mistakenly but inevitably imagine some undifferentiated origin (the body without organs):

> The body without organs is in fact produced as a whole alongside the parts—a whole that does not unify or totalise them, but that is added to them like a new, really distinct part ... The organs–partial objects and the body without organs are at bottom one and the same thing, one and the same multiplicity ... The body without organs is the matter that always fills space to given degrees of intensity, and the partial objects are these degrees, these intensive parts that produce the real in space starting from matter as intensity = 0. The body without organs is the immanent substance, in the most Spinozist sense of the word; and the partial objects are like its ultimate attributes, which belong to it precisely insofar as they are really distinct and cannot on this account exclude or oppose one another (Deleuze & Guattari 1983, p. 327).

Not only do we need to free ourselves of the illusion that forces, powers or desires have some ultimate underlying origin or substance, we also have to look at the political and historical productions of this ultimate ground or body without organs. This is where Deleuze's insistence on positive difference—a difference that is productive, plural and ungrounded—leads directly into a political theory and a historical program. If we can think the flows of difference itself and not reduce difference to a difference between terms or the differentiation of some substance, then we will liberate thinking from its moral foundations.

Durations

When we think or act we tend to divide continuous flows of difference into separate objects or static quantities. In order to move around in the world we code the fluxes of perception into distinct and recognisable objects, and we accept a single point of view or world within which all difference is located. This is the plane of transcendence, which leads us to believe that all difference can be traced back to some identical origin or ground. We situate becoming, for example, within a single line or plane of history. But Deleuze insists that becoming does not extend along one line; there are, rather, thousands of 'plateaus' or planes of different durations. By what right, for example, do western cultures refer to other cultures as 'developing', 'post-colonial' or 'pre-industrial'? Only by taking one line of historical development (that of the west) and measuring other histories within this plane. By contrast, Deleuze refers to historical planes in geological terms, so his use of the term 'primitive' does not refer to an absent past but to a still-present tendency. There are still primitive investments in capitalism; certain religious events still invest in a sacred and intensively experienced body. Capitalism is a plateau that intersects and overlaps with other lines of time, such as the primitive and despotic. (There are traces of barbarism in the current use of the death penalty in western cultures, and hints of capitalism in primitive cultures and their tendency to exchange.) The stakes of different durations go beyond human life. For Deleuze, time is not a way of measuring and connecting equivalent points. Each being has its own rhythm or temporality. Human life, for example, has developed technologies of memory which enable it to slow down its responses to life—memory enables me to act on the present with greater consideration. I can deliberate what to do now by referring to a series of possible outcomes; I anticipate a future by referring to a past and thereby act with greater slowness. A molecule, by contrast, does not deliberate or choose its response; it operates at a different speed. Deleuze seeks to expose an inhuman time that will open thought up to a future, a future that is no longer grounded on the unfolding of human history. It is this aspect of Deleuze's thought which has been expressed most clearly in the recent work of John Rajchman, who argues for the essentially creative potential in Deleuze's concept of time: 'Deleuze thinks only this differentiating or singularizing time that precedes us, and that exposes us to another logic of individuation and invention, is capable of freeing us from an "original" nature, contract, or law we must imitate or obey, and so allows us to really experiment with ourselves' (Rajchman 2000, p. 111).

The history that Deleuze and Guattari compose in *A Thousand Plateaus* places human becoming alongside other planes of becoming. Within human life there are flows of varying speed and slowness—varying degrees of habit, memory, promising and desiring—while there are also the speeds and flows of non-human becomings (including animals, machines, molecules and languages). This intersects with two of Deleuze's key concepts: desire and the fold. The idea of the fold helped Deleuze to think of various ways in which life produced an inside and an outside: the 'eye' of the human body produces an inside of mind set against an outside reality, but there are other folds. Molecules responding to light, heat or moisture create an inside of a cellular organism and an outside of environment. Thought in this way, as a plane of infinite foldings, we can also think life as desire. It is not that there are beings who then desire what lies outside them. Life is just change, becoming or creation, producing further lines of change and becoming by creating ever more complex folds. This means that life is always active and creative, affirming the power to become. We can use the word 'desire' to describe this whole of creation and foldings precisely because desire is not a thing or being but a relation or force. A fold in being is created through a response or interaction: light interacting with a cellular organism. It is in the striving to respond to the light that the cellular organism becomes what it is; like all life it *is* its desire, its power of change. Far from thinking of the world as a collection of beings who then have desires, Deleuze insists that life begins from flows of becoming or desire, which then produce relative points of stability.

In order to live we organise the flows of becoming into identifiable beings. We tend to begin our thinking from organs and organisms, especially the organism of 'man'. For Deleuze, philosophy and creative thinking need to work against this tendency. We should not begin our thinking from already defined terms. This is the mistake of theories that commence with the question of how minds or subjects can know a world; it is also the mistake of beginning our thought from simple propositions or common sense. Common sense and ordinary language have already divided the world into subject and object, noun and verb, inner experience from outside world, or the eye that observes the body. Common sense and ordinary language produce a plane of transcendence, some set of objects or being over against which thought is set. We usually begin our thinking by assuming that there is some separate or differentiated object that is there to be viewed by some subject. Against this acceptance of differences being already given (or transcendent), all Deleuze's work was geared towards understanding how differences emerge. That is: what is the real difference from which we abstract differentiated (and therefore identifiable) beings and terms? How is it that we separate a perceiving mind from some outside world that is there to be perceived? How is it that certain points within the thoroughly immanent plane of life—such as the 'self' or 'man'—are abstracted and used to judge life? Why do we think of the durations and flows of life in terms of equivalent points (the uniform 'nows' of time or the regular 'points' of space)? How did we come to think of 'mind', 'man' or 'matter' as nouns or separate substances that might be used to explain the whole?

Philosophy, art and science need to confront immanence, the difference or flow of life that has no single centre, foundation or outside point from which it might be judged or defined. But this means that Deleuze has to write in such a way that his own thought does not provide yet one more foundational term. If he wants to get away from a history of thought that has tried to explain all that 'is' by subordinating it to a single term, he can not just substitute another term. He must write in a way that confronts the limits of propositions, terminology and thinking. Most importantly, he tries to avoid both metaphors and representative examples.

Against representation

'Kill metaphor' (Deleuze & Guattari 1986, p. 70). What's wrong with metaphor and representation? Well, the very idea of metaphor is that there is a literal, present, simply objective world that we then think about through an image or figure. (Deleuze also rejects the idea that 'all we have are metaphors', for this suggests that there is a real world lying forever out of reach of the images we have of it.) Instead of accepting that there is an actual world that we then represent in virtual figures or metaphors, Deleuze sees the virtual (or the power of imaging) as primary, as productive of the actual: 'Metamorphosis is the contrary of metaphor. There is no longer any proper sense or figurative sense, but only a distribution of states that is part of the range of the world' (Deleuze & Guattari 1986, p. 22). Deleuze argues that the very idea of metaphor or representation has underpinned thinking and philosophy. We act as though there were a literal world that then needs to be conveyed by the metaphors or representations generated by minds. Philosophers see themselves as using metaphors to describe an objective world—if a philosopher wants to describe time, for example, he might ask us to think of a line, or a river, or a series of points that are joined together like links in a chain. But this suggests that there *is* time and that we then think of this real time through a variety of secondary images. Alternatively, a philosopher might ask us to imagine mind as a camera, window or mirror. This metaphor also prompts us to think that the thinking subject is simply there, and that we then use certain figures and images to re-present it. This would mean that images were passive replications of the world, added on to already differentiated beings. And it would also suggest that the world existed in itself, without images.

If, however, we refuse to see the world as some external and static object or collection of objects, then we have to accept that thinking of the world or 'imaging' the world constitutes the world. (Further, we also have to acknowledge that imaging is not the privileged activity of human minds; when a plant turns towards the sun it 'perceives' or has an image of what is not itself, but does so with its own style of perception.) Deleuze argues that the world is nothing other than an interactive plane of imaging or series of images, with each event in the world imaging or responding to every other. The world is not an already given whole of points or beings that then interact through perception and imaging; rather, a specific point is actualised only through the event of imaging and perception: 'There are images, things are themselves images, because images aren't in our head in our brain. The brain's just one image among others. Images are constantly acting and reacting on each other, producing and consuming. There's no difference at all between *images, things,* and motion' (Deleuze 1995, p. 42).

This is not an anti-realist theory. Deleuze is not arguing that reality is 'just an image' or is constructed by mind. On the contrary, reality in all its difference and complexity cannot be reduced to the extended images 'we' have formed of it. Nor can the mind be seen as the author or origin of all images. Reality itself is an infinite and inhuman plane of imaging: when one cell responds to another, or when a plant grows toward the sun, or when a virus mutates, we can refer to each of these as imaging. One event of life has apprehended a different event, creating two points, and each point of imaging has its own world. There are not subjects who then perceive; there is an impersonal plane of perceptions from which subjects are folded. It is from the specific manner of perception, its style or inflection, that the point of view of the soul or subject is effected:

> ... the whole world is only a virtuality that currently exists only in the folds of the soul which convey it, the soul implementing inner pleats through which it endows itself with a representation of the enclosed world. We are moving from inflection to inclusion in a subject, as if from the virtual to the real, inflection defining the fold, but inclusion defining the soul or the subject, that is, what envelops the fold, its final cause and its completed act (Deleuze 1993, p. 23).

Human life or thought is just one type of imaging or perception among others; the error has been to think that the world is simply there, or transcendent, only to be viewed by the human knower. If we begin from immanence then there is no privileged point— such as mind, thinking or representation—that can adopt such an external point of view.

When we think about the world we actually give it form or, as Deleuze termed it, 'consistency'. Thinking is an act of creation and transformation; it takes the dynamic flow of life and produces its own concepts, images and the idea of extended matter. (Thinking is not the separate and autonomous act of mind set over or against a transcendent or outside world. Thinking realises itself or becomes through perceiving, allowing something like a thinker to be formed in response to what is thought. Thinking is the connection of one flow with another.) The problem with representation is that it assumes the distinction between mind (which represents) and world (represented). The problem with metaphor is that it leads us to believe that 'we' think by likening one thing to another, as though thought were simply a form of recognition and comparison added on to an already objectified reality. But reality is far richer than this. What is real is a plane of infinitely differing and eternally becoming life. Images and the power of imaging extend well beyond the range of everyday language and representation. True thinking should confront all those bizarre and inhuman modes of imaging, from human stupidity and art to animal life and cinema, that create new perceivers and new worlds. Common sense and ordinary language work by metaphor and example, comparing and contrasting one thing with another. But philosophy, art and science need to break with these habitual modes of thinking, in order to confront just how it is that from the chaos of life and difference identifiable things— such as subjects and objects—emerge. (We also need to think of chaos, not as the negation or absence of order and difference, but as differences that have not yet been thought or encountered.)

For this reason Deleuze's writing is essentially difficult. Philosophy is creative and provocative, taking thought beyond recognition and common sense. In particular, philosophy requires stylistic invention. Examples and propositions tend to leave thought where it already is. We remain within the rigid style of subject and predicate sentences. But if life is itself style, where each event of life bears its own inflections or manner of including its world, then we also need to confront this life stylistically: 'Language must devote itself to reaching these feminine, animal, molecular detours, and every detour is a becoming-mortal. There are no straight lines, neither in things nor in language. Syntax is the set of necessary detours that are created in each case to reveal the life in things' (Deleuze 1997, p. 2). Complex and indirect sentence forms enable us to think of the world not as a domain of facts and truths awaiting presentation but as a dynamic openness that constantly requires new thought and renewed confrontation. The western model of representation has always assumed the opposition between being and representation, between life and the knowledge or thought we have of life, between the actual world and its virtual copy. Against this Deleuze insists on one plane of immanent life, where the virtual and actual are both fully real. Thought is not the virtual representation of life—it is part of life's infinite and open becoming.

This is where the broad relevance and influence of Deleuze's work resides. He presents a challenge to all those literary and social theories that reduce difference to an identity. (We often think that it is mind, language, culture or human history that differentiates the world, as though there were a privileged being that accounts for becoming, as though we could explain difference by referring it back to some undifferentiated origin.) If we accept Deleuze's notion of univocal being then we can no longer explain the difference of life according to a privileged or elevated being (such as the human being). If there is only one being then human life is an event within this plane of immanent difference, not its condition, origin or end.

4

'Doing philosophy': Interdisciplinarity

Deleuze's writings cover an enormous number of disciplines, topics and other writers, and a vast array of cultural phenomena, such as cinema, sexual perversion, crowds, animals and technology. His encyclopaedic approach culminated in the incredibly difficult and wide-ranging books that he co-authored with Félix Guattari. Their final work, *What is Philosophy?* (1994), presents the complex relation between art, science and philosophy and draws upon mathematics, evolutionary theory, the history of philosophy, contemporary art and literature and their own idiosyncratic vocabulary. Deleuze's early works, by contrast, were more conventional, philosophical and exegetical, explicating the specific projects of key figures from the history of philosophy. For the most part, Deleuze chose to work on those philosophers who also affirmed the immanence or 'univocity' of being. The turning point, if there is one, is *Difference and Repetition* (written in 1968, translated in 1994), the first work in which Deleuze considered himself to be 'doing philosophy' rather than working with the 'history of philosophy'.

'Doing philosophy'

Even in his earlier historical studies Deleuze had a quite unique take on what it meant to approach a philosopher historically.

In his first book, on the eighteenth-century Scottish philosopher David Hume, he argued that the history of philosophy is not about listing opinions and sorting out arguments, but about seeing how philosophers create new problems through new concepts (Deleuze 1991). In a much later reflection Deleuze described this approach to the past in even more novel terms:

> I myself 'did' history of philosophy for a long time, read books on this or that author. But I compensated in various ways ... I suppose the main way I coped with it at the time was to see the history of philosophy as a sort of buggery or (if it comes to the same thing) immaculate conception. I saw myself as taking an author from behind and giving him a child that would be his offspring, yet monstrous (Deleuze 1995, p. 6).

Philosophy is not a question of assessing the correctness or accuracy of a philosopher's propositions so much as coming to terms with the specific problem that each philosopher responds to. (Deleuze saw life, not just human life, as an active response to problems; genetic or evolutionary mutations are responses to 'problems' of existence.) A great philosopher does not just tidy up errors in our thinking; she creates a new style of thinking by forming new problems. So, before we have the explicit questions of philosophy—such as 'Do foetuses have a right to life?'—we have broader problems which are the medium of thinking and questioning. Before we can ask whether certain beings do or do not have rights we must have produced the problem of rights; we must have thought about human beings in terms of rights, and we must have created rights as a way of thinking the moral problem. Thinking about a philosophy should not remain within a question, but should look at how a philosophy can produce its questions. We do not, for example, take a general question such as 'What is the good?' and then see who has answered this question most effectively. Rather, we need to see why Plato was motivated by the question of the good and why, by contrast, Kant began with the question of knowledge. (If we took this approach to Deleuze we might come up with a number of questions, but the very title of one of his last writings, *What is Philosophy?*, indicates that for Deleuze we no longer have questions within philosophy; rather, we need to ask just what we are doing when we 'do' philosophy, or art or science.)

In his early works Deleuze chose the philosophers he wrote on quite carefully, selecting figures whom he felt challenged the very idea of what it means to think, and who did so by asking quite different questions. Imagine the state of philosophy today. Perhaps one of its key questions is whether a machine will ever be able to think like a human. We are dominated by questions of artificial intelligence or, more broadly, just what constitutes the boundary of human life. Issues of cloning, genetic engineering, artificial intelligence and even animal rights all concern the borders of human life. We need to sort out just what passes as legitimate human practice and what falls outside the limits of humanity. How far ought we to go with cloning or genetics? Is a foetus a human being? Philosophical debates tend to take place within this question, disputing what does or does not count as an instance of the human. Most philosophers accept the questions of their time but some, Deleuze argues, are capable of forming new problems; such philosophers are 'untimely'. Deleuze, for example, spent a lot of his own philosophy overturning the very problem of humanity. What interested him was not the border between the human and the inhuman. Philosophy and literature had, he thought, been far too concerned with the limits of human life: the limits of language, consciousness, representation and history. Deleuze felt that new questions could only be asked if we looked at other differences and other limits—such as the differences between types of image and perception that cut across human and animal life. For there are different styles of perception and even 'language' that extend beyond the human domain. We should not accept the questions of our time, such as 'What is man?'—we should form new problems that transform our time. For Deleuze, this meant asking 'What is life?' or 'What is thinking?' or 'What is time?'—life, thinking and time in general and not human life, human thought and human time. (This meant writing in ways that many have thought to be quite unphilosophical, and possibly inhuman or unreadable.)

But Deleuze did so only after a quite careful apprenticeship in philosophy (Hardt 1993). Having written books on Hume (1991), Nietzsche (1983), Kant (1984), Bergson (1988) and Spinoza (1992), Deleuze then presented his own encyclopaedic work, *Difference and Repetition* (1994), his first work 'doing philosophy' rather than writing a history of philosophy. We should get away from the idea that Deleuze is just one more post-modern philosopher who does away with essences and arguments in order to overcome philosophy (Lucy 1999). Deleuze insisted on the affirmative and essential nature of philosophy. When we ask what the essence of something, such as philosophy, is, then we should not point to any of its instances or examples and say 'This is philosophy'. Essences are not things that we can point to as already determined; the essence of philosophy is not what philosophy *is* but its specific mode of becoming. 'Doing philosophy' does not mean copying a previous philosopher; it means activating all the forces and differences that produce philosophical events. There are essences, but essence should not be confused with the things that embody essence: 'It is not the individuals who constitute the world, but the worlds enveloped, the essences that constitute the individuals' (Deleuze 2000, p. 43). The essence of thinking or philosophy is not given in any one act of thought or any philosophical text; it is only by thinking of how thinking and philosophy are produced that we will grasp their essence. While Deleuze did refer positively to the existence of essences, he tended to prefer talking about distinct powers or singularities. A power or singularity is a potential to become in a distinct way. We should not see the essence of philosophy in what philosophy already *is*, but in its power to become. Looking at a philosophical text creatively means grasping its singular power, the specific way in which this thinker added to life by creating a new problem.

'Doing philosophy', according to Deleuze, is an act of creation and affirmation. In *Difference and Repetition* Deleuze sets himself two broad creative projects: the construction of new concepts of difference and repetition and the production of a new image of thought. (This new image of thought, he argued, would not be just one more way of defining thought; it would allow us to imagine thought as not tied to any specific image.) *Difference and*

Repetition is one of Deleuze's most difficult texts. Where his early works adopted the vocabulary and questions of the specific writers concerned, *Difference and Repetition* moves through the history of philosophy (from Socrates to Heidegger), mathematical theory, linguistics, psychoanalysis, literature and fine art. At the same time Deleuze begins to formulate his own vocabulary, drawing and adapting terms from all these disciplines and anticipating the thoroughly idiosyncratic terminology that will dominate his later works. In *Difference and Repetition* Deleuze mentions 'planes', 'immanence', 'singularities', 'nomadism', 'intensities' and 'assemblages'—terms that his later works will expand, clarify and complicate. He also starts to open up to the vast range of interests that characterises his later works. In many ways this text is the key or opening to all Deleuze's later thought, although it is perhaps only readable after coming to terms with his subsequent projects. In *Difference and Repetition* Deleuze moves from Freud and death to mathematics and perception, and then back to Dostoevsky and stupidity, often shifting from topic to topic and author to author within a single paragraph. But it is just this very way of writing that confirms his approach to life and thought in general. We shouldn't be producing *books*—unified totalities that reflect a well-ordered world, we should be producing texts that are *assemblages*—unexpected, disparate and productive connections that create new ways of thinking and living.

Rhizomatics

Deleuze eventually affirmed this disruption of the notion of the book in the later works he co-authored with Félix Guattari, especially *A Thousand Plateaus*, the second volume of *Capitalism and Schizophrenia*. Not only do Deleuze and Guattari insist that this work's apparent dual authorship is actually multiple—because each writer or person already includes a large number of personalities (Deleuze & Guattari 1987)—they also insist that writing ought to be rhizomatic rather than arborescent. An arborescent book is modelled on a tree, with a unified centre and structure and subordinate branches. Even the great modernist works that are supposedly multiple are still centred on the all-inclusive personality of the author (Deleuze & Guattari 1987, p. 6). Against the 'great book' Deleuze and Guattari put forward the rhizome—not just a proliferating network of branches but a chaotic root structure: connecting every point to every other point, moving in every direction, branching out to create new directions. Whereas the tree grows upward, suggesting a hierarchical structure with a ground and elevated upper branches, the rhizome is one of Deleuze's many figures that describes movement along a single surface, that then stratifies or creates surfaces: no point elevated above any other, and no foundation or surface upon which movement and activity takes place, just movement and activity itself. A conventional book has a meaning and a subject which it represents or expresses; a rhizomatic text does not have a meaning—it *is* itself a work, event or production.

Even Deleuze's earlier, more philosophical works affirm this principle; his books on the great philosophers try to recreate those figures in terms of the present. Writing about the past does not just mean retrieving an object from the archive. If we actively engage with a past philosopher it will help us to rearrange the present: the past plus the present will then give us a new future. (The past is not some static being, and it is not a previous present, nor a present that has passed away; the past has its own dynamic being which is constantly renewed and renewing.) Writing should be about making unexpected, difficult and almost unmanageable connections, leaping into a past that is not just another variation of the present. Furthermore, Deleuze is not just an inter-disciplinary writer, using the insights of economic theory to illuminate certain literary texts, for example. He aims to transform each discipline through each encounter. Philosophy does not use metaphors or information from contemporary science or cinema; philosophy will be quite a different mode of thought after it has confronted the events of genetics and avant-garde cinema. This also means that each mode of thought also has its own specific difference: the concept of 'multiplicity', for example, possesses a different resonance in science from its sense in philosophy.

Philosophy and other powers of production

Deleuze has been criticised for flagrantly misappropriating and misconstruing complex developments in science and mathematical theory (Bricmont & Sokal 1999). Such an attack assumes that there is one correct mode of thinking, the scientific, to which other disciplines ought to defer. Against this, Deleuze insisted that philosophy could confront science and art, but it then needed to think in a specifically philosophical mode. A scientist thinks in terms of states of affairs, or a particular set of objects that can be ordered and regulated. Science, for example, abstracts from the flux of experience and forms a view of the world that remains stable across different instances; this is how sciences, such as physics, can be used to build bridges or manage reality. A science must give order to the chaos of life, whereas the task of philosophy is to think and confront chaos (Deleuze & Guattari 1994, p. 133). A philosopher thinks in terms of concepts—concepts that aim to think, not of this or that object, but of the plane of all objectivity, subjectivity or being.

While Deleuze writes books on cinema, literature, psychoanalysis and fine art, he nevertheless insists on a specifically philosophical nature of approach. The books on cinema, for example, negotiate just how we think or conceptualise time and movement; this is what makes them philosophical, for philosophy is the art of concepts. But cinema, Deleuze argues, also allows for a renewal of philosophy. It is only after modern cinema has aimed to capture an image of time that a philosopher can conceptualise the very relation between time and images: 'Cinema itself is a new practice of images and signs, whose theory philosophy must produce as conceptual practice' (Deleuze 1989, p. 280). Thus when Deleuze approaches a film, a novel or an artwork he does not do so to offer examples. This would suggest that a novel or painting is an instance or example of literature or art, so that the philosopher might then provide a general definition—but each instance or particular case demands a re-conceptualisation of art, literature or whatever is under consideration.

Cinema, for example, provides images of time and movement; but each type of cinema (realist, expressionist or impressionist) provokes a new path towards the concept of time. Deleuze always begins his philosophical conceptualisations from singular cases: how does the very difference, specificity or singularity of this particular author produce literature? This is the flip side of univocity. If there is just one immanent domain of life then we can never arrive at a final concept of art or literature. (There can be no finality, no end-point or centre from which particular cases might be judged.) An immanent plane is necessarily open to re-conceptualisation, for there is no privileged point from which we might form *the* concept of art or *the* concept of literature. And if the plane is immanent, it also has no outside end or finality that would allow us to close questions of just what this immanence *is*. Each instance of art, science, literature or cinema forces us to rethink the concept of art, science, literature or cinema.

Deleuze's work is therefore truly inter-disciplinary, not just a 'theory' that can be applied to the arts and sciences. Each event in art and science is itself an opportunity to reinvent the whole process of thinking and living. There is no single ground of production—such as the production of language, concepts or even material production—that explains the other levels of production that constitute life. In both *Anti-Oedipus* and *A Thousand Plateaus* Deleuze and Guattari describe the history of production: this production is at once genetic, economic and socio-historical, referring to the production of organisms, of material objects, of social structures and ideas. The point of this inter-disciplinarity is not just that we can use the insights or metaphors of genetics to explain social forms. Deleuze is not saying that societies are like organisms. His radical insistence is that the productions or changes at the level of genetics intersect with and transform the productions of societies, which in turn connect with and transfigure the productions of bodies. Deleuze and Guattari use the notion of production to describe the inter-secting but different series of life: inorganic life, organisms, technical machines, societies and fantasies. There can be no separate point of view of 'theory' that could provide a general form for dealing with specific events and disciplines. This does not mean that we just accept the relative borders of each discipline and that there is no truth in general. On the contrary,

philosophy is only philosophy if it confronts the plane of immanence—the site of production in all its different forms. Philosophy
should not accept already given definitions and models for
thinking; it should continually take thought beyond itself to its
real conditions. So, while distinct from art and science, philosophy nevertheless engages with what is not philosophy—the
affective productions of art and the objective productions of
science—in order to transform itself.

Deleuze was adamant that the continual rejuvenation of
thought would only be possible if disciplines remained open to
the outside. The 'universal history' that he wrote with Guattari
takes psychoanalysis and Marxism and uses them to account for
the emergence of science and politics from primitive and animal
life. Being inter-disciplinary does not just mean combining literary
insights with philosophy, or using anthropology to enhance
psychology; it means accounting for all the different ways in
which thought produces order out of chaos. It means expanding
Marxist economic theory in order to explain not just how capitalism emerges but how it is that societies begin to form systems
of exchange in the first place. It means expanding psychoanalysis
not just to account for the fantasies of the individual but how we
came to think of ourselves as individuals with families and
desires. It requires thinking globally: not remaining within any
one discipline, and not just combining disciplines, but crossing
from discipline to discipline, to continually open and renew the
very medium or 'milieu' within which we think.

Subjectivity

Through crossing between disciplines, Deleuze's project continually attacked the notion of the autonomous thinking subject
which, according to him, is *the* dogma of the western tradition.
We begin philosophising or theorising with some pre-given image
of a thinking self, some notion of common sense that we recognise as properly human, universal and self-evident (Deleuze
1994). Against this, Deleuze wrote a quite radical history of
thought that is not just a history of opinions or a history of ideas

but an attempt to show that what thought *is* is the outcome of divergent series of events. Thought is the result of violent confrontations; it is a response to problems. Thought emerges from chaos and difference. If we want to understand what it is to think we need to think the genesis or emergence of thought from its prehuman and inhuman origins. This means confronting the noise, chaos, stupidity or inhuman element from which thinking and subjectivity emerge. Speech, for example, is not reducible to the noises made by the mouth as a part of the body, but the sense of speech does emerge from the non-sense of the mouth (Deleuze 1990). Writing is not just a set of material markings, but it does result from 'primitive' systems of inscriptions, such as tattooing, body-painting, carving and even the torture of bodies (Deleuze & Guattari 1987). Even the notion of the person, ego or individual is the historical outcome of the increasing organisation, or territorialisation, of life.

If we accept univocity and immanence then we cannot begin with the notion of the thinking subject, for this would assume that there were simply some separate and already identifiable being that could then judge and account for being in general. But if being simply is *what is*, in all its complexity and infinite becoming, then we need to explain just how something like the modern subject or individual is differentiated from this plane of immanence, and then how this subject elevates itself to be the origin of all difference: man as the origin of thought, language and representation. Deleuze diagnoses the emergence of the subject in several ways. His writings on psychoanalysis with Guattari trace the history of desire: how life moved from tribal and collective assemblages to the individual and 'his' family. He uses Marxist economics to explain how production and desire eventually become measurable through the quantitative units of capital (money and labour). Deleuze also writes on the history of philosophy to describe the ways in which philosophers assume or effect an underlying 'image of thought', such that each philosophical problem already responds to some norm of what constitutes good thinking.

Difference and Repetition theorised difference directly, but all Deleuze's other works are motivated by the question of difference. How is it that from the univocal plane of difference the centred subject was formed as some type of foundation or ground? This problem is philosophical because it is an attempt to grasp the plane of immanence from which specific beings are identified; but a philosophical problem also demands a consideration of science, literature, art, economics and psycho-analysis.

Intensive difference and difference itself

Deleuze begins 'doing philosophy' in *Difference and Repetition* with an attempt to confront difference itself. This is not the difference between one thing and another. It is an active difference that differentiates things, that allows recognisable and repeatable identities to emerge. This difference does not take a single form; the mutations of viruses are not the same as the differences in the particles of a language, which are different again from the differences effected in thinking. It is not that we have a world of things, already objectified and identical, and that difference merely relates one thing to another. (This would preclude univocity; we would begin with more than one type of being, or 'equivocity'.) Difference in itself is radical and primary; it is from difference that different beings are subsequently identified.

Think, for example, of the colour spectrum. Let us imagine one single colour, such as blue. From the darkest blue to the lightest there is an infinitely divisible series of difference. Zero intensity would be no blue at all, and then we would move towards the darkest and most intense blue. In order to think and act around this intensive series of difference we tend to differentiate it into points or units; we cut up the pure flow of intensity into recognisable and perceptible differences. (The difference between very light blue and light blue, and then the difference between light blue and a not-so-dark blue, *could* be seen to be the same; we could say that they both differ by one 'shade' or one 'degree', but this is so only if we compare the two differences in terms of some common measure.) A colour chart from a paint shop gives us perhaps twenty or so points, and it represents these points extensively, through spatially divided coloured squares. In order to manage intensities like the colour spectrum we reduce difference and subject it to a uniform scale of measure; we do not recognise all the barely perceptible or imperceptible shadings. And we see the shades as differing by equivalent degrees or quantities (as though the quantities were the same). We say that one colour is four shades lighter or darker than another. We take a differing intensity, which is never the same at any two points (precisely because it is not really a series of points so much as a differing flow), and manage all these points as though they were simply increasing in terms of equivalent units (plus or minus so many shades or degrees). Now we all know that it is not just that blue goes from lighter to darker; there are different qualities of difference: red-blue, iridescent blue, as well as differences that have to do with other quantities, such as texture. Practically, we have to organise all these series of differences into manageable points. But intensity is far more complex than the extended and differentiated points or units we abstract from it.

Further, the differences of intensity themselves emerge from 'pure' difference. It is not just that blue differs in intensity, or that blue differs from red; there is also the pure difference, which allows the intensity of blue to differ from the intensity of red. Colour, experienced as intensity, is the outcome of the difference of white light, which is the real condition for the intensities of the colour spectrum. We might say, then, that we begin from pure difference—the differing power of light—which diverges into tendencies: the tendency of becoming different through colour, or the tendency to become different in sound waves.

The colour spectrum is just one instance of difference. There is also the power of genetic difference, which then gives us the various potentials of DNA. But Deleuze argues for infinitely diverging series of difference of a far more complex nature:

> No doubt differentiation comes from the resistance life encounters in matter, but it comes first and above all from the internal explosive force that life carries in itself ... [V]irtuality exists in such a way that it realises itself in dissociating itself, in such a way that it is forced to dissociate itself in order to

realise itself. Self-differentiation is the movement of a virtuality which actualises itself. Life differs from itself, so much so that we find ourselves before divergent lines of evolution and, on each line, before original procedures; but it is still only with itself that it differs, such that, on each line we will also find certain apparati, certain identical organ structures obtained by different means (Deleuze 1999, p. 51).

We tend to think of life in terms of persons or bounded organisms, and we think of difference as the difference between extended units, such as men and women, or men and animals. But even here we have to see that the subject or 'man' is the outcome of a history of reducing intensive differences—all the possible genetic variations—into some form or recognisable image. We tend to think that there is something like the category of the 'human', which then differs according to race, class, sex and so on. But Deleuze argues the reverse. Life is a flow of complex differences, but we have imposed the category of 'man' or 'humanity' onto a widely divergent field. We have taken all the flows of human becoming—lines of memory, habit, conceptuality, sociality and fantasy—and produced the extended object of 'man'.

The task of thinking should be to step back from the extended image of human life and first to think of intensive differences as the manifestation of tendencies. That is, the human as a recognisable form shares many similar lines of difference with animal life, but has become distinctly human through the power to write, remember, imagine or produce societies. Instead of accepting what human life actually is, we can ask how it has become from all its virtual potentials. What is the style of becoming that produces the specific differences of human life? (Animals also have a tendency to become 'conscious' but it has not become in the same way.) Second, human life is not a static and already given thing; it is a form of becoming. It has its own tendency to become, and all these tendencies of life can be referred to, not as human being, but as becoming-human. We have, however, always defined the human as the subject, or as that which underlies or grounds becoming, that which remains the same. For this reason, Deleuze and Guattari say that we need to begin with becoming-woman, or what is other than man, and that there can be no becoming-human (Deleuze & Guattari 1987, p. 276). Deleuze also refers to a becoming-inhuman, which would be directly tied to the power of thought, the power to imagine what is not ourselves:

> It's not a question of being this or that sort of human, but of becoming inhuman, of a universal animal becoming—not seeing yourself as some dumb animal, but unravelling your body's organization, exploring this or that zone of bodily intensity, with everyone discovering their own particular zones, and the groups, populations and species that inhabit them (Deleuze 1995, p. 11).

Philosophy, as an activity of the human brain, is different in kind from other actualisations of becoming-human precisely because it creates concepts that enable us to think of the very difference of all becomings. So, while all life is becoming and creation, philosophy can create concepts that lead us to think of creation. It is the philosophical concept that, unlike the everyday concepts of common sense which recognise objects, creates a new way of thinking life as such. Deleuze's concepts of the 'fold', or 'desire', for example, helps us to think the very difference or power of life; the concept is an event of life and difference that confronts, thinks or gives consistency to difference.

Before philosophy can think this pure difference it needs to free itself from all the dogmas of subjectivism. We need to get away from the idea that there is a subject or 'man' who thinks, and that life remains something that we think or represent. Thinking is a creative event within life, and it is the event or act of thought that produces subjects. Thought is not just the passive repetition of already differentiated beings; thought is itself a becoming or difference that creates concepts that enable us to consider difference in itself. So, if Deleuze begins with the question of difference in itself, it is not surprising that *What is Philosophy?* is one of his last works. Philosophy is one of the ways in which we have taken the infinite intensity of thought and life and measured it according to some standard, such as the 'subject' or 'man'. We need to understand how philosophy has subjected difference to a single image, and then we need to see if philosophy might form an image that does not 'crucify' difference. How is it that one event of difference—the brain—manages to provide itself with an image that explains the whole of difference? For Deleuze this is philosophy: a way of giving consistency to, or confronting, an eternal, prehuman, chaotic and violent difference. Deleuze's task is to think the plane of immanent difference without providing yet one more image that would explain difference in general.

Becoming different: Intensity

In *Difference and Repetition* Deleuze comes as close as possible to offering a concept of difference without actually doing so. And this is why the language of this book is extremely abstract, devoid of concrete examples and metaphors. The difficulty lies in the fact that we have always likened the dynamic intensities of life— space, time and their differences—to static units or concrete examples. We think of space as a container or field of points; we think of time as a series of 'nows' or presents, and we think of difference as the relation between things. This may be necessary for practical day-to-day life, but it is not really thinking. Real thought does not order what it perceives according to ready-made units and measures but allows itself to be violated, confronted and transgressed by intensive differences. *Difference and Repetition* tries to think difference and thinking as such, independent of all the common-sense images and dogmas we have of them.

Difference is so important for Deleuze because he believes that western thought has been dominated by the privileging of identity over difference, a privilege that has political, aesthetic and ethical consequences. Politically, we tend to begin our theories from notions of ideology and interests. We assume that there are 'human' interests and that these may then be misrepresented by competing ideologies. If we accept a more radical theory of difference we have to question the notion of general human interests.

This is why Deleuze and Guattari described their project as a 'micropolitics': how is it that we form recognisable human interests from prehuman collections of intensities? (Think of the human as formed from whiteness, maleness, the domination of the face and the phallus.) How have we organised or coded the infinite differences of life into a single norm of 'man'? How have we come to think of a general human subject that is representative of us all? We need to attend to all those molecular or pre-individual intensities that make up the image of 'man'.

We can understand this by seeing how political or cultural characters are produced from intensities. An intensity is not a differentiated thing or object, which then possesses qualities. Broadly speaking, an intensity is an experience, feeling, perception or event—not so much located within an ordered time and space as being one of the many flows from which time and space are discerned. Life just is a 'swarm' of intensities—colours, gestures, tones, textures, movements—from which we then order or perceive extended things. Our perception of a person and their individuality, for example, is a composition of fluctuating intensities which are otherwise impersonal. We abstract the character or person not from their fixed body, but from the styles of their movement and speech, and what we expect or anticipate of them. A character is something that is multiple and becomes, through time, a collection or multiplicity—not of things but of intensities such as styles, gestures, tastes and quirks. Further, these intensities can also be perceived regardless of any person or identity who holds them. Think of how a television character can be marked by a certain hairstyle, which then becomes fashionable, repeated and separated from any meaning of character. The style can then sum up a decade, so that our desire or investment in the 1960s draws upon impersonal nuances—the Elvis Presley hairstyle that reaches an exaggerated pitch that not even Elvis would have worn. Film stars, politicians and literary characters are compositions of style, gesture, tone and mood. James Dean is a hat, a swagger, a sense of rebellion, a pair of jeans and a hairdo. Shakespeare's Macbeth is the conjunction of power, murder, hubris, a wife with bloodstained hands, daggers, witches and Banquo's ghost. We experience Heathcliffe in *Wuthering Heights* through the darkness of his physical features, the coarseness of his speech, his wanderings across the moors and the marks of labour scarring his body. Many US presidents have become 'presidential' by drawing upon the gestures or mannerisms of their predecessors. Bill Clinton did not repeat the beliefs of John F. Kennedy, but his speeches used Kennedy's rhythms, pauses and cadences.

Against the idea of representation—that there are persons or things that we come to know through qualities—we can say that there is a world of perceptions, intensities or varying qualities from which we produce extended things or an underlying human nature. This means that cultural or artistic works do not represent an already given human nature so much as produce general interests from intensities. Western 'man', for example, is a 'molar' formation that begins from the specific investment in (molecular, or pre-individual) intensities. 'Man' is a collection of intensities that has now been taken as exemplary of the 'human'. For Deleuze, though, real thinking demands that we take any general category or molar formation (such as man) and look at the molecular intensities from which it is composed. Molar formations are formed from varying investments in intensities, which have less to do with belief or meaning so much as the elevation of specific qualities. We could therefore look at the distinct ways in which political machines produce the general concept of 'man'. This micropolitics or schizoanalysis would be different from analysing sexist beliefs or ideology; it would look at the images that allow those beliefs to be formed. Think of the way advertising in the 1990s repeated the image of a muscular male abdomen, usually emphasising a tanned whiteness, set alongside certain textures such as the whiteness of sheets or overalls and the viscosity of dark grease or body oil. This contrasts with earlier productions of 'man' from other intensities. In the 1950s there was an investment in quite different body forms—the hips and denim jeans of Elvis and James Dean, a certain highly maintained hairstyle—and a different image texture—such as black and white film as opposed to glossy billboards or magazines. Intensities are not just parts of objects; they are tied to affect. These perceptions of western man were clear, distinct, bounded and ordered, whereas what is inhuman has a whole different style of perception.

Animality and foreignness, for example, are often presented in dark, chaotic and unbounded images: think of the deliberately disorganised presentation of the 'masses' of foreigners, often using dark, uncut and blurry footage. Western man, by contrast, has a long history of being presented in clear, individual outlines, well-illuminated. The whiteness of an image is not just something that we perceive; it has its own intensity of perception. Whiteness, line and light have a certain effect on the eye, producing an affect. (We see extreme versions of this in horror films, where the visual data can be so bright or fast-moving that the eye is violated or forced to turn away, regardless of the violence of content. Contrast this with the softness of focus of Romance cinema.) So our shared experience of 'man' comes about not through perception of some pre-given object, but the coding and organisation of our perceptions through specific intensities. Persons in film, literature and philosophy are outcomes of the synthesis of intensities. In addition to philosophy, in which we create new paths of thought by exposing the dogmas in thinking, art can create new styles of perception by exposing the rigidity of our styles of perception.

Art and signs

When Deleuze looks at an artist or writer he negotiates the singular ways in which art confronts difference. The philosopher might confront the plane of immanence, but the artist begins from the smallest of differences, specific or singular intensities. In Deleuze's book on the French novelist Marcel Proust, it is the notion of signs which creates a path to difference (Deleuze 2000). We can understand all life as a series of signs. The animal finds its food by following signs. I know there is a fire because I 'read' the sign of smoke or the smell of burning. I discern that you are upset by 'reading' your gestures. When a virus mutates by leaping across to another species it 'reads' its new environment. But there are certain signs that lead us to the intensity of life itself. This is the path of signs that Deleuze finds in the novels of Proust, where he describes four levels of signs.

For the most part experience takes the form of 'worldly signs' (Deleuze 2000, pp. 6–7). We look at things in terms of some other thing. Bodies are the signs of a certain character; clothes are the signs of class, occupation or gender. 'Worldly' signs relate differences back to some meaning that a complex of signs might share: a curvaceous body, diaphanous clothing, high heels and a delicate walk might enable us to recognise 'woman'. This process of recognition and interpretation enables us to act and make our way in the world. But, according to Deleuze, Proust also describes signs of love. Here, we do not interpret the sign in order to recognise what lies behind the sign; the sign does not lead us from one thing to another. In love, the sign halts interpretation. The beloved's body, style, dress and movements signal what cannot be recognised or simply known. When we love someone we do not incorporate them into our world of things, and we do not regard them as something to enable action. The person we love is the 'sign' of an entirely different world, an experience that is not ours (Deleuze 2000). So, while worldly signs pass from thing to thing within the world—from smoke to fire—the signs of love lead us to another world: the world the beloved perceives that I can never know. Her face, the face of the one I love, is a sign of what can never be experienced or perceived by me. Thus the signs of love open out to the virtual, what is not given but only anticipated. Even more complex are what Deleuze, through Proust, describes as 'sensuous' signs; these are material and are unique to art. The redness of a painting is a sign, not because it represents an object we can use (worldly signs), nor because it indicates the experience of another person (signs of love), but because it embodies 'redness'. Art expresses material or sensuous signs independent of objects or persons. Again, this opens to the virtual. What I see here is not just this actual paint on the canvas; I get a sense of colour or visuality—what it is 'to see'—above and beyond this particular instance. 'What is an essence as revealed in the work of art? It is a difference, the absolute and ultimate Difference. Difference is what constitutes being, what makes us conceive being' (Deleuze 2000, p. 41). It would be a mistake to *interpret* art for some actual hidden meaning—what the author wanted to say, or the message coded in a text—as though art were a worldly sign that just led us from one thing to another (from picture to meaning). Art gives us material signs: *this* redness in all its singularity and specificity, which is not tied to any actual thing or meaning but presents us with the very possibility or potential of colour, the power *to be* red in this way. These sensuous signs then lead us to the final level of essences, which Deleuze regards as the ultimate level of signs. If we are confronted with the very materiality of *this red*, then we are on our way to experiencing the very essence of redness: no longer subordinated to meanings, actions or persons. And once we have experienced art in this essential way we see the truth of experience in all its difference. This is not a truth tied to an object, opinion or a state of affairs; it is the truth of the whole or possibility of experience: experience as an impersonal and differential flow beyond any of our actual or finite perceptions. The truth of experience is its power or capacity to extend beyond any actual image we have of it. Art, like love but in a far less personal way, leads us out of ourselves to impersonal experience. This can then lead us to the sense of experience as such, to the truth of life as one impersonal whole, well beyond any located or human perception of judgement. Essences for Deleuze are not general categories or meanings that lie behind experience; they are unique possibilities which are actualised in any experience. In perceiving red I can both see this red here *and* think of it as an expression of the essence of colour: 'What can one do with essence, which is ultimate difference, except to repeat it, because it is irreplaceable and because nothing can be substituted for it?' (Deleuze 2000, p. 49).

For Deleuze, then, essences are singular and absolutely contrasted with generalities. We usually move about life using the worldly signs of generality: this is a chair; this is a table; this is a carpet, which happens to be red, like the red chair. But art confronts us with the singularity of essences; *this* red here is material and sensuous, and is different in its singularity. It is the sign of the ideal essence of a singular redness. And so the experience of art will then transform all our other signs. Once we are taken out of our selves and the generalities we habitually impose on the world, we can perceive the world in its intensity, as a proliferating expanse of differences that we necessarily 'forget' in order to live with distinct persons and things. We realise that worldly signs, the signs of love and sensuous signs are all contractions of an intense difference, a difference that disrupts thought over and over again, opening a multiplicity of worlds. We cannot rest with any single sign that would represent this essential difference; we must continually recreate the sensuous signs of art in order to re-encounter difference in all its singularity: 'Art is a veritable transmutation of substance. By it, substance is spiritualized and physical surroundings dematerialized in order to refract essence, that is, the quality of an original world' (Deleuze 2000, p. 47).

In his book on Proust Deleuze (2000) expresses his affirmation of difference and repetition from the particular understanding of signs created by the novelist. Proust writes a novel that allows present experiences, say the feeling of a napkin, to recall a past experience, which leads to a sense of the specificity of each sensual event. The specificity of the past disrupts the order of the present, and does so because these sensual essences—such as taste, touch or the shade of a certain light—have an essence quite independent from the narrative order we impose on life. All art, for Deleuze, has this power of invoking essential singularities. In a painting, each singular event of redness repeats the essence of redness, the capacity for red to vary, multiply and constantly be repeated in different ways. The essence is repeated or affirmed, not by a repetition of something that is the same; repetition is difference. For what we repeat is the power of each event to affirm itself over and over again in different ways. Art is crucially tied to difference and repetition.

Art is not the repetition of the same: it is not the production of endless sequels, copies or imitations. We wouldn't refer to an Elvis impersonator, for example, as the next Elvis. To really repeat the essence of popular music would require repeating all the shock and transformation of the first Elvis. The student sitting in the academy faithfully copying the old masters is not repeating Monet. And the art critic or cultural studies commentator who tells us what Monet or Elvis signified or meant is certainly not repeating the essence of art or music. The contemporary garage band or installation artist is closer to the repetition of Elvis or Monet, only insofar as they affirm differences of sound and visuality with the same (and therefore different) force of the 'original': 'the most exact, the most strict repetition has as its correlate the maximum of difference' (Deleuze 1994, p. xxii). To really repeat an event is not to repeat the worldly image we have of it, but to grasp its transcendental condition of difference: what was the force of difference and invention that Monet or Elvis affirmed? Art is the repetition of singular differences, not just the differences of sound, tone, colour and other sensibles, but also the differences of affect—of love, horror, fear or pleasure.

Deleuze, in general, argues against interpreting another thinker or artist. We should not look for some meaning that the work expresses; works of art are creative of differences. Rather, we should try to understand the specific ways in which difference is encountered in their work. Proust's novels created layers of signs in order to present signs that opened up to the very essence of different singularities. When a philosopher like Deleuze looks at an artist or writer like Proust, he does not offer philosophical background or explanation. Nor does he give a philosophical version of what the artist expressed aesthetically. Neither art nor philosophy has some independent content that is then expressed in different styles: say, the propositions of philosophy and the metaphors of art. Art gives us sensibility in all its singularity, liberated from the generalities and comparisons that we impose on it for the purposes of practical existence. Philosophy gives us concepts that help us to think the plane of all these singularities. In the case of Proust, Deleuze uses the concepts of 'sign', 'essence', 'truth' and 'monad' to re-create Proust's own search for difference in itself. Philosophy is different from art in that it conceptualises, or tries to grasp in itself, what art will present in singular fashion. Art will give us the essence of 'redness' by presenting this particular red in its singularity; we will no longer subordinate red to some object that is red, or some meaning symbolised by red. While philosophy does not begin from this or that singularity or sensuous sign, its project of thinking difference in itself will nevertheless always work with specific revelations of difference, such as those offered by art and other philosophers, and it will then try to think just how such singularities emerge.

Reading difference

Deleuze's own work continually creates different terminologies, different strategies and different questions. While Deleuze is clearly critical of a static theoretical system that might then explain specific events, his thought is relatively unified by the affirmation of difference, an affirmation that takes on different forms depending on the problem or writer addressed. 'Form' is not a word Deleuze would use in this sense, as it suggests a distinction between form and matter—where there would be a formless matter that then takes on specific forms. He uses the words 'manner' or 'style' instead. Matter itself is different and becomes in its own different styles. For there is no difference in general independent of its specific, singular and different expressions. 'Pure difference' is virtual; in actuality there are only specific differences. Deleuze's theory of intensive or positive difference is not so much a theory, an overarching explanatory rubric, as it is a constant and eternal challenge: how do we think the specific difference of each event, each writer, each artwork and each perception?

Of course, the problem with any introduction to Deleuze is that it will have to use all those methods, of metaphor, generalisation and example, against which his thought was directed. But Deleuze provides a way of dealing with this. We always begin from our own world or way of approaching difference. We do tend to think difference itself in terms of some different thing. There is nothing wrong with proceeding this way. (In fact, a lot of the problems arise when philosophy starts to moralise about thinking, condemning forms of error or judgement.) The idea is to see our examples not as specific cases of some general truth about difference, thinking that we can grasp generalities behind particulars. Rather, we should go on to re-create further differences: so the cases we begin from are not examples of a difference in general, but instances of a difference, which will be different each time according to the way in which we approach it. There cannot be a general difference that we can grasp once and for all. We have to assess the different ways in which each work of art, each concept and each scientific discovery transforms the ways in which we think.

If we have been thinking about univocity, immanence and difference, how might we give some explication of these concepts? Consider 'The Sick Rose', a short poem by the early Romantic William Blake (1757–1827):

O Rose, thou art sick!
The invisible worm,
That flies in the night,
In the howling storm,

Has found out thy bed
Of crimson joy;
And his dark secret love
Does thy life destroy.

If we 'interpret' the poem, we ask what it means, we find some sense behind the words on the page. This poem is often read as an ironic expression of attitudes towards life and desire. The speaker can only see desire as a form of corruption, and so he ties love to secrecy, destruction and darkness. We could read the poem as an example or expression of some more general meaning (pious eighteenth-century moralism). We often think that there are certain meanings, ways of thinking or certain types of speaker. In the case of Blake's poem, we would say that it represents the repressive attitude to the body and life that characterised the eighteenth century.

Deleuze, however, asks that we read immanently and intensively, asking how a text works and what it does or produces, and not what it means. He wants to argue that there are not meanings or senses or even speaking subjects that are then expressed through language. Subjects are formed through their ways of speaking. Sense is an event that emerges from language, rather than lying behind language and requiring language only for its communication (Deleuze 1990). Sense is not reducible to the material words on the page, but each event of sense is produced from material non-sense. We begin with the event of style, an expression (in the case of writing) of the materiality of syntax. This means that style is not an ornament that we place over our meanings; there is a style from which meaning and sense emerge. You can only have a moralising subject if there are certain ways of speaking, a border created between the one who speaks and judges and the object that is judged. This also creates sense, sense being the virtual, non-actual or immaterial element of language. But art is not about the presentation of sense or meaning; it is about the emergence of sense or the virtual from the actual or sensible. (Remember that it is from percepts and affects—presented impersonally—that subject positions or subjectivities are produced.)

In the case of Proust, for example, Deleuze argues that the novelist presents 'sensuous signs'—the experience of sensation—but this is part of an affirmation of how, from the sensuous, certain styles of character and life are formed. From the sense of the world, all its meaningful signs and purposes, we are presented with those intensities which make up the specific style of persons, characters and places. Blake's poem, therefore, can be read not just as a comment on morality but as a presentation of the style of morality, the way a certain type of person is formed from a manner of language. First, there is the intensity of the poem's rhythm. The monosyllabic diction and the short clipped phrases produce a rhythm of simplicity, of delineated units, of tidy contrasts. This produces a certain syntax of thinking, of simple oppositions and clear judgement boundaries, as though the world were a collection of objects to be sorted between positive and negative. The poem also takes the form of simple pronounce-ments, as though it could adopt a diagnosing point of view: 'O Rose, thou art sick!' Indeed, this poem comes from a series called *Songs of Innocence and of Experience*, many of which begin in this style, with simple declarative pronouncements and descriptions. We can only have a moralising subject through specific types of rhetoric, such as the speech acts which diagnose ('thou art sick'), judge ('Does thy life destroy') or interpret to find some hidden corruption ('The invisible worm … Has found out thy bed'). Morality also has a certain speed and rhythm. Not just in Blake, but in proverbs and everyday dogma, morality operates by singsong repetitions and short, fast pronouncements. (Think of the way in which the dogmas of common sense and infantile moralism are often presented: 'what goes around comes around'; 'no pain, no gain'; 'out of all things comes some good'.) Blake is presenting the style or materiality of the sense of moralism. The *Songs of Innocence and of Experience* are short verses with simple rhythms, presenting the non-sense at the heart of morality, its dependence on a style of rhyme, rhythm and metre: 'Then cherish pity, lest you drive an angel from your door' ('Holy Thursday'); 'Where Mercy, Love, and Pity dwell / There God is dwelling too' ('The Divine Image'); 'So if all do their duty they need not fear harm' ('The Chimney Sweeper'). To say that 'The Sick Rose' is not an example of repressiveness is to say that repression is nothing other than a specific and singular style. There is not a general mood (repression) which can then be depicted in a style; all our moods and meanings are produced from styles.

The poem does not represent repression or morality; it shows how repression and morality emerge from manners of speaking. It looks at language positively, not as the reflection or representation of a world but as the creation of a world. 'The Sick Rose', like so many of Blake's *Songs of Innocence and of Experience*, shows how a world of corruption, fallenness and destruction is effected from quite specific ways of speaking. In order to think non-repressively or non-moralistically, we would have to imagine a far more complex style: not reducing thought to simple phrases, identities and judgements. This is indeed what Blake's later poetry tried to do (which is why, like Deleuze perhaps, he is also so difficult to read.) The minute we take any voice as exemplary we have elevated one particular mode of thinking and speaking as a general model. We have ceased to think.

5

History of desire

Desire as production

How we think desire and how we think difference are closely tied. Deleuze expressed his project of positive difference by reading through a number of authors, but it is in his critique of psychoanalysis with Félix Guattari that he politicises the issue of difference through the notion of desire. The standard notions of desire, and the psychoanalytic explanation, tie desire essentially to lack, negation and the subject. It is usually thought that I can only desire what I do not have, and so desire is understood as the external relation between two terms: the desiring subject and the desired object. For psychoanalysis this goes even further. I can only be an 'I' or subject through this essential lack of desire. Imagine the child at the breast, with all its needs fulfilled. It has no sense of self, no sense of world, and no difference. It is only in being other than this pure fulfilment that there can be a sense of self at all. So it is in its differentiation from its desired origin that the 'I' emerges. For the rest of our lives, psychoanalysis argues, we desire this original presence and plenitude, but to achieve such plenitude would also be a loss of self, or death. (This is why psychoanalysis posits a 'death drive' as the very essence of selfhood; desire strives towards overcoming all difference or lack, and therefore desires its own end.) On the conventional and psychoanalytic picture, difference and desire are essentially negative.

In order to understand how we arrive at this miserable story, Deleuze and Guattari write what they refer to as a 'universal history'. In *Anti-Oedipus* this history describes how we move from a difference which is intensive and positive to a difference which is extensive and negative, with psychoanalysis emerging at the end of a long history that negates desire by interpreting it. From Plato to Freud, Deleuze argues, desire has been seen as other than life, or as something to be interpreted; we desire what we do not have, and our desires are mere 'images', 'fantasies' or 'representations'.

For Deleuze and Guattari, however, desire is not a relation between terms—the desire of the subject and the absent object, which they lack; desire is production. All life is desire, a flow of positive difference and becoming, a full series of productive connections. (The hand that touches the breast is desire and connection, and so is the mouth that attaches to food or even the virus that alters in a new organism, for desire is just the creative striving of life in general.) There is, then, just one immanent plane of life as desire, and not desiring subjects set over against an inert and lifeless object world. Prior to Deleuze, there had been radical political uses of the concept of desire, most of which derived from Hegel and Marx and were rigidly humanist. Alexandre Kojeve, whose reading of Hegel was crucial for the generation of French writers prior to Deleuze, argued that desire was human and negative. Only human life can represent what life *is not*; it can have an image of what is not already present, and this desire can cause it to act on the present. Desire is other than life, and this is because life, in itself, has no reference to a future or what is not given. Deleuze, by contrast, frees desire from representation: desires are not images we have of what we lack; desires are positive events—including all the perceptions and sensible encounters of all bodies. Once we free desire from representation, once we see desire as the act of a body itself and not the representation or wishful hallucination of an act, then we can also free desire from the human. Humans, as speaking beings, are no longer the only sites for desire. On the contrary, speech does not represent our desires or what we lack. Speech and language— the noises of the mouth, the inscriptions of signs, the marks or codes of a culture—emerge from desire. Life in general produces all sorts of marks, noises, inscriptions and codes; this is part of its productive creativity. We turn against life when we imagine one form of desire—rational man—as the origin and explanation of desire. There is one ever-differentiating and productive plane of desire. Distinct terms—such as the human—emerge only in the organisation of desire: that is, the coding of flows of desire into distinct organisms.

All life is therefore a desiring flow towards ever-proliferating differences and productions. What is originally desired, Deleuze and Guattari insist, is not the personal maternal object but a pre-personal 'germinal influx of intensity' (Deleuze & Guattari 1983, p. 164). Desire is the tendency towards flow and difference, which also means that desire is inherently revolutionary or destructive of any closed order. Desire begins not as the desire for some object by some person—rather, there is a flow of life, an impersonal differentiating 'sexuality', which produces bodies and organisms. So, before there are any subjects who desire, there is the production of desire.

In *Anti-Oedipus* Deleuze and Guattari refer to this production in the first instance as the connection of flows. The difference between one flow and another, or one becoming and another, can be understood in terms of cut and connection. A plant turns to the sun; an insect flies to a plant; a human body hunts an animal—each connection is the becoming of a flow of life, but it is not an isolated becoming; it becomes only through connection with another becoming. It is this connection or synthesis that allows two intensities to be 'cut' from the flow of life. A mouth seeks a breast; it must connect but it must also meet with resistance. So a flow continues and becomes only in being connected, but any connection also cuts into the first flow. The two intensities—mouth and breast—become only in being connected. *The* flow of life, the flow that we imagine to be at the origin of all these specific intensive flows, does not actually exist; it is the virtual whole of interconnecting and interrupting intensive flows. These intensities emerge from difference itself.

Becoming inhuman

Life is the production of difference, or the actualisation of tendencies to differ. But Deleuze and Guattari's emphasis on desire as production also marks a distinction from the usual notion of possibility. We tend to think that there is an actual world that then bears certain possibilities: to become in one way rather than another. Typically, they reverse this account. Life is the potential to differ, which produces actual beings. The mistake comes in when, from our own point of view and our own world, we imagine possibilities as based on the actual world. For example, once a being has been actualised—say, modern man—we then limit becoming to that image; we think of other histories or cultures of man, all the possibilities for human life. We do not see the more radical, open and not-actualised potential for becoming something quite other than man. In order to uncover this productive power of difference—the power to become other than the actual world and its present possibilities—Deleuze and Guattari trace the productions of desire back to their more open emergence.

The differences of life are not possibilities that proceed from an already determined actual object. The pure difference that gives tendencies to differ in specific intensities is virtual rather than possible. The difference from which actual life emerges is not already given as a completed set. It is virtual or open, with each actualisation of difference producing new possibilities:

> The whole is not a closed set, but on the contrary that by
> virtue of which the set is never absolutely closed, never
> completely sheltered, that which keeps it open somewhere as
> if by the finest thread which attaches it to the rest of the
> universe ... The whole creates itself, and constantly creates
> itself in another dimension without parts—like that which
> carries along the set of one qualitative state to another, like
> the pure ceaseless becoming which passes through these
> states (Deleuze 1986, p. 10).

Deleuze and Guattari apply this problem of open becoming to the understanding of human life, or the relation between the social machine and desiring machines, in *Anti-Oedipus*. Ultimately their critique comes down to the ways in which one actualised and extended (or transcendent) object—the human—is used to explain and ground virtual difference. From all the genetic differences that open out into human life we eventually form the image of man (the historical result of the colonisation of all tribes, races and sexes by the western individual). We then take this object of man and use it to describe the emergence of difference: all the races, sexes and tribes are seen as differing from some underlying human form or essence. The idea of a humanity that we all share is yet one more way in which immanent difference is subjected to a plane of transcendence: one differentiated thing—man—has become the origin of all difference. But this error of transcendence has a social history, which can be explained by two regimes of the same process of difference: desiring machines and social machines.

Deleuze and Guattari's historical account is immanent and can be thought of on the model of a single plane. (So this is not a history of man—not a history grounded on some transcendent term—but an analysis of life from which the very possibility of history, culture and politics emerge.) To undertake this immanent analysis, we can imagine a field of force, with no fixed terms, operating by attraction and repulsion (or territorialisation and deterritorialisation). Or, instead of force we can think of a process of 'machinic assemblage': moving in one direction towards organisation and in other towards free flow. In *Anti-Oedipus* Deleuze and Guattari describe the immanent production of human history, leading up to the point in capitalism and modernity where we can recognise the desire or difference that has produced all the political illusions of transcendence: the illusion of those single terms (such as man, the State or law) that would ground politics and history. They begin with the notion of desiring machines in general, prior to their organisation into human organisms.

Desiring machines

Desiring machines are productive and connective: a mouth connecting with a breast, a wasp connecting with an orchid, animals collecting into packs. These connections are not connections between terms; they need to be understood as the expression of a flow of life from which extended terms can then be abstracted. Sexuality, for example, is best understood not as one person desiring another, but as the way in which life produces and continues—with bodies being the points through which this impersonal life flows. Distinct bodies would be intense affirmations of virtual differences or tendencies. We can see masculinity and femininity, for example, as two of the responses or creations that life produces in order to continue; such sexually distinct bodies are specific ways in which life becomes. There is a flow of life that affirms and expresses itself in different ways, such as sexually different bodies. But the general notion of male and female as two sexes is the result of reducing a far more complex political history that begins with the differentiation of genetic flows into larger territories.

The problem with our usual account of desire is that we begin from the family triangle: child, mother and father. All desire is explained from this model. We assume the extended unit of the individual. We pass from a flow of life that is intensive (the 'intense germinal order') to the representation of extended bodies (the 'regime of somatic generations'). Desire, however, is not originally between persons. In fact, by the time we have come to think in terms of 'persons', desire has already been repressed. We have moved from the impersonal flow of desire—the intense germinal implex—to distinct persons who then have desires:

> The *somatic complex* refers to a *germinal implex* ... Incest as it is prohibited (the form of discernible persons) is employed to repress incest as it is desired (the substance of the intense earth). The intensive germinal flow is the representative of desire; it is against this flow that the repression is directed (Deleuze and Guattari 1983, p. 162).

In *Anti-Oedipus* Deleuze and Guattari challenge the psychoanalytic and structuralist argument that culture begins with the prohibition on incest, the idea that it is only in prohibiting the mother as an object of desire that we are forced to marry, exchange and organise. It is not, they insist, incest that is prohibited or repressed. Incest is a relation between persons—mother and child—but desire is pre-personal; it does not desire an other person but only its own continued flow and production. This is why desire itself is revolutionary; it is essentially alien to structure, organisation and extended systems. Deleuze and Guattari also continually argue that desire only works when it 'breaks down'. A 'successful' desire—when a man marries the woman of his dreams—is a pale image and repression of desire. It is only when desire goes haywire—refusing any recognised object as its supposed fulfilment—that it is really at work. For desire is just this flow that passes across, destroys and dissolves structures, terms and identities. (The feminist who says, 'Yes, that's me, I *am* woman and fully human', has subjected her desire to an image. The feminist who says, 'No, I am not one of your kind', keeps desire open.)

Anti-Oedipus

Deleuze and Guattari's critique of modern oedipal man is not just an attack on Freudian psychoanalysis. Their account itself is indebted to psychoanalysis, by insisting on the primacy of desire, but they also see psychoanalysis as a symptom of a tendency of a greater historical tendency. Just as life tends to organise itself into relatively stable points, so human history has tended to reduce its own life to the already formed productions of desire. An attack on the picture of the Oedipus complex—the picture of the human self that enters culture by repressing 'natural' desires for the maternal origin—frees desire and life from such supposedly fixed instinct. We are repressed by the very idea that we have a natural object—the mother or the origin—that we must renounce to become human. In telling us that we must not desire our mothers, western culture presents desire as that which was first directed towards the mother. The prohibition produces the person.

This means that before there is lack there is an event of creative force: the prohibition or idea that we must repress desire for our mothers—an act of force—produces us as repressed and desiring subjects. Thus prohibition, force or punishment is productive. Describing desire in terms of persons and incest, as psychoanalysis does, represses desire by organising it into human terms. Further, the mother as an extended term from which all relations are explained is produced through the fantasy of prohibition. It is in being told not to desire one's mother that desire is objectified, socialised and humanised. It is only by telling us that incest is prohibited that the social machine (and psychoanalysis) produces an image of desire as familial. The oedipal story of a desire that emerges from the family reduces desire to a personal and private complex of extended terms. And once these extended terms (mother–father–child) have been marked out, desire is explained as the (disjunctive) relation between one term and another. The child must accept paternal authority or fall back into unmediated maternal death:

> It is the great nocturnal memory of the intensive germinal filiation that is repressed for the sake of an extensive somatic memory, created from filiations that have become extended (patrilineal *or* matrilineal) and from the alliances that they imply ...
> The system in extension is born of the intensive conditions that make it possible, but it reacts on them, cancels them, represses them, and allows them no more than a mythical expression. The signs cease to be ambiguous at the same time as they are determined in relation to the extended filiations and the lateral alliances: the disjunctions become exclusive, restrictive (the 'either/or else' replaces the intense 'either ... or ... or ...'); the names, the appellations no longer designate intensive states, but discernible persons (Deleuze & Guattari 1983, p. 160).

By contrast with the personal oedipal account of desire and difference, Deleuze and Guattari want to show how desire has an intensive and political history, which culminates in capitalism and the (psychoanalyst's) individual. This political theory will begin from pre-personal desire. Pre-personal desire is simply the flow and force of life, prior to any organised identity or hint of stability.

Synthesis

Deleuze and Guattari describe various historical stages of the political theory of desire, each of which has its own dominant form of synthesis or production. *Anti-Oedipus* is a history of desire and its syntheses. (The quotation in the section above refers to the second 'disjunctive synthesis', which in its intense form is inclusive—one can desire this or this or this—but in its oedipal and extended form is exclusive: choose either your father or your mother.) Deleuze had already placed a great deal of importance on the positive notion of synthesis in *Difference and Repetition,* where the argument was tied to the history of philosophy. In order to have a world or an experienced and ordered domain of objects, philosophers like Hume and Kant argued that there needed to be a process of synthesis (Deleuze 1984, 1991). We need to connect our perceptions into spatial and temporal continuities; we order the world causally and logically. The world is the effect of a process of synthesis. For the most part, Deleuze accepts this argument but he makes two distinct points. First, there is not *a* world but worlds resulting from all the different syntheses that make up life. Alongside the synthesised worlds there is also the 'chaosmos', 'the intense germinal influx', the plane of immanence, the body without organs or the 'mechanosphere' (depending on which of his books we are reading.) This plane upon which syntheses take place is itself a production or synthesis; it is produced alongside. That is, there is a process of synthesis and connection; this produces relations and terms, and we then imagine some pre-synthesised, disorganised or chaotic origin or plane from which synthesis emerged:

> The plan(e) can always be described, but as a part aside, as ungiven in that to which it gives rise … Life plan(e), music plan(e), writing plan(e), it's all the same: a plan(e) that cannot be given as such, that can only be inferred from the forms it develops and the subjects it forms, since it is for these forms and these subjects (Deleuze & Guattari 1987, p. 266).

If there is a One or Totality it is not some actual ground or being that precedes different parts, nor some organism that unites parts into a more meaningful whole. It is the virtual space produced through and alongside the events of connection and spatialisation (hence the idea of a 'plane'). So, the 'body without organs' is not a general undifferentiated ground, but is specific to the events or organisation or assemblage from which it can be intuited:

> The BwO is the egg. But the egg is not regressive; on the contrary, it is perfectly contemporary, you always carry it with you as your own milieu of experimentation, your associated milieu. The egg is the milieu of pure intensity, spatium not extension ... the egg always designates this intensive reality, which is not undifferentiated, but is where things and organs are distinguished solely by gradients, migrations, zones of proximity (Deleuze & Guattari 1987, p. 164).

The three historical syntheses: Connection, disjunction, conjunction

The first synthesis of connection, with life producing distinct intensities by one flow of desire intersecting with another (mouth/breast, not yet organised into persons or full objects), can also be thought of as territorialisation: a tribe gathers on the earth through a collective and connective ritual of marking, where each body is scarred or marked by a tattoo. This is also a process of coding: cutting the flows of intensity into body parts or specific intensities.

Then there is the second synthesis of disjunction, with one intensity set against another; one body can be elevated above another, such that there is a distinction between two levels. Here, the connections are referred to some ground or order. There are the marked bodies or connections and the body of the despot who allows these marks to be seen as signs of some law or order. This can also be described as deterritorialisation— the groupings or coded collectives are distributed across a common surface; the occupied territories are ordered by some overarching or transcendent power. It is also a movement of overcoding; it is not just the immediate mark or scar on the body—the shared affect or intensity—that organises the tribe. The mark or scar (the code) is read as a sign of subordination to the power of the despot. The pain is no longer a collective ritual of intensity, but the threat of the despot's power. (The pain has become more than itself, producing a surplus value.)

Then there is the third synthesis of conjunction. The flows are explained or referred back to some ground, reason or logic from which they emerged. We see the connections as governed, say, by some general law of nature. The cruelty of tribal inscription is not just ordered by the terror of the despot; the law is no longer a transcendent and explicitly overpowering terror. It becomes the internal and immanent law of life. Instead of one body or investment overcoding the whole explicitly with the threat of terror, all life is decoded into one single immanent flow. All life is labour and capital, not subjected to any outside order or value. The third synthesis of conjunction refers all the flows back to some general abstract essence, such as the flow of capital. The order of connections is not imposed from without (the body of the despot terrorising the tribe); it is produced from the ground—all connections and disjunctions, all differences or flows, are read as instances of, as signs or expressions of, some underlying whole. It is through this third synthesis that we can imagine that virtual whole of difference which possessed the tendencies from which difference emerged: the body without organs, the chaosmos, the plane of immanence, life, virtual difference.

From cruelty to terror

One example of the three historical stages or regimes of synthesis can be drawn from Deleuze's contemporary Michel Foucault, although the main difference between Deleuze and Foucault lies in the first stage. Foucault does not consider life before the disjunctive synthesis; a point where life was nothing more than its open connections would not be thinkable. We would need to have some disjunctive point, such as the self, from which we can think. Deleuze thought it was possible to write and think about power before its political overcoding; he referred to a pre-personal desire not yet recognised in terms of human sexualities. By contrast, Foucault wrote about the second and third regimes of desire, where desire is explicitly regulated by external force, such as tyrants or despots (Foucault 1979), followed by modernity where desire becomes self-subjecting and referred back to the subject (Foucault 1981). Foucault did write about the 'body and its pleasures' prior to any general code, but he insisted that—even in Ancient Greece—desire could be thought only through norms and regularities.

We can think of the three stages that *Anti-Oedipus* describes as primitive (cruelty), despotic (terror) and capitalist (cynical), through the notion of immanence and transcendence. In cruelty, or the primitive social machine, power is immanent; tribes are organised through the circulation of forces, a mark on one body affirms the force of the whole, and bodies are only organised, collected and separated (or assembled) through the action and reaction of forces. There is always a tendency for one of those bodies, the body of the chieftain, to transcend and organise power from above, but this tendency is warded off by further acts of force and investment, such as investments in impersonal forces that cut across bodies: sacrifices, totems, animal intensities.

In the second (despotic) stage, desire or force is subjected to some transcendence; the marks on the body are seen as punishments inflicted by the 'enjoying' eye of the despot. Deleuze and Guattari made these three stages explicit in their work, but the idea of a pre-modern regime of terror was also explored by Michel Foucault.

Foucault's *Discipline and Punish* (1979) describes just such a regime of terror or spectacle, and how this spectacle or enjoyment of the eye produces the transcendence of power. Forces are no longer operating through action and reaction, but are organised by a body that presents itself as the origin or law of force. A body is tortured publicly for having committed the crime of regicide. A system of debt is produced because we can see the suffering of this body as a payment for a crime. This equation is only possible through disequilibrium: one body—the body of the king—must represent a law that measures, distributes and judges the force of all bodies. The disequilibrium or emergence of a separate transcendent power is achieved through spectacle. Instead of a tribe viewing the marking of a body and investing the organ collectively where all bodies will be cut and scarred, a body is displayed for torture with the law overseeing what has now become punishment. The other bodies of the socius look on and are ordered by terror, the threat of the law—or the eye of the king—that may always extract punishment as a debt. The elevated body that issues the law or punishment must be capable of overseeing a measurement. It is in the public display of the marked body that the process of cruelty becomes one of terror. The body is not just being marked but punished. The torture of the criminal body 'equals' payment for transgression of law. Law begins positively and excessively: it is by exerting more force that the despot's body is elevated and produced; more social energy and power are gathered at a certain point, creating a disjunction. This contrasts with the oedipal account where law emerges from lack; it is because we are other than the origin or mother that we must imagine a law or father that robbed us of our original desire. Foucault and Deleuze's accounts are anti-oedipal precisely because they see law as secondary to production and excess. The original joy in cruelty, and then the excess of cruelty in the despot's overseeing enjoyment and terror, produces social distinctions and law.

It is in Foucault's described modern regime of power as 'discipline' that we see a new relation between immanence, transcendence and spectacle, and it is here that his account of the subject dovetails with Deleuze and Guattari's history of oedipal man. In *Discipline and Punish* Foucault describes how the actual and elevated enjoying body of the terrorising despot becomes a virtual power of subjection. A body in prison is being 'viewed' by a central tower; whether the warden is in the tower or not is immaterial. The prisoner is disciplined by the virtual gaze, or the possibility, of being viewed. Power no longer acts on the body materially but immaterially or virtually. When prisons then use all the machinery of the human sciences—criminology, psychology and sociology—to ask about the intentions and psyche of the criminal, they produce an immaterial power that installs itself within the body. The practices that seek to 'know' man—the human sciences—actually produce man as an object to be viewed. (In modernity there is no longer some separate point of power; power flows through all the bodies as a micropolitics through the very notion or concept of man as subject.) In examining, knowing, questioning and making a problem of the criminal, the prisons, courts and human sciences produce the object 'humanity'. In modernity it is through knowing ourselves—especially through questions of sexuality—that desire is subjected to one of its own produced and transcendent terms. The law is no longer attributed to a punishing despot, but to the soul that lies within us all. This new regime of power and spectacle reaches its pitch in the very notion of the modern sexual individual. What do I want? What is it normal or human to do? Who am I? What is my sexuality? Psychoanalysis takes the force that was once circulating primitively and then attributed to the body of the despot, and installs it within the soul of the individual. (So we get a conjunction of all the flows to one point—the medium of human life or 'man'. What is my sexuality? What do all these desires mean?)

We have become self-disciplining precisely because we have repressed the historical and political syntheses that produce bodies and individuals. We have installed a soul or individual as the origin and ground of all the syntheses; the flow of life is normalised and interpreted—referred to some underlying substance. The task of *Anti-Oedipus* is to explain the syntheses that produce human bodies as social individuals, and then to explain how these syntheses have become subordinated to one of their transcendent productions: familial man.

Immanent and transcendent use of the syntheses

Each form of synthesis, Deleuze and Guattari argue, has its legitimate (immanent) and illegitimate (transcendent) uses. This, the crucial distinction for their political theory, requires a redefinition of desire and difference, and also enables a new mode of political critique. A legitimate understanding of the syntheses does not ground the production of desire on some prior term. Immanent connection, for example, would understand intensities or 'partial objects' as produced from flows: it is the intersection of the mouth and breast that produces the pleasure or intensity of two surfaces. A transcendent understanding, however, begins with already synthesised terms, explaining desire from one of its effects. Psychoanalysis explains desire from the relation of the mother to the desire of the child. But, as Deleuze and Guattari insist, such 'global persons' are themselves effects of intensities. Being a 'mother' is possible, not only after the connection with the child's mouth, but with a series of other intensities (including the formations of separate tribes or lines of alliance), such that the 'mother' is a social–political function. The mother is the one whose body is prohibited as an object of desire by the chieftain, and the chieftain's power is achieved through the investment of intensities. It is this body (of the chieftain) that gathers the forces of production, enjoying more than the other bodies. The organising power of the social machine is achieved with excess and surplus value: by enjoying more of the forces of production the body of the despot becomes a point of power and law. This then allows for the creation of social orders; by prohibiting certain bodies for enjoyment—such as the body of the mother—something like a family is created. Families are created through social machines, and such social machines can only operate by coding desires. The breast begins as an organ of production, as does the hand, whose material goods are abstracted by the chieftain. We are not yet in the regime of private persons but of collectively invested organs.

So the first synthesis of connection (mouth and breast) becomes socially recorded in disjunction. The productions are divided, distributed and separated into a surplus. Society, Deleuze and Guattari insist, does not begin with scarcity but excess. A social machine is formed when the excess of production, such as the productions of the hand that are not consumed, or the enjoyment of body parts that exceed the needs of life, are 'drawn off' by a locus of anti-production: the chieftain who enjoys the labour of bodies while not producing.

Thus the first two syntheses of connection and disjunction

have an immanent and transcendent use. It is the transcendent use that produces the social machine, and accounts for the way desire becomes limited by its own productions. Immanent connection begins with the flows of desire from which persons are formed as organised 'zones'. Connection is then subjected to the illusion of transcendence when we locate these zones of intensity on pre-given extended objects; we imagine connection as operating between persons; we begin analysis from already synthesised terms. The second synthesis of disjunction also has an immanent and transcendent use. Immanent disjunction is inclusive. The flow of desire includes all the points through which it passes; the mouth of the child is at once also the breast to which it attaches; its body at one with the toys it handles, the images of animals with which it is fascinated. It is psychoanalytic interpretation that understands disjunction exclusively; and this is where transcendence emerges. Desire must be either for the mother (anti-social and regressive) or for the father (social and self-productive). The child, for psychoanalysis, is both radically other than its object of desire (the breast) and disjoined from the body part that organises desire (the father's phallus). Child, mother and father become exclusive positions ordering the flow of desire from without: either identify with your father or fall back into the pre-oedipal undifferentiated night of the maternal.

In social–political terms, Deleuze and Guattari describe the illegitimate use of exclusive disjunction: one is either white or black, male or female. Immanent disjunction is inclusive: 'I am male and female, white and black, all the sexes and all the races of the world.' Exclusive disjunction is produced by a distinction between ordering law and the series of objects: you must be one or the other.

The third synthesis also has its immanent and transcendent uses. We understand conjunction immanently if we see the body without organs as a totality or One that is nothing more than its parts, produced alongside those parts. The body without organs is the imagined whole, thought from the point of view of a specific desire or production. There is no whole or ground in general, only perceptions of the whole from singular events. So, it is not that there is a ground or body that is then divided or separated into parts. Rather it is from the connections and disjunctions of parts that we discern the body without organs that is nothing more than the plane of all syntheses and intensities; it does not exist independently or prior to these syntheses. Immanent conjunction is an understanding of the intersection of all these flows in a 'substantive multiplicity'. That is, even if all the flows can be discerned as a whole this does not mean they are unified by a single measure. It is conjunction that enables us to think the body without organs. From all the partial objects, intensities and body parts that are produced through connections we can imagine that uncoded, disorganised flux that allows itself to be coded. This multiplicity or conjunction is nothing outside of itself, not organised by a common measure or ground: 'a multiplicity is defined not by the elements that compose it in extension, not by the characteristics that compose it in comprehension, but by the lines and dimensions it encompasses in "intension." If you change dimensions, if you add or subtract one, you change multiplicity' (Deleuze & Guattari 1987, p. 245). In the transcendent use of conjunction the multiplicity is subjected to some ordering principle: the body without organs is interpreted as the social body or origin from which difference and law derive. Desire is referred back to human nature; social organisation and exchange is referred back to the law of capital.

Immanence and passive synthesis

It is the transcendent use of synthesis that allows us to judge life from the position of one of its produced terms: man, society, or even human sexuality. Immanent synthesis refuses to locate desire within persons or agents of intention. The syntheses of desire, if understood pre-personally and without meaning or intent, open up a political theory of intensities, rather than values or ideology. Political critique would begin with schizoanalysis: look at any moral opposition—such as the opposition between good and evil, law and its others—and examine the process of differentiation that allows life to be ordered by a seemingly transcendent principle.

The processes of synthesis cannot be located within the human subject, and so Deleuze makes much of these syntheses being passive and pre-personal. This is where the history of synthesis links up with the history of desire. Desire is production and synthesis itself, and it is from desire and its productions that the individual is ultimately produced. There are passive syntheses within the human body (the beating of the heart, the contractions of muscles, and even the activities of the brain that give thought), and there are also inhuman passive syntheses (genetic, molecular and animal becomings). In *Anti-Oedipus* and *A Thousand Plateaus* the syntheses are trans-human: the productions of social machines and the investments in intensities that are not decided by individuals.

In *Difference and Repetition*, and in many of his other works, Deleuze refers to passive synthesis. We usually conclude that because our world is made up of meaningful and ordered (or synthesised) units that there must have been some subject who synthesised, and we usually think of this subject as the human mind or ego. But synthesis, Deleuze insists, is passive and can only be explained if we do not locate desire within organisms but think of desire as life itself, which then synthesises or connects and produces organisms. (Traditional evolutionary theory suffers from the same failures that plague western metaphysics: of thinking difference extensively. It explains life from bodies or species that survive, respond and adapt. To think creation intensively demands that we see evolution as a process that flows through bodies, so that genetic creations are neither bounded by organisms, nor can they be explained as adaptations or responses to some outside world.)

There is a creative genesis that produces borders between insides and outsides through the formation of strata. The development of vision, for example, is a creation that can be affirmed in the becoming of a number of species in different ways; it is a tendency in life which can manifest itself or be actualised in different types of organisms. It is not that the organism offers a response to an outside world. It is from a responsive life in general that the eye–light assemblage can be formed. There is, in life, already a virtual tendency for vision to be actualised, and it can be actualised through different lines of development. The tendency or becoming is not owned by the organism; the organism is the vehicle or passage through which the becoming flows.

The history of thought has tended to ground synthesis on some subject, such that becoming or desire—the very production of life—is interpreted as the activity of some being. Again, this is the error of transcendence: attributing becoming to one of its effects. It might seem strange at first, but it is only if we think of synthesis as passive that we can really affirm desire. If synthesis were active it would be the activity of some thing, being or subject; it would relate, then, to what it is not. The subject would synthesise its world; mind would synthesise its experiences. But passive synthesis just means that there is production and connection, without being grounded on some prior agent or subject.

Think of it at the human level first. I can think of desire negatively, as striving to achieve what I do not have. This would mean that desire would be explained from the starting point of a subject. Alternatively, desire can be thought of affirmatively. It is not that 'I' have desires; it is from desire that an 'I' or subject is effected. Desire will be nothing more than the development, production or assertion of what 'I' will be or can become. The notion of desire as productive means that desire does not result from something not having what it wants. Desire is the affirmation or production of difference—all the while bearing in mind that difference is different in each of its becomings. But we also need to think this affirmative notion of desire alongside a prehuman and passive synthesis. Take an example from evolution: organisms are formed or synthesised by following the possibilities or pathways that increase their power. These are not conscious or active syntheses, they are not acts of mind, nor are they decisions. But we can see them in terms of desire, for the creation of life is the affirmation of a force or power. Different organisms are not the result of a uniform life that splits into species. The syntheses of life—the differences and repetitions from which organisms emerge—are productive and infinitely richer than the closed forms we seem to perceive. A being evolves, not by unfolding what it *is*, but by selecting and actualising a multiplicity of its virtual powers to become. Thus becoming is not the action of an agent responding to an object world, becoming is desire and synthesis. The 'who' or 'what' that desires (the distinction between inside and outside) is produced in and through the production of relations. Further, the relations and connections, or syntheses, of life are secondary to the affirmations of the singular powers from which distinct beings emerge.

To see the synthesis of life as passive is to recognise its thoroughly open and immanent nature, not subordinated to any originating ground, prior intent, being or form. Desire is just this affirmation and production of life from itself, towards no end other than itself. Desire is not the desire of either some agent or some object:

> ... there is a pure plane of immanence, univocality,
> composition, upon which everything is given, upon which
> unformed elements and materials dance that are
> distinguished from one another only by their speed and that
> enter into this or that individuated assemblage depending on
> their connections, their relations of movement. A fixed plane
> of life upon which everything stirs, slows down or
> accelerates. A single abstract Animal for all the assemblages
> that effectuate it (Deleuze & Guattari 1987, p. 255).

It is from the productions and syntheses of desire that there are agents and objects, and these productions derive from difference itself. (Thinking this 'difference itself' is to think the body without organs; it is the imagined or virtual whole that encompasses all differences.) So to say that life is passive synthesis is to insist that it does not proceed from agents, and that agents and subjects are productions of the singular becomings that cannot be reduced to some general ground or uniform difference:

> Desire is the set of *passive syntheses* that engineer partial
> objects, flows, and bodies, and that function as units of
> production. The real is the end product, the result of the
> passive syntheses of desire as autoproduction of the
> unconscious. Desire does not lack anything; it does not lack

its object. It is, rather, the *subject* that is missing in desire, or desire that lacks a fixed subject; there is no fixed subject unless there is a repression. Desire and its object are one and the same thing: the machine, as a machine of a machine (Deleuze & Guattari 1983, p. 26).

Surplus value

Even before Deleuze teamed up with the psychoanalyst Guattari he had already taken the logical discourse of philosophy and argued that our mental operations were manifestations of the impersonal syntheses of 'life'. The syntheses of connection ('and') or disjunction ('or') can be understood not just logically but also genetically: connection of one flow of genetic material with another ('and'), and the processes of selection through which genetic mutation passes ('or'). The syntheses can also be referred to socio-economically: connection begins as the production of life, with human bodies producing in order to remain alive, while disjunction refers to 'recording', so that the goods produced can be distributed among the group. The final synthesis of conjunction refers to consumption, such that there are now collective or individual subjects whom the system of production seems to serve. In all these cases of the syntheses—the logical, genetic and economic—Deleuze refers to 'surplus value'. Desire is flow. But the flow of desire does not precede uniformly. The flow is unbalanced, producing disequilibrium, or points where more energy or quantity alters the very function of the system. In the case of economics, surplus value is just that element of production that exceeds the direct needs of human production and allows for disequilibrium of power. If the chieftain of a tribe gathers the excess of the harvest, then this produces a point outside the chain of production that can govern the whole. So, social power begins with excess of force and enjoyment, and not with scarcity and fear.

Surplus value can also be understood genetically; if two lines of genetic code intersect, there is always an excess element that produces a radical indeterminacy in development such that evolution cannot be predicted as the simple addition and

118

accumulation of data. Two simple chains of code can, through 'misfirings' or 'drift' (or even the 'leaps' of viruses), create mutations and transformations far in excess of the original quantities. Surplus value also has its psychoanalytic resonance. The mouth that connects with the breast sustains the production of life but there is also an excess pleasure drawn off from the production: the pleasure of the surface of the lips forms a zone outside production (the infant's pleasure in sucking independent of any nourishment). Finally, there is surplus value at the level of code in general; if a flow of graphic material or writing is taken to mean something, then there is a sense established outside the connection of signs. The signifier, for Deleuze and Guattari, is therefore the very form of transcendent or despotic power: the way in which a code or flow of data is subjected to some point of interpretation. When a mark becomes a signifier it becomes more than its actual force; we ask what the signifier means. We are subjected to one element in the code that seems to offer the law of code in general—the signifier overcodes.

Overcoding

It is through the particular synthesis of human marks and sounds—what Deleuze and Guattari refer to as the voice–graph system—that a surplus value of sense is produced. The marks are not just immanent, actual and material forces, but produce an incorporeal transformation. A virtual world of sense is created alongside the actual world. A knife may cut a body, but when we call this event a punishment we create a whole new (incorporeal) world of morals, crimes, criminals, laws and judgements. (For an extended analysis of the politics of incorporeal events of sense see Patton 1996.) In *The Logic of Sense* (1990) Deleuze regards the capacity of language to produce incorporeal transformations as the very opening of creative thought. Sense does not just perceive the actual world; it also opens out to the virtual. It is a surplus of perception. The clearest case of this is the sense of the problem: an organism can do this or that, or say this or that, but in thinking or deliberating these possibilities it must locate itself in a problem.

119

All life is productive or open through the problems it poses, and the incorporeal transformations of sense—our words and signs—allow us to extend and magnify problems.

In *Anti-Oedipus* Deleuze and Guattari describe the way the incorporeal transforming power is subjected to the despotic signifier. The signifier presents itself not as the production or synthesis of relations and transformations but as the representation of some preceding meaning. Western culture in general suffers from this 'interpretosis'. That is, there is a power to produce sense—that which is more than the signifier or sign itself. We react against this when we think the signifier does not produce but stands in for, or replaces, a meaning or sense that was there all along and which is now lacking or hidden. Rather than looking at the way marks produce sense (how do inscriptions work and transform bodies?), we ask what signifiers mean. We subject force to some supposedly underlying law or power; we do not see power at the immanent level of forces themselves. In the case of psychoanalysis we interpret desires to disclose an oedipal unconscious—so this is what you must have wanted, the meaning that was there all along, behind all the signs of your desire.

What makes the signifier despotic is just this capacity, through synthesis, to produce some transcendent or incorporeal power that appears as the very law of synthesis. Whereas the despot or king directly controls the flows of bodies through gathering the material surplus of production, the signifier allows life to be subjected immanently. To take a mark as a signifier is to posit some sense behind what it says. The system of signs is referred back to some meaning which it then re-presents. 'Behind' all the signs is the speaking subject. Against representation and interpretation, Deleuze insists that we should not be referring signs back to the sense they express; rather, we should see the content that is expressed as the effect of productive syntheses. This means that we should not be subjecting the divergent series of syntheses to the signifier; we should not be asking of life: what does it mean? To do so is to treat all life as the sign of some underlying law. We need to assess the syntheses and forces themselves. So, presented with an action we should not posit some moral meaning behind the event: is this good or evil? (Is this film sexist or feminist?) We should be looking at what those forces do: what relations and terms are created? (Does this film create possibilities for thinking or does it reduce becoming to already given terms?) Against overcoding—trying to find the sense and underlying meaning for the events of life—we should decode, or assess, the singular forces that produce systems and regularities. The problem of capitalism is that it decodes—seeing all religions, cultures, meanings and values as lacking in any specific power or meaning—but then 'axiomatises' all these codes through capital. Capital can allow the flow of any language or system as long as it is quantified and circulating through the system of exchange. The only way to overcome this homogenising power of capital, which decodes only to reduce difference, is to decode the syntheses and open up their power to produce difference—the power of desire.

Synthesis is the very form of life. By arguing that politics, genetics, economics and desire can be explained by the formal operations of synthesis, Deleuze transforms the very status of theory: we do not just use logic to analyse social or biological data. We have to see the way our logic or forms of thought are themselves instances of the impersonal syntheses of life. 'Desire' refers to this impersonal and universal synthesis which produces organisms, societies, economic and linguistic systems and selves. No object—neither consciousness nor language, genetics, politics, history or the economy—can be positioned outside the chain of production to act as an explanatory point. We can only begin with process: the formal operations of desire or the syntheses. The analysis is therefore immanent; no transcendent point or context grounds the whole. There are coexisting 'planes' of genetics, linguistics, history, politics and logic.

The history of desire

What now needs to be understood is how Deleuze and Guattari historicise and politicise the three modes of synthesis: connective, disjunctive and conjunctive. This accords with three historical and political formations: the tribal/primitive, the barbarian/despotic and capitalist. Before we consider this history we need to understand what Deleuze and Guattari refer to as machinic production. They insist that the word 'machine' is not a metaphor, which means that they want to begin with the literal notion of life as machine, and not as organism or mechanism. A machine operates by the connection of parts. Unlike an organism or a mechanism it has no final or bounded form; it is pure production in and for itself without governing intention. Desire, therefore, is not the effect of differentiating a subject from an object (as in psychoanalysis or structuralism). Desire is machinic and productive.

Connection

The first synthesis is connective. Imagine the pure flow of intensive life. In order for any mode of difference to become, it will connect with other becomings. A wasp connects with an orchid; in so doing both the wasp and the orchid become different in their own way, and this difference is both an affirmation of their own power and a creative response to another power with which they connect. All life works this way, with one machine connecting to another, one flow connecting with another flow. Deleuze refers to the becoming of 'machines' rather than things or beings, because a machine is a process, not a pre-given substance, and a machine is devoid of any purpose or governing intention other than its own operation or power. Of course, we do end up with organisms and mechanisms—such as human beings and the system of capital. The point of *Anti-Oedipus* is to write a history of desire and its syntheses, showing the emergence of organisms and the production, also, of a body without organs.

The first thing to note about the structure and terminology of both *Anti-Oedipus* and *A Thousand Plateaus* is that Deleuze and Guattari refer to these processes of synthesis using a collective and political terminology. Whereas previous philosophers had argued that the world was synthesised by subjects—who formed the world through connections of time and space—Deleuze and Guattari take all the categories of logic and render them directly political. Consider the connective synthesis. In terms of logic we use the term 'and', and we might say that it is the most basic synthesis for the formation of the world. Deleuze and Guattari do two things to this synthesis. First, connection is described as a process of territorialisation, and so it occurs through a directly political collection of bodies in space. At its simplest level we can think of a territorialisation as the connection of bodies into a tribe. This connection or production is not the connection of named units (it is not 'the Australians' who connect), it is the synthesis of connection that forms the territory; the bodies connect and so *become* bodies ('we are of this tribe') and the territory becomes what it is through this connection ('the land of this tribe'). So the first synthesis is social and political, not because it takes place within the polis or society, but because it forms a 'social machine'. In tribal forms of the socius the system is one of cruelty: it is in the marking or scarring of bodies that groups are formed. (Imagine a scene of ritual and collective tattooing; it is pain that produces a surplus value. We look on and wince or flinch as the young boy is initiated through a cut into his body; it is this surplus pain or the affect on the eye that collects the tribe.) There is only a socius or collection of bodies after certain connections, and connections are produced through the affirmation of force.

Disjunction

The processes of the connecting machines are inscribed or marked, and this leads to the next synthesis, which is the disjunctive. While connection is the logic of 'and', disjunction is the logic of 'or', so in disjunction one machine can be contrasted with another (Deleuze & Guattari 1983, pp. 12–13). The marks on the body or the inscriptions can be referred to a higher machine: rather than collective inscription, where the intensity of pain is spread across the territory, the pain is enjoyed by the despot. The marks inscribe a terror; the body is subjected to the possible vengeance of the despot. Societies are not stable systems of exchange, or collections of bodies, but rely on disequilibrium or surplus value. It is only if one point on the system is the locus of more force than the others that the system is given some sort of organisation. When the despot looks on and enjoys the marking of bodies, the social production of energy is referred to some point outside the chain of connection. So, while primitive social regimes operate by connection across the body of the earth, barbarian regimes add a disjunction which orders the spaces on the earth by the despot's body being elevated above the other bodies: 'For the first time, something has been withdrawn from life and from the earth that will make it possible to judge life and to survey the earth from above: a first principle of paranoiac knowledge' (Deleuze & Guattari 1983, p. 194).

The despot appears as the representative of law and force, descended from the gods and bearing a higher power. The crucial thing to note is the transition from immanence to transcendence: from a power that operates on bodies across a space or territory, to a power that organises that territory from some position outside or above that territory. The transition from immanence to transcendence is explained, by Deleuze & Guattari, economically and immanently. Social life begins with positive cruelty, and this cruelty is nothing more than the affirmation of force: 'So much is pain part of an active life and an obliging gaze' (Deleuze and Guattari 1983, p. 191). The production of a law, which will govern this cruelty, is achieved by a surplus value of enjoyment. When the despot looks on and enjoys the marking of bodies, a position is generated from within force that seems to govern and order force. This is the beginning of the State, and the beginning of the political problem. How does desire enslave itself, react against itself and turn against itself? The affirmation of cruelty is interpreted as originating from some higher law, and can be so interpreted only because one of the bodies attracts the forces to itself. So, disjunction or the distinction between the marked bodies and the enjoying gaze of the despot also creates social time or social 'recording'. The marked body operates as a threat: if my body is marked then there must be some power or terror that can extract revenge. The despot's enjoyment of pain creates a social memory and a system of debt; the pain of the body refers to a power that may always extract force. Terror—or the anticipation of force (virtual force)—subjects bodies to a position outside the chain of production.

Conjunction

Production is being inscribed or recorded. When this happens we can imagine that there must have been some common ground or surface that was divided; this is the 'full body' of the socius. In the case of tribes and territories we imagine a pre-existing earth which is distributed among the territories. In despotic/ barbarian societies it is the body of the tyrant that operates as the ground of law and politics, and in modernity it is capital. That is, once connections and disjunctions organise bodies we subsequently presuppose a body without organs, which now seems to be the cause of all these connections. Deleuze and Guattari are here offering a political version of their argument of immanence. All life is act, event and flow, but we never experience life in all its infinite difference and production. The whole is never given. We order, synthesise or organise life into organisms and subjects. We do not think difference immanently; we ground difference on some being. Politically and socially, this necessary illusion takes the form of a production of a 'full body'. Desire assembles into tribes, states and persons; through synthesis and production it forms assemblages. But it is after the event that we imagine that there must have been some substance or ground which was assembled, some substance in itself. In modernity this is the myth of capital. We imagine some homogenous quantity that was divided up by synthesis. (We explain all social life as having emerged from the need to exchange.) But the opposite is the case; it is synthesis and desire that forms intensive quantities into bodies or units and then imagines that these bodies are instances of some general substance (capital, humanity).

Capitalism and schizoanalysis

There is a more specific problem with capital, however. All the other produced surfaces, in primitive and State forms, explicitly displayed the force of power in all its positivity. The problem with capital is its supposed immanence. There is no longer an external figure of law that openly exerts force, such as the despot or the

125

king. Capitalism no longer abstracts units (such as the bodies of subjects), which are then coded by some higher law; there is no law outside the unit of capital itself. Capitalism is immanent and axiomatic. We become self-subjecting—and this is because of the third or conjunctive synthesis. If the first synthesis is connective and forms assemblages, the second is disjunctive and allows these assemblages to be mapped in relation to each other, ordered by some external law or 'terror'. We could also describe this as a process of territorialisation (the connection into tribes), followed by deterritorialisation (the relation of these tribes to each other across the space of the earth, and then the overcoding of these positive inscriptions by the figure of law or State). In the third synthesis of conjunction we explain or organise the first two syntheses by positing some cause, origin, ground or subject. This, according to Deleuze and Guattari, explains the modern oedipal individual. First, there is a pure flow of intensities. From this flow assemblages or territories are formed. Then we imagine that these territories or assemblages were the differentiations of some undifferentiated absolute (the body without organs that is produced alongside production). Finally, we give an interpretation to this distribution: there must be some law, agent or subject from which this differentiation emerges. There must be some law—the king—that authors and legitimates the process of inscription. In capitalism, 'man' and capital become the point of conjunction. We begin with codes, the marks on bodies (cruelty). This is then overcoded by an external power; the marks are attributed to a punishing external power or law (terror). Capitalism is a radical decoding. There is not an external authority that overcodes or that allows each unit and event of exchange to be subjected to the threat or terror of power. Every point and force of capital is rendered equivalent; life is nothing more than exchange and flow, but this is a flow of capital. So there is at once a radical decoding and deterritorialisation; we no longer allow any impediment to the flow of capital. But it is now the flow itself which comes to govern and subject desire: we work, not for some enjoying despot, but just to keep the flow of capital moving. It is no longer a surplus value of code that forms the social regime (no longer an excess of goods or enjoyment around a body to create a disequilibrium).

Capitalism is a surplus value of flows; anything is allowable and permissible if it can be translated into capital flow. It is not a transcendent State or ideology that subjects human life to some overarching code or belief. It is the immanence of flow. Any practice, technology, knowledge or 'belief' can be adopted if it allows the flow of capital. There is therefore a reterritorialisation, not because a part comes to govern the whole, but because the whole is subjected to an axiom: 'It is at the level of flows, the monetary flows included, and not at the level of ideology, that the integration of desire is achieved' (Deleuze & Guattari 1983, p. 239).

Economic exchange before capitalism, Deleuze and Guattari argue, always 'warded off' the unimpeded flow of exchange: the despot or authority enforces an external limit and draws off surplus value. Flows are subjected to a higher authority. There is an element of deterritorialisation, such that the marks on bodies refer to some higher social system of debts and punishments, or the possibility of a terror that may always be inflicted. But deterritorialisation is kept in check through the figure of an external law or elevated body (disjunction); flows are organised and subjected to a higher point that governs the code. In capitalism it is the third synthesis and decoding that takes over. The third synthesis posits a uniform and undifferentiated full body behind or beneath the connections and disjunctions. In capitalism the codes are no longer subjected to an external authority; it is the unit of code itself that governs life.

We can look at this in abstract terms. We need to organise the intense flux of life into extended matter. We then think that there was some (transcendent) matter which our experience merely re-presented or encountered (the illusion of transcendence, or the explanation of life from two of its terms: mind and matter). But the real problem arises when we take some generalisation or abstraction of all these extended bodies and posit something like matter in general as the very origin of all being. Politically, the error takes the following form: we use some measure, such as money, to allow the exchange of different terms, but we then assume that this measure was the very origin and essence of exchange. In capitalism the system circulates and exchanges, not so that any desire can be realised, but because there is just the desire for capital flow. The signifier that was produced in order to allow exchange (capital) becomes the very axiom of exchange: all relations and productions are valued and ordered by their capacity to generate and move capital.

Prior to capitalism, then, the codes always allowed the flow of some content—such as women, food, goods or symbols—and the codes seemed to be regulated by some higher point outside the code: the terror of law or the body of the despot. The pure flow of life that is organised by the social machines is always relatively territorialised and deterritorialised. Bodies must be marked, and goods must be quantified (territorialisation), but they must also be allowed to interact and produce, and produce a surplus value that enables subjection (from the sumptuous feasts of kings to the display of military power). In capitalism there is a radical deterritorialisation and decoding. The flows of exchange are no longer impeded by an external authority, so deterritorialisation is no longer limited from without. Capitalism works by allowing maximum exchange without subjection to a higher law. More significantly, though, there is a radical decoding. Capital is not the measure or quantity that allows the exchange of goods. It is capital itself that is exchanged and flows. (Think of the way one can live as a sharemarket trader; the flow of capital is not used to translate one set of goods into another, but only to increase capital flow.) Not only can everything become capital (think of the way the avant-garde, punk, feminism, and post-colonialism all become marketable images), but power is produced by the flow rather than a surplus value of code. It is not that there is some external authority that governs the flow of code; it is the imperative of the flow of capital that governs life. Politics is no longer a question of the State, some position or law elevated above the flow of life—political power is immanent. (We all know today that it is the power of capital that selects, decides, gives power and distributes.) It does not matter what is exchanged and quantified; indeed, it is not that there is a substance that is quantified. It is the unit or measure of exchange that has become the immanent authority. Transcendence has now been installed within immanence. We use a measure such as money originally to exchange goods; but now it is money itself, the flow of money, its capacity to decode every other code, that is the very power of capitalism. If marking bodies was cruelty, and over-coding those marks with a law was terror, then the capitalist reign is one of cynicism. Capitalism does not work by ideology or belief; capitalism is not a set of moral or political values. This is why capitalism can allow for all forms of art, knowledge and belief. We can watch the feminism of *Thelma and Louise* at the cinema, affirm the multiculturalism of indigenous art works in galleries, have corporate sponsorships of gay pride festivals and have university scientists and intellectuals working on radical knowl-edges. There is no meaning or message that can transgress capitalism, for capitalism is no longer a morality or code. It is the capacity or power to allow all codes to flow as capital. Any 'belief' can circulate if it sells, and any science will be supported if it produces a further flow of capital.

Axiom and Utopia

We are enslaved by the very axiom of capitalism, and yet for Deleuze and Guattari this also signals a utopian possibility. Both capitalism and psychoanalysis have the radical power of decoding; they allow us to recognise that authority and power are strictly questions of synthesis. It does not matter who or what is in power—the despot, the king, the State or 'man'—what does matter is the production of these authorities through the syntheses of desire. The syntheses are used illegitimately or tran-scendently when one of the synthesised units is placed outside the chain and used to explain or govern the whole. What makes capitalism so insidious and so inescapable is that we no longer posit some external authority that would organise the process of coding; we allow the abstract and uniform process of decoding to operate as an immanent limit and subjection. The radically free flow of code that would destroy all subjection and let desire run riot is impeded only by subjection to the very abstract essence of flow (capital). What prevents capitalism from becoming a utopia of desire is that once we get rid of all external authorities—the despot, the king, God—we become enslaved to the abstract quantity of the syntheses. We imagine that there is some real unit (capital/desire) that provides the foundation or origin of the syntheses.

This is what allows economists to speak of the 'laws' of capital, and it is also what allows modern individuals to recognise and interpret their desire. We imagine—from the free flows or syntheses of capital and desire—that there must have been someone or something from which the syntheses originated. We subject the flow as process to an abstract substance (capital or man). This is what makes the third synthesis of conjunction illegitimate and transcendent, and what distinguishes the full body of capital from the absolutely deterritorialised body without organs. The open totality of flows of divergent series of difference (the body without organs) is organised from within by the axiom of capital:

> Here we discover a new determination of the properly
> capitalist field of immanence: not only the interplay of the
> relations and differential coefficients of decoded flows, not
> only the nature of the limits that capitalism reproduces on an
> ever wider scale as interior limits, but the presence of
> antiproduction within production itself. The apparatus of
> antiproduction is no longer a transcendent instance that
> opposes production, limits it, or checks it; on the contrary,
> it insinuates itself everywhere in the productive machine and
> becomes firmly wedded to it in order to regulate its
> productivity and realize its surplus value (Deleuze &
> Guattari 1983, p. 235).

In capitalism, the unit of exchange or code (money) no longer signifies some possible object, body or power. It is the pure flow of code or flux itself that produces power. We are subjected, but not to the body of the king or despot or the threat of law, someone or something that might abstract a debt or punishment. The debt and guilt become infinite: capital is never 'cashed in'. It does not represent a desire that can be fulfilled or discharged; it is representation itself, the capacity for all codes to become capital.

Capitalism is also the conclusion of the logic of the signifier. Prior to capitalism we can imagine social regimes of interacting and competing codes and flows—flows of goods, bodies, women and the codes of life in general. But with the idea of the signifier comes the idea of the subject and capitalism. There is one system—language, signification, the signifier—which stands in for and represents an otherwise uniform, undifferentiated and meaningless life. The very idea of the signifier is tied to decoding; all life can be referred to the system of signification. The signifier creates a separation between one regime of signs (language/code) and the world that exists there to be coded. All other codes—genetics, marked bodies, gestures—can be reduced or translated to the system of signification.

But the despotism of the signifier lies also in its emptiness; it does not represent some quantity or quality but is that which allows for the translation and relation of all other quantities. The structure of signifiers, like capital, is relational, uniformly differential. Codes are no longer governed by some voice, law or content; the signifier is nothing more than a differential relation. We speak or are subjects only insofar as we are subjected to this system of the exchange of signifiers, and the meaning or value of any signifier is nothing more than the difference of all other signifiers. We are therefore essentially castrated, for the presence or phallic power that would open the law of the system of signifiers is itself the effect of signification: 'This common, transcendent, absent something will be called phallus or law, in order to designate "the" signifier that distributes the effects of meaning throughout the chain and introduces exclusions there' (Deleuze & Guattari 1983, p. 73).

Deleuze and Guattari argue that this is what ties capitalism to structural psychoanalysis and Oedipus. We are enslaved not because we are subjected to this or that law or authority, but because of the very structure of desire and signification. It is because I speak that I am subjected to a system of signification; the oedipal fantasy is merely the representation of this structure of subjection. The father of the Symbolic order, the mother of the prohibited desire and the child's desire are effects of the system. The despotism has become internal and I am enslaved precisely because I see desire as representation: as what must be expressed through speech rather than as positive production. The 'graphism' that in tribal or primitive societies marked, scarred and tattooed bodies as a process of positive difference gives way to a 'writing' that represents the voice. The signifier is not a direct bodily inscription but the sign of some subject. With the notion of the signifier we are landed into the logic of capital and Oedipus; we imagine all desire as passing through a shared system, and we imagine this system to be sustained by the general speaking subject. Law and alienation are no longer located in the transcendent figure of the despot or king. We now accept law and subjection as our own.

The only way out of this is to push the deterritorialising tendency of capitalism and psychoanalysis to its limit. If all life is flow and synthesis then we need to undo the illusion that such flows can be generalised into a single system that can act as the axiom for all flows. Rather than seeing difference as the system of signification that codes and orders all other differences, the very notion of the 'speaking subject'—or 'man' as the locus of economic and sexual difference—is actually the effect of inhuman, divergent and positive becomings.

Schizoanalysis

Let us begin by positing, at one end of the spectrum, a flow of life that is purely nomadic, not occupying any specific ground and moving freely. Before it is humanised, life is actually char-acterised by a complex flow of highly differentiated genetic material. Certain networks or connections of genetic similarity and difference can be socially coded, or inscribed, into specific groups, such as tribes, kinship systems and families. It is only when all these specific and determined codes are decoded (in modernity) that we can 'recognise' that all along they were instances of life prior to all coding. We imagine a 'man' or 'humanity' in general that was then differentiated into tribes or races. Deleuze and Guattari argue the opposite: that tribes and races organise a genetic flow which becomes increasingly more uniform or overcoded in modernity. An immanent and schizo-analytic method would trace back from the coded units to a pure flux of 'schizzes' or molecules. The transcendent and illegitimate method traces back from the determined units (the specific and determined tribes and codes) to the abstract essence of 'man'. The immanent method sees man as the production of specific intensities: how certain bodies—white, male and able—came to signify life in general. We tend to see social organisation (illegitimately) as issuing from persons, rather than being the syntheses of pre-personal flows. Before there can be families—the recognition of mother–father–child units, or lines of filiation—the intense germinal influx needs to be organised into bodies occupying separate tribal territories, or lines of alliance. This means that the father is always the contraction or abstraction from a social and political field; the father is constituted through a much larger organisation than that of the personal family. Before there can be the triangle of sexual difference in the family, there are racial, tribal and political lines of alliance: 'The first things to be distributed on the body without organs are races, cultures, and their gods' (Deleuze & Guattari 1983, p. 85). These alliances are overcoded by a political line of filiation: the despot as son or descendent of a god organises the various chains or series.

From a general, constantly shifting and highly differentiated genesis of human life, social coding creates relatively stable, divided, social units (such as tribes which are relations of alliance): 'It is alliance that represses the great, intense, mute filiative memory, the germinal influx as the representative of the noncoded flows of desire capable of surveying everything' (Deleuze & Guattari 1983, p. 185). Life in general is a process of pure becoming and differentiation which, for the purposes of social action, is stabilised, identified and coded. Interests, classes and groups are an effect of what Deleuze and Guattari refer to as 'social production'. One cannot use the units of class or persons to transgress social oppression, for it is the very coding of life into such territories that engineers oppression. Revolution, therefore, is not about transgression or overthrowing the law—revolution comes from confronting the syntheses of desire that produce law.

The difference between psychoanalysis and what Deleuze and Guattari refer to as schizoanalysis lies in the relation between immanence and transcendence. Psychoanalysis begins with the psyche: the child in relation to the mother who will identify with the threat of the father. We take extended terms and then explain politics and social power: I obey the law because I have internalised the image of my father. All political life will be the substitution of figures of authority, according to the structure of this originating triangle. Schizoanalysis, by contrast, begins with the partial objects or pre-personal differences from which the familial triangle is formed. Tribal connections occur in the marking of bodies or investment of organs, which means that body parts or 'partial objects' are directly political. There is only a phallus rather than a penis, through the process of collective inscription. The tribe might be formed by a public ritual of circumcision. It is when the despot gathers the force of these body parts that a disjunction between immanent force and political terror is produced. It is through prohibition that persons and kinship structures are produced. To say, 'You must not marry your mother or your sister', actually creates lines or distinctions between one tribe and another, and creates the family identity. The despot extracts a surplus value by being the one who *can* commit incest, by being excepted from the very prohibition that produces persons and law. Thus law is not a question of imposition but of distribution; and law is positive. The law does not impose itself on individuals and families; it produces families as part of a much larger social machine. The family is not the unit from which social organisation begins. The family is a contraction of social organisation. It is the immanence of law in capitalism that reduces the family and man to a universal function. Psychoanalysis begins from the function: All your paranoid fantasies are extensions of your father; your dreams of God, of the king or of Hitler are extensions of paternal identification. Deleuze and Guattari's schizoanalysis, by contrast, undertakes a transcendental critique of the family. The oedipal man who has internalised the father and law is the consequence of a political history. The father, they argue, is the conductor of a political field. 'Male authority' begins as tribal authority—the body of the despot who extracts enjoyment or surplus value from the bodies of the primitive socius. The modern State is a further abstraction. The idea that we are governed by what is moral or 'human' merely internalises the body of the despot; there is now the white, bourgeois male within us all. Sexual difference, as the relation between 'man' and 'woman', is a contraction and normalisation of tribal difference. We have reduced the intense flow of life to two extended bodies. The despot's body, which the socius once invested through terror, has become 'man' or humanity, which we imagine lies above and beyond all the differences of race, sex, class and history.

The task of schizoanalysis is then to take this image of universal man and disclose its specific political and historical formations. It is not that there is a relation between sexes (man and woman) that is then organised into social groupings. There are tribal and then social groupings that eventually produce a State. The State is the site of deterritorialisation, a point within desire that elevates itself to be the law of all desire. This transcendence, in capitalism, becomes nothing more than the abstract essence of man in general.

This is why all becoming, according to Deleuze and Guattari, begins with becoming-woman. 'Man' or 'humanism' is the culmination of the reaction of desire. One of desire's active effects—the abstract image of the human—is read as the ground and law of desire. Desire actively produces, but one of its terms—first the body of the despot, then the State, then 'man'—turns back and governs desire from within. Reaction turns the act of desire—persons produced from desire—into a law of desire: it is because you are a person that you desire. Your desire therefore takes this human or oedipal form. Schizoanalysis opens the familial field out into the social, political and historical field:

> It is strange that we had to wait for the dreams of colonized peoples to see that, on the vertices of the pseudo triangle, mommy was dancing with the missionary, daddy was being fucked by the tax collector, while the self was being beaten by a white man. It is precisely this pairing of the parental figures with another nature, their locking embrace similar to that of

wrestlers, that keeps the triangle from closing up again, from being valid in itself, and from claiming to express or represent this different nature of the agents that are in question in the unconscious itself.

... The father, the mother, and the self are at grips with, and directly coupled to, the elements of the political and historical situation—the soldier, the cop, the occupier, the collaborator, the radical, the resister, the boss, the boss's wife—who constantly break all the triangulations, and who prevent the entire situation from falling back on the familial complex and becoming internalized in it (Deleuze & Guattari 1983, pp. 96–7).

Reading through schizoanalysis

As an example of schizoanalysis we might consider two ways of approaching Sylvia Plath's (1932–63) great poem, 'Daddy' (Plath 1981). The poem uses the diction of fascism and Nazi politics, the father being identified not just with Germany but also with the German tongue and a 'Meinkampf look'. The daughter/speaker of the poem suspects that she might be a 'bit of a Jew'. The poem begins by addressing 'Daddy' as a 'black shoe / In which I have lived like a foot / For thirty years, poor and white'. One obvious, tried and tested way to read this poem is to begin from the biography and sexuality of Plath, such that the origins of the poem's sense would be psychological. If we begin with biography we would note Plath's own psychic fragmentation, and see this reflected in the way this, and many of her other poems, present persons through scattered body parts, items of clothing and machines. Plath uses the images of God, the fascist, a giant statue and even the trains that 'chuff' the Jews to concentration camps to describe her father. Such images could be read as metaphors, ways of describing the tyrannical hold her father has on her being, such that she is not so much a person as a foot in a shoe, bereft of psychology or height—contrasted with her father's elevation as a 'Luftwaffe' or 'ghastly statue'. We can radicalise this reading by extending biography into sexual politics. Plath uses the relation between a daughter and a father, and the metaphors of fascism, to align sexual oppression with political oppression. Plath is to her father as the Jew is to the Aryan Fascist German. Plath, we might say, shows the sexuality at the heart of politics: subjection begins sexually, from the relations between fathers and daughters. However, a reading of this nature raises the question of the order of metaphor and likeness. Is Plath using the metaphors of Nazi politics to describe a sexual oppression? Or is this a poem about political repression, or repression in general, using the figure of the father?

A schizoanalytic reading proceeds by an entirely different and historical path. Far from seeing the poem as a way of drawing analogies between private, familial sexuality and historical politics, it is a diagnosis of investments. To begin with, Nazism is not an ideology or belief, but a series of part objects and intensities: the 'Ach du', the swastika, the barbed wire, the Luftwaffe and the 'Aryan eye, bright, blue'. The poem pulls the father apart, such that 'Daddy' is no longer a figure of law, nor a familial figure, but is opened out into a political field that is also sexual, although this is no longer a personal sexuality. It is a sexuality that has invested all the force, cruelty and terror of Fascism. The father *is* a Nazi, precisely because the familial/sexual figure of the father is only possible from the contraction of politics into the figure of the brutal man who is at once father, lover, husband and fascist: 'Not God but a swastika / So black no sky could squeak through. / Every woman adores a Fascist, / The boot in the face, the brute / Brute heart of a brute like you.' Far from being a personal poem, 'Daddy' begins with personal pronouns, 'you' and 'I', only to dissolve persons into collections of bodies, nations and territories. The personal becomes familial, then political and eventually multiple: 'I thought every German was you'. At the close of the poem, it is not the daughter who kills the father. His death is described as an object, not an action:

> There's a stake in your fat black heart
> And the villagers never liked you.
> They are dancing and stamping on you.
> They always knew it was you.
> Daddy, daddy, you bastard, I'm through.

The poem concludes with the daughter's hatred becoming that of the villagers dancing over the grave of a deposed vampire. The personal pronouns have become a dancing 'They'. The father is a 'bastard' and the 'I' of the poem is 'through'.

Deleuze and Guattari reject metaphor as a way of analysing investments in power. It is not that the father is likened to a Nazi, nor that the speaker uses the Jew as a metaphor for persecution; the father and the larger political reality have the same paranoid structure and condition of possibility. What Nazism and familialism share is the attribution of power to an invested voice, a single authority. A reactionary revolution merely shifts the terms of the structure around and maintains the same coded interests: don't call me Jewish, I am one of your kind. The revolutionary schizophrenic position refuses to recognise the purity of kinds: I am a Jew, a gypsy, a villager. And the father becomes an intensity, a swastika, a boot in the face. The poem takes the paranoid investment of law—the law as image of the father—and distributes it to its part objects, the father's voice being reduced to a disembodied machine: 'The black telephone's off at the root'. And the poem's own investment is far from being an appropriation of paranoia (or the centring of power on a single voice). It does not demand power, inclusion and recognition; indeed it expresses disgust for having been 'pulled ... out of the sack ... stuck ... together with glue'. The poem's voice is schizoanalytic, in Deleuze and Guattari's sense, dissolving into all the dispossessed races of the earth: 'With my gypsy ancestress and my weird luck / And my Taroc pack and my Taroc pack / I may be a bit of a Jew'.

But it's not just the content or sense of Plath's poem that can be opened out through such a reading. The poem's very construction, diction and style resist metaphorical or analogical— and even psychological—readings (although the history of Plath scholarship would indicate otherwise). Like most literature, and certainly most poetry, Plath's poem is not given in subject/predicate propositions. It is not as though there is a speaker who is judging some outside world. The poem collects objects, parts of persons, proper names, using words as though they were found objects rather than expressions. Even the word 'I' becomes noise and repeated sound, like so many of the poem's other reiterated monosyllables: 'Ich, ich, ich, ich'. The repetition of words also refuses any development of description. Rather than attaching a series of descriptives that would develop character, the word 'brute' is repeated as both noun and adjective (and alongside 'boot'), robbing what it describes of any depth: 'The boot in the face, the brute / Brute heart of a brute like you'. This is not a poem of metaphor and symbol, but an array of words and things placed across a surface, such that no one thing can be said to be the likeness or image of the other. It is not so much what this poem means but how it works that is important: the connections it makes between the familial and the political, and the destruction of a person—the father—into objects and intensities.

The point of such a reading is not to say that a poem that seems to be about pain and fragmentation is really about celebrating difference. The point is just to question the use we make of metaphor and analogy in reading and literature. It is not that we use political images to describe familial relations, or vice versa. The family is a contraction of the political, with the father being a 'conductor' for the politics of capitalism, representing the figure of 'man' to whom we are all subjected by identification. The political is and always has been sexual; we desire the fascist because politics is nothing more than the direct and desired investment in elevated bodies. So while all the biography and personal psychology of Plath may refer the poem to a relation with her father, a schizoanalytic reading asks how the father is possible. What are the social political units, the investments and intensities, that make up the relations between persons? A feminist reading must always, therefore, be a reading of racial difference, for any image of 'man' is the image of the white, western bourgeois man of capital. But a political reading is always no less a sexual reading; for the figure of law is always the consequence of investments, in bodies, intensities and (paranoid) modes of desire.

6

Perception, time, cinema

Rather than looking at perception as the way in which one term (the eye) grasps some content (the image to be interpreted), Deleuze's politics of immanence extends to the micropolitics of pre-personal perceptions. There are non-visual, inhuman and even molecular perceptions. We need to understand how it is that the human eye has come to be taken as *the* subjective starting point for perception, and we also need to forge a 'perceptual semiotics' (Deleuze & Guattari 1987, p. 194) that explains how subjects and objects are formed from perceptions. Perception is used by Deleuze in its broadest possible sense, as a connection, interaction or encounter within the plane of life. (Thus we could regard the attraction and repulsion of molecules as an event of perception.) Perception is one of the ways in which we can understand how the immanent force of life produces relations between terms. It is also here, in the confrontation with an impersonal perception, that Deleuze and Guattari use the notion of 'haecceity', so important in *A Thousand Plateaus*. We might think of haecceity as a 'whatness' or unique quality that is not yet grounded in a subject or thing, such that perception creates subjects and objects from the interactions of haecceities (for example, vibration of light and a pulsation in the retina open the perception between eye and image):

> Perception will no longer reside in the relation between a
> subject and an object, but rather in the movement serving as

the limit of that relation, in the period associated with the subject and object. Perception will confront its own limit; it will be in the midst of things, throughout its own proximity, as the presence of one haecceity in another, the prehension of one by the other or the passage from one to the other: Look only at the movements (Deleuze & Guattari 1987, p. 282).

Codes and assemblages

Deleuze's understanding of perception is one of the ways in which he strives to free thought from its foundation in distinct terms (such as the perceiving eye of man) in order to think the differential plane from which such terms emerge (all the micro-perceptions that make up life). Let us begin by going back to the notions of territorialisation and codings. In *Anti-Oedipus* Deleuze and Guattari used these terms to refer to the ways in which social machines organise the flow of genetic life, rendering it human, political and collective. In *A Thousand Plateaus* they use a similar (expanded) vocabulary to refer to molecular life and its synthe-ses. Territorialisation can now refer not just to human bodies and political groupings or assemblages but to chemical processes and genetic processes: the ways in which proteins and nucleic acids become, or the ways in which organs, such as the hand, deter-ritorialise to become tools. Molecules territorialise and deterritorialise by creating ever-new groupings (territories) and then branching off into other possibilities (deterritorialisation). Organs such as the hand territorialise the earth by working and transforming it, but then deterritorialise when those same func-tions leave the body to become detached tools. So, 'below' the level of political territories (such as tribes or States) there are also pre-personal assemblages (everything from micro-organisms to languages).

This reference to pre-personal and molecular becomings has a twofold significance. The first has to do with method. When we refer to 'code' we often think of a language, such that an element of a code is the sign or signifier for some pre-coded content; the word refers to a thing. Once we have this idea of the signifier we then tend to think all life in 'biunivocal' terms:

as strictly divided between a content and its expression. We think of matter plus mind, the actual world and its virtual representation, bodies and speech acts: we think of the code as a virtual order imposed on actual life. We fail to see how the actual and virtual, or content and expression, are infolded and always crossing over into each other, each with their own forms and deterritorialisations. What is a signifier at one level (such as the smoke that signifies fire) can become a signified at another level (the word 'smoke' is the signifier for the signified smoke). So, against the idea of a world and then its signification in a single set of signifiers, such as language, Deleuze and Guattari see all life as one univocal plane of codings, each point in life reading or perceiving its own world. In contrast with the signifier's strict distinction between the code and what it signified, Deleuze and Guattari begin *A Thousand Plateaus* with non-signifying codes. A genetic code, for example, does not convey information: the interactions and connections are direct. DNA does not represent content; the units of a genetic chain *are* its content. So there is a methodological significance in beginning with non-signifying codes. There are also relays of codes that do not mean anything. Deleuze and Guattari can now refer to territorialisations and deterritorialisations at the molecular, or purely machinic, level. Any two connections of code—this chemical with that chemical—can create a territory, but this will also be accompanied by relative deterritorialisation or a line of flight: the outcome of the interaction is not fully determined and there will always be a drift or tendency to further becomings. (For the implications of the notion of 'line of flight' in political theory, see May (1991, p. 32), who argues for the power of local groups to produce unforeseen freedoms.) At the level of molecular life there is an element of freedom, if not free will. Even if we knew all the present elements we could never determine the outcome, for it is the interaction of elements that continually opens new becomings. The formation of 'collectives' in *A Thousand Plateaus* now refers not just to social and human assemblages but to prepersonal processes. So by beginning with non-signifying codes Deleuze and Guattari enable a method that can approach life non-interpretively.

We do not posit some sense or law behind the codes which would be their truth or order. We begin with forces rather than substances. This fulfils the requirements of immanence; we begin not with an originating, fixed or privileged term (or terms) but with the dynamic forces within which we are located. Analysis looks at how these forces produce terms. We do not begin with a moral image of man or human freedom; we rely on the examination of syntheses, interactions and the openness of life to a not already-given future. We begin, therefore, with perception: not a subject who perceives, nor an object perceived, but an interaction or event of perception which then creates a relation, territory or machine of two responding terms.

Second, as well as being important for method, the insistence on a purely immanent becoming—that is, a plane of perception not enclosed within the mind of man—is accompanied by an explanation of the emergence of the human mode of desire from the 'prebiotic soup' (Deleuze & Guattari 1987, p. 49). All life is a plane of interacting codes—genes that read or decode other genes or environments—but there are also stratifications. The connection of two codes can form a 'higher' and 'lower' element; the eye that reads the animal's tracks creates a distinction between perceiver and perceived, code and what is decoded. Indeed, *A Thousand Plateaus* delineates three modes of 'stratification'. The first is at the level of chemical life, the second at the level of organisms (Deleuze & Guattari 1987), while it is the third stratification of language and overcoding that constitutes the human. The earlier strata were 'homoplastic'—one code interacts with another through a like response (such as the virus that reads and adapts to the body it invades). But the human code, or language, creates a distinction between code and coded, between sign and world, such that language can now be used to translate and refer to any other code (we can talk about genes, cultures, gestures, chemical process and evolution in one encompassing code). It is by taking the codes as signifiers of some meaning that human life is stratified:

> There is a third major grouping of strata, defined less by a human essence than, once again, by a new distribution of

content and expression. Form of content becomes 'alloplastic' rather than 'homoplastic'; in other words, it brings about modifications in the external world. Form of expression becomes linguistic rather than genetic; in other words, it operates with symbols that are comprehensible, transmittable, and modifiable from outside. What some call properties of human beings—technology and language, tool and symbol, free hand and supple larynx, 'gesture and speech'—are in fact properties of this new distribution (Deleuze & Guattari 1987, p. 60).

We have passed from molecular perception to human perception. Perception needs first to be grasped at the molecular level, as the way in which one series of code connects with another and, through the process of perception, creates and affirms the becoming of life: 'That there are molecular perceptions no less than molecular reactions can be seen in the economy of the cell and the property of regulatory agents to "recognize" only one or two kinds of chemicals in a very diverse exteriority' (Deleuze & Guattari 1987, p. 51).

Human perception is a stratification of a 'cerebral-nervous milieu' (Deleuze & Guattari 1987, p. 64). The perceiving eye or the nervous stimulus does not respond or connect immediately but allows the brain to introduce a delay: which path? which action? what should I do? And this brain that installs delay or slowness is not some human essence of freedom but itself the outcome of highly complex connections: 'The brain is a population, a set of tribes tending toward two poles' (Deleuze & Guattari 1987, p. 64). It is language or the signifier that allows this biunivocal tendency, or a stratification between the hand that acts and the eye that perceives, the sense of the world.

Eye and signifier

If both *Anti-Oedipus* and *A Thousand Plateaus* refer to the 'despotism' of the signifier, this is because the signifier requires and institutes a certain regime of vision. Recall that it is the enjoying eye of the despot that allows the marks on bodies to be interpreted or overcoded as punishments or acts of terror. The marks are no longer just marks; they are signs or signifiers of a law or threat. But the signifier as such is a more radical deterritorialisation and is tied to a dichotomy of vision. A signifier is only a signifier if I assume some sense behind what is said or written. This is what makes a word different from noise, so a signifier essentially refers to what it is not—what is absent or signified. Now this means that the signifier is also tied to the function of the subject. Only if we can think of what lies 'behind' the sound or signifier can there be an act of signification. I must take the noise that issues from your mouth as the expression of someone who speaks. So, at the level of the signifier, we have moved from the primitive regime of marks that is the imposition of the despot's terror to the regime of subjects who speak. Codes are now the expressions of subjects. It is not the enjoying eye of the despot that overcodes the forces of difference and inscription; it is the function of the speaking subject.

In *A Thousand Plateaus* Deleuze and Guattari argue that this regime is only possible with the 'bi-univocalisation' of the perception of the face (Deleuze & Guattari 1987, p. 176). They describe this as a 'black hole/white wall' assemblage. The face is the white screen whose surface conceals some sense; the eyes are the black holes that lead to the depth of consciousness. Only the face allows the 'redundancy' of the signifier; the signifier must refer to what it is not, to the sense behind it:

> Significance is never without a white wall upon which it
> inscribes its signs and redundancies. Subjectification is never
> without a black hole in which it lodges its consciousness,
> passion and redundancies. Since all semiotics are mixed and
> strata come at least in twos, it should come as no surprise
> that a very special mechanism is situated at their intersection.
> Oddly enough, it is a face: the *white wall/black hole* system ...
> The face is not an envelope exterior to the person who
> speaks, thinks, or feels. The form of the signifier in language,
> even its units, would remain indeterminate if the potential
> listener did not use the face of the speaker to guide his or her
> choices (Deleuze & Guattari 1987, p. 167).

145

There can only be a signifier—a sound that refers to a subject who expresses some content—if there is this complex of the face. The face is not a 'head'—just one body part among others—it is a body part that allows the body to be organised as human, as meaningful, as expressive.

Human perception

Human perception—a perception that grasps the world and others as there to be interpreted—relies on a slowing down of molecular perceptions. If all life is perception—producing and connecting by attraction and repulsion—then certain assemblages are formed when perception slows down. In the case of the face, human bodies are not just interacting forces but become surfaces to be interpreted, depths to be read, sites of significance:

> The black hole/white wall system must already have gridded all of space and outlined its arborescences or dichotomies for those of the signifier and subjectification even to be conceivable ... One can form a web of subjectivities only if one possesses a central eye, a black hole capturing everything that would exceed or transform either the assigned affects or the dominant significations ... A language is always embedded in the faces that announce its statements and ballast them in relation to the signifiers in progress and subjects concerned ... Doubtless, the binarities and biunivocalities of the face are not the same as those of language, of its elements and subjects. There is no resemblance between them. But the former subtend the latter (Deleuze & Guattari 1987, p. 179).

There is now a double articulation between the nervous responses of the body (content) and what the body can express. The face, for example, is not taken just as a body part but as the expression of a person. Human perception, in this stratification, becomes overcoded—this is a question of speed. A molecular perception connects and territorialises without the delay that characterises the stimulus–response circuit of the human brain.

The peculiar speeds and slownesses of human perception are not just biological but directly political—for in not acting immediately in a relay of actions and attractions, human perception 'decides' or localises. The face and self are produced as a certain speed, as a 'What does this mean?' or a 'What does this express?', thereby slowing down responses. This person or subject is the effect, and not the ground, of a territory of perception: a territory made possible through the image of the human.

The brain, Deleuze and Guattari insist, is a 'tribe'; its complexity consists in its inclusion of a virtual collective. (The body thinks of itself as an 'I' or singular body only when forces between bodies can mark out surfaces—only when, for example the tribal ritual of tattooing marks 'me' as one of our kind.) Deterritorialisation is therefore essential to the stratification of human life, which moves from the territory or the marking out of bodies to the deterritorialised notion of 'a' body, 'my' body, 'the human' or 'man' in general. Such deterritorialisations also rely on a slowing down of perception. It is when the hand becomes a tool that it is deterritorialised—no longer responding immediately but creating a practice or know-how which can be repeated over time—and we can say the same about the mouth when it becomes an organ of speech. These technical machinic developments allow for the social machines of memory, and it is memory that constitutes the essential speed of human perception.

We need to begin, then, with the idea of perception as the interaction or connection of forces or codes; it is from this general becoming or molecular perception that we can then separate or articulate a perceiver from a perceived, a content from its expression. The idea of an underlying matter that is there to be expressed or perceived is the effect of perceptions. So there is perception (or perceptions) which subsequently produces the whole or totality that is there to be perceived.

Human perception is the outcome of a series of molecular perceptions of increasing complexity, gradually creating an essential distinction between content and expression. It is through the human assemblages or territorialisations that perception slows down; the vast flux of data is coded into extended bodies and things. The human does not just act or react but delays, remembers, anticipates and interprets. The physical world can become a signifier or sign of some sense or meaning. The face can express a subject or person, and all the codes of life can be translated or overcoded through human language (Deleuze & Guattari 1987, p. 63). This gives Deleuze and Guattari two directions to pursue. First, we can move 'downward' to the molecular level, looking at all those pre-personal forms of life from which human perception in its social–political aspect emerges. (This is the direction of *Anti-Oedipus* and *A Thousand Plateaus*: how does 'man' come to perceive himself as the origin, centre and ground of life?) Second, we can move 'upwards' to that point in history (in philosophy and cinema) where human perception can free itself from technical requirements—imagining the virtual whole of life, or difference as such. Human perception may begin with a delay in action, enabled by the development of technical machines: it is the complexity of the hand that allows human life to develop a social machine that then allows it to perceive the face of another's body as the expression of another life. But once these technical machines develop to a greater and greater degree we can plunge back into the very essence of perception. We no longer perceive in order to act, but perceive in and for itself. This brings us to the 'percepts' of art—perceptions that are no longer of this or that thing, but are the experience of the perceivable as such.

Percepts and affects

It is through philosophy that language can be used to grasp the very plane of becoming from which all codes emerge. But it is through art that we grasp the singular perceptions or affects from which general perceptions or signs are drawn. The cinema, for example, might begin its history with the presentation of narratives whereby the stimulus–response circuit still dominates; the images are part of a story with characters interacting for some overall end or function. We see a train hurtling towards us and we leap back; we see a blinding light and we shut our eyes; similarly, we see a standard form of narrative cinema and we respond at the level of action. We identify with the characters, desire their outcomes, grip the seat when they are threatened; here, the eye is still engaged to action and perceives a world of bodies in cause–effect relations. Everyday perceptions occur as actions and reactions of forces, creating a relation and the terms related. Perceptions, we might say, are territorialised or synthesised into meaningful and personal human units. We take the mobile flow of life and see the world in 'snapshots' of immobilised images. This is what enables human action; we have to slow down the intense flux of data into extended images. We then see movement as a passage from one of these images to another, or from one point to another.

Cinema: The movement-image

What makes cinema valuable, according to Deleuze, is its capacity for mobilising perceptions. Deleuze wrote two books on cinema, the first (1986) looking at images of movement, and the second (1989) looking at images of time. We tend to immobilise the flow of life in order to act. Cinema, however, begins to open up perception by presenting flows of movement, a moving camera following another moving body. Whereas we tend to think of time as the linking up of immobile points (or we see time as that which flows from an immobile point of view), cinema frees point of view from the single immobilised viewer. For Deleuze this gives us the cinematic art of the movement-image, not a thing which moves, but movement itself. (In this sense, cinema is not just one more art form; it allows us to think the truth and art of life as movement which we have subsequently immobilised in our perceptions):

> The shot is the movement-image. In so far as it relates movement to a whole which changes, it is the mobile section of a duration. Describing the image of a street demonstration Pudovkin says: it is as if you climbed on a roof to see it, then you climb down to the first floor window to read the placards, then you mix with the crowd … It is only 'as if'; for natural perception introduces halts, moorings, fixed points or separated points of view, moving bodies or even distinct

vehicles, whilst cinematographic perception works continuously, in a single movement whose very halts are an integral part of it and are only a vibration on to itself ...

What counts is that the mobile camera is like a *general equivalent* of all the means of locomotion that it shows or that it makes use of—aeroplane, car, boat, bicycle, foot, metro ... In other words, the essence of the cinematographic movement-image lies in extracting from vehicles or moving bodies the movement which is their common substance, or extracting from movements the mobility which is their essence (Deleuze 1986, pp. 22–3).

According to Deleuze early cinema was governed by the movement-image: time was presented from the movement of mobile sections. In its usual human form perception is governed by movement or purposeful action, but we tend to view movement as a relation between bodies from an immobilised point of view. We get a sense of time or history from movement, as that which unites actions and purposes, so that time is understood from the drama of human action. This can still happen within film and narrative: we see characters and actions governed by some purpose, and cinematic images and effects serve that purpose. For the most part, we view film in the same mode as everyday life, where movement seems to be nothing more than the movement of fixed things, and where time is just the connection or sequence of all these movements into one whole. Thus we tend to view film in terms of some single progression of movement. The affect and perceptions are received in terms of the meaningful whole of action: 'What will he do?', 'How will this be resolved?', 'I fear for his life', 'I want them to get back together'.

But art and cinema can develop to create perceptions that are different in kind from those of the everyday stimulus–response mechanism. Cinema interrupts or dilates vision, freeing it from action and actualised images, multiplying points of view and presenting movement itself—not a movement governed by the purposes of fixed terms. The movement-image, for example, would be a camera following the movement of one character, then another, and then perhaps the flow of time presented as the movement of clouds across the sky. In the movement-image we no longer see movement as a shift from one point to another in an already given and homogenous space; it is no longer a movement within an immobile space. Space itself is an open and mobile whole:

> By producing in this way a mobile section of movements, the shot is not content to express the duration of a whole which changes, but constantly puts bodies, parts, aspects, dimensions, distances and the respective positions of the bodies which make up a set in the image into variation. The one comes about through the other. It is because pure movement varies the elements of the set by dividing them up into fractions with different denominators—because it decomposes and recomposes the set—that it also relates to a fundamentally open whole, whose essence is constantly to 'become' or to change, to endure; and vice versa (Deleuze 1986, p. 23).

Cinema: The time-image

If early cinema for Deleuze is governed by the movement-image, which presents time indirectly, modern cinema creates the time-image. In modern cinema we do not see (moving) things or objects, or even the movement of the camera itself, but are invited into the virtual. For the freed percept or affect allows me not just to view 'this red' or 'this space' or 'this point in time'; through complex processes of resonance I can think time as such, sensibility as such. This means passing from actual perceptions (or what is given) to their virtual possibility—not colour as it is viewed by me here now, but the very possibility of colour; not this temporal series but the very flow or duration of time which is never actually given.

Consider the way standard narrative cinema ties perception and affect to motor response. In a suspense-horror film we see the walls torn off an aeroplane in mid-flight. We grip the cinema seat in anticipation and fear; the images of flames, blood, bodies

151

and light make us turn away or scream, in spite of ourselves—even if we 'know' it is only a movie. Our body is engaged to act—even if only to suppress a gasp or start—and this is as though by habit, as if some machinic intellect were operating. This is a form of habit-memory that is responding to generalised perceptions. I perceive the images on screen not for their singular affect—the light, tone and colour—but for what they represent for a brain that has learned patterns of motor response. The affects that bombard us are attributed to action and life, to a sequence of events governed by humanised needs, fears and interests. (Some of us read novels this way: we can't put *Adam Bede* down, for we just have to know whether Adam marries Hetty or Dinah. We read in terms of expectations, formal requirements and resolved endings.)

Now the value of cinema in its early stages, according to Deleuze, was its capacity to present 'mobile sections'. Rather than perception being prompted to respond or move by some stimulus point outside itself, the flow of movement itself could be presented without being located within the point of view of an engaged viewer. It is in his first book on cinema that Deleuze explores this movement-image, and his argument goes well beyond cinema. This is because western thought has tended to think of a fixed and actual world which then goes through time and movement. We have also tended to think of time from movement (time as the hands of a clock, or the moving light on a sundial or the progress of the sun across the sky). It is as though there were a world with movement added on, and then as though time were the adding-up or measurement of those movements. Against this image of time is the linking-up of fixed points or moving things, Deleuze argues that cinema's movement-image frees movement from fixed points. This is done because the camera's 'eye' can itself move across movements, and can also multiply points of view (such that the eye that looks is no longer fixed within movement but is itself open up to a plane of movement). By presenting movement itself, the very image of movement—and not the movement of a thing from a fixed point—early cinema transforms the possibility of thinking. Time is no longer just the connection or sequence of actual things; we get an indirect image of the real virtuality of time: time as the flow, movement or becoming of the world from which we then perceive fixed bodies.

Early cinema therefore goes part of the way towards liberating perception from the fixed images it imposes on the world in order to act and work. But the image of time is still only indirect; from all the flows of movement we can think of time as the power of difference from which movements are impelled. We do not see time itself but we do see flows rather than things, sections of mobility rather than a simple sequence of events. Modern cinema, by contrast, is dominated by the time-image rather than the movement-image. ('Modern' is used by Deleuze to refer to post-war cinema, but it describes not so much a historical marker as a possibility realised by certain developments in film.)

Time in standard cinema is derived from movement, and this is also the case with everyday perception. Just as we need to slow down the vast influx of perceptions and intensities to experience a world of ordered and extended objects, so we tend to see time as some homogenous form that links or contains one action or object to another. We do not experience the flow or becoming of time; we see time as that line or unity within which our actions and experiences are located and ordered. Time is, usually, derived from the actual and extended objects of ordered and slowed down perception. The whole of time is then seen to be a unity derived from extended parts; it is the result of connecting. So in standard cinema we are given actions and events, with time or history providing the unity or field within which they are located. It is the Civil War, for example, that unifies all the narrative moments of *Gone with the Wind*. We know that it is the 'future' that allows all the events of *Alien* to cohere into a unity of plot and action.

It is the human ordering, abstraction or contraction and contemplation of perceptions which slows down the flux of movement to give a world of things upon which we can act. However, an even greater slowing down would allow human perception to surpass or short-circuit action altogether and attain a perception not of actual objects for action but of intensities or percepts. While a microbe responds immediately, being nothing more than its perceptions, the human agent allows a delay in order to decide how to act, but an even 'slower' perception would allow the visual (or perceptual) to flow in and for itself. No longer would images be subordinated to a time derived from action; we would be given an image of time itself: the virtual. The actual world is a contraction of the virtual, for there are actual and extended things only through the reduction of differences into relatively stable assembled points. In the case of human visual perception this is also so, but an expansion of perception opens vision out into the unseen or virtual difference—the pure flow of time or differing difference:

> Movements, becomings, in other words, pure relations of speed and slowness, pure affects, are below and above the threshold of perception. Doubtless, thresholds of perception are relative; there is always a threshold capable of grasping what eludes another: the eagle's eye ... But the adequate threshold can in turn operate only as a function of a perceptible form and a perceived, discerned subject. So that movement in itself continues to occur elsewhere: if we serialize perception, the movement always takes place above the maximum threshold and below the minimum threshold, in expanding or contracting intervals (microintervals) ... What we must do is reach the photographic or cinematic threshold ... (Deleuze & Guattari 1987, p. 281).

Time and the virtual

It is from time or duration—differing difference—that all perceptions are possible. It is this difference itself that for Deleuze is the virtual; any world or things is the actualisation or concretion of a flux of difference. Worlds and things are constituted from intersections and connections of different perceptions of this difference. A plant perceiving the sun is the interaction of two speeds: all the light rays that emanate from the sun connecting with the differences and responses of the plant. The human perceives the sun at a different speed, allowing the light to also be discerned as an extended object. The scientist who theorises the flow of heat and light operates at a different speed again, no longer just responding to warmth and light but allowing a perception of those flows or differences that produce heat and light.

But it is art that brings us to the essence of perception and virtual difference. One of the ways this is possible is through the presentation of time, not a time that is merely the link between one action and another (actualised time), but the differing time that allows us to perceive the actual at all. This is just what happens in literature in an epiphany, which moves from the perception of viewing subjects to a virtual perception, viewed by no one. Deleuze refers to Marcel Proust and James Joyce and their use of epiphany (or revelation), but one of his other frequently cited authors is Virginia Woolf. Her short story 'Happiness' is a classic example of epiphany in literature. (For the most part Deleuze's celebrated authors were modernists or early twentieth-century writers rather than post-modernists. This is probably due to the fact that modernist authors, like Deleuze, were concerned with grasping the pre-personal and essential differences of life from which persons and objects were contracted. Deleuze would have had little sympathy with post-modern meta-fiction, or stories about stories, precisely because he believed the task of art was not just the reiteration and parody of received forms, but the renewal of form from the very depths of life. He was a philosopher of essences and singularities, not of social constructions and received ideas.) Woolf's story opens with a character's everyday conversation and events being disrupted by the smallest of experiences. The character is transported away from his personal concerns towards the singularity of experience, 'freed ... from all dependence upon anyone and everything' (Woolf 1989, p. 180).

Becoming, for Deleuze, is not a relation between two terms. Becoming-animal is not a human being impersonating an animal; becoming-woman is not a transformation to a pre-given image of what woman is or should be. Becoming is a direct connection, where the self that contemplates *is* nothing other than the singularities it perceives. (To become-animal is thus to perceive the animal is if one were perceiving 'its' world. To become-woman is to create what is other than man and fixity, or to become as such.) This is why literature, for Deleuze and

Guattari, is essentially tied to becoming and becoming-woman. The notion of the underlying subject who precedes all perceptions and remains the same (the 'man' or 'human' for whom there can be no true becoming) is undone in a literature such as Woolf's, where the self is nothing more than the fluidity of its perceptions. In the following epiphany in 'Happiness' the main character, Stuart Elton, is no longer a personal self, but becomes the very sensible intensities that he beholds:

> As Stuart Elton stooped and flicked off his trousers a white thread, the trivial act, accompanied as it was by a slide and avalanche of sensation, seemed like a petal falling from a rose, and Stuart Elton straightening himself to resume his conversation with Mrs Sutton felt that he was compact of many petals laid firmly and closely on top of each other all reddened, all warmed through, all tinged with this inexplicable glow. When he was young he had not felt it— no—now aged forty-five, he had only to stoop, to flick a thread off his trousers, and it rushed down all through him, this beautiful orderly sense of life, this slide, this avalanche of sensation, to be at one, when he stood up again—but what was she saying? (Woolf 1989, p. 178).

Like the literary epiphanies that Deleuze draws from Proust, the character in Woolf's story takes a moment from the present and refers it to a past experience; a sensation now is compared to a sensation drawn from the past. (Here, Stuart Elton realises that the sensation he views now was not experienced in all its intensity in the past; the present renews a past that was not lived fully.) But this resonance between past and present makes possible a virtual perception of the very essence of the sensation: the sensation as it is there to be viewed beyond any personal past or present. We are in the realm of difference and repetition: the difference of this event as it is there to be repeated in each of its different actualisations, all the rose petals and glows to come. A literary epiphany takes the experience of an event from a specific point of view, and then shows how that particular experience can disclose what is viewed as if it were viewed by no one; it is the experience in its virtual or essential dimension, there to be actualised by any subject whatever. We move from the world of objects and things in terms of life-narratives and purposes to the sensible and singular essences which are actualised in each life and narrative.

This expansion of perception for Deleuze is at one with ethics and joy, no longer judging the world in terms of the goods or evils it holds for the finite self: 'What we repeat is each time a particular suffering; but the repetition itself is always joyous, the phenomenon of repetition forms a general joy. Or rather, the phenomena are always unhappy and particular, but the idea extracted from them is general and joyous' (Deleuze 2000, pp. 73–4). With expanded perception we realise the innocent forces from which all terms emerge, and it is from this pre-personal dimension of joy—or in Woolf's terms, 'happiness'—that we can open a positive ethics and analysis. This is not a personal happiness that elevates one, in a priestly manner, above life. It is an impersonal happiness that produces a freedom that is at one with the very becoming of life:

> In happiness there is always this terrific exultation. It is not
> high spirits; nor rapture; nor praise, fame or health (he could
> not walk two miles without feeling done up), it is a mystic
> state, a trance, an ecstasy which, for all that he was
> atheistical, sceptical, unbaptised and all the rest of it, had, he
> suspected, some affinity with the ecstasy that turned men
> priests, sent women in the prime of life trudging the streets
> with starched cyclamen-like frills about their faces, and set
> lips and stony eyes; but with this difference; them it prisoned;
> him it set free. It freed him from all dependence upon anyone
> upon anything (Woolf 1989, p. 180).

If there are limited terms that seem to judge and contain life, or turn the forces of life away from their activity—such as the image of the good moral self who ought to obey his human nature— then only the reactivation of virtual differences prior to their extended terms can re-open thinking and perception. Deleuze's method of intuition aims to discern the imperceptible differences that make up a perceived and organised whole.

Cinema's virtual difference

We can begin to bring this discussion even closer to the notion of the virtual and the time-image by thinking of films that operate directly by thematising the flow of time. There have been time-travel narratives since the very beginnings of cinema, but more often than not the traveller moves along a line of unified time. In the 1960 film version of H.G. Wells's *The Time-Machine*, for example, the central character played by Rod Taylor moves back and forwards through history, as though the events of time were so many actual and already-given objects, with time being the chain upon which they are linked. A more complex version of this is still maintained in the more recent series of films, *Back to the Future*. The main character, played by Michael J. Fox, travels back to the past and nearly disrupts the romance that is forming between the two people who will later become his parents. The more he interferes with events of the past, the more his own image begins to disappear from the family photo that he has carried with him. Again, in both films, it is as if time were a single plane, with past and future in a linear causal sequence. Time is presented as nothing more than an actual series of events, with the future being the playing out of the possibilities in the past. The future can only be changed through an alteration in the actual events of the past.

Deleuze's notion of the time-image was a very strict one, which occupied his second book on cinema, and which challenged the actualised order of temporal events in order to think the virtual power or flow of time. As an example we can think of Alan Resnais' film *Hiroshima Mon Amour*, a film about a French actress's love affair with a Japanese man while she is making a film in post-war Japan about the bombing of Hiroshima. This film in general draws on themes of witnessing and the composition of history. The French actress claims to have seen and experienced the trauma of Hiroshima through her experience of museums, memorials and documents. The Japanese man, however, insists that she cannot have seen such an event. The monuments and memorials we compose in order to remember the trauma of the past will necessarily miss the violent irruption, difference and event of the past. The key moment in the film occurs when the actress views the Japanese man's hand in slight movement; the film 'irrationally' (without order or sequence) cuts back to another hand also moving slightly. This turns out to be the remembered hand of the actress's former lover who had died a traumatic death. This intervention of a past-image does not take the form of a remembered flashback; it has no narrative sequence. When it appears it disrupts the point of view of the present. The hand viewed seems to recall another world, another time; the actual hand intersects with what is not present, not perceived here and now. Now, the point of this as a time-image lies in the following: when we see actions linked up into an ordered sequence, then time is tamed, ordered and spatialised—but when, as in *Hiroshima Mon Amour*, an image of the past disrupts the present sequence of images, we see time not as an ordered sequence but as a virtual whole. The past, other narratives, other viewpoints, and other lines of time all co-exist but are ordered by our day-to-day perceptions. In the time-image cinema allows for past perceptions to cut into the present, displaying the very potential of time: time as disruption of what is (the actual) by difference.

The time-image is, for Deleuze, a potential of cinema which tells us something about perception and difference in general. We order time into a single line of events and objects, but such an ordering is only possible because of the flux of images and difference within which we breathe and move, the difference which we 'are'. The time-image presents this flux of difference itself: no longer a spatial or ordered image of time, but time as the power of imaging:

> Becoming can in fact be defined as that which transforms an empirical sequence into a series: a burst of series. A series is a sequence of images, which tend in themselves in the direction of a limit, which orients and inspires the first image (the before), and gives way to another sequence organized as series which tends in turn towards another limit (the after). The before and after are then no longer successive determinations of the course of time, but the two sides of the power, or the passage of the power to a higher power. The direct time-image does not appear in an order of coexistences or simultaneities, but in a becoming as

potentialization, as series of powers … Beyond the true or the false, becoming as the power of the false (Deleuze 1989, p. 275).

The importance of Deleuze's definition of modern cinema does not lie in the standard post-modern line that everything is unreal and that we are not sure what reality is any more. Cinema of the time-image, for Deleuze, is a transcendental analysis of the real; it explores all those virtual planes and differences from which actual worlds are possible. There is only a real (actual) world of extended action and narrative logic if there is a reduction of the virtual, a contraction of perceptions into a single line of time and affect. By destroying that line of time, logic and action, the time-image disrupts the sensory-motor apparatus. The images no longer present events to which bodies (either those of characters or viewers) respond by habit. The images are disengaged from action, presented as images, as visual affects which both characters and viewers have to organise.

Not only does Deleuze want to explain how meaningful human life emerges from meaningless prehuman connections and syntheses, he also wants to confront the ways in which forms of perception in art and cinema allow us to re-think the emergence of the human. Language may begin as a technical and social machine, but it can also deterritorialise to the point where it can create concepts that allow us to think the absolute deterritorialisation of all machines and connections. (This is the task of philosophy.) Perception may begin at the molecular level as the stimulus–response articulation of life, but it can also deterritorialise to cross a threshold such that we can perceive sensibility itself. (This is art and cinema.)

Conclusion
Virtual freedom

Series and sequence

Deleuze's project of immanence demands a redefinition and a reaffirmation of perception. The illusion of transcendence—that there might be some external point from which life could be judged—is tied to the problem of point of view. Throughout his work Deleuze refers to the ways in which western philosophy has privileged a certain 'optics'. Western thought begins from a subject who views the world, assuming a strict distinction between viewer and viewed. There is *a* world, which is then perceived from a number of viewpoints, and these pictures or representations of the world can be assessed according to their correctness or fidelity. We might say, then, that western thought produces a proper order or sequence for thought. The world is actual and original, and this is followed by representations or copies, which are virtual and secondary. Deleuze makes two important responses to what he refers to as this 'dogma of representation'. First, we need to think about series rather than sequence. Second, we need to affirm the positivity of the virtual.

First, let us deal with series and sequence. The traditional sequence of world plus representation, or original plus copy, gives images a proper or moral relation. The copy is judged as inferior, while an original is established as the measure for all subsequent repetitions. This dogma of representation is tied to transcendence:

one point can act as a foundation or beginning for some other point. There is a world and then its representation. Representation is also a commitment to equivocity (two types of being, the real and its representation). And it is a refusal of immanence, for if we accept the thesis of immanence, that there is only one univocal plane of being, then how can we differentiate some already present world from its secondary and subordinate representation?

In his book on Spinoza, Deleuze argues that an ethical view of the world will have to replace this moralism (Deleuze 1992). The moral distinction between good and evil depends upon privileging a restricted point of view; a thing can be viewed as evil only from the point of view of a limited being who judges an affect as damaging or pernicious. (Arsenic is an evil or poison only for the body who would be damaged; in the total view of the universe there is nothing evil about the power of arsenic.) Similarly, the distinction between original and copy relies on one image being privileged as the good and proper origin of another. If we accept one plane of being (as Deleuze suggests we do), the actual cannot be given a grounding or originating position in relation to the virtual, for this would distinguish between two orders of being. Rather, actuality and virtuality coexist. There is no proper sequence by which we could see the virtual as secondary or caused by some already given, self-present and undifferentiated actual being. Rather, we need to think of the flows of series—with no privileged order, origin or goal. These series interconnect, transform each other and constantly create new possibilities for a further branching out or line of flight. Western thought has privileged the proper order of the sequence: the line of time that branches out from some origin towards some end. By contrast, Deleuze demonstrates all manner of groundless series: the proliferating differences of art, genetics, perception, images and 'worlds'. Whereas representationalism argues that a natural priority must be given to the thing itself, while the copy or image is an effect, the idea of series argues for any number of possible relations. This idea of series is therefore tied in with the 'image' and 'simulacra'. A copy will always be the copy of some thing or original, but Deleuze argues that the image or simulacra is appearance itself. Life just *is* appearance: a plane of images or simulations. The supposed 'real thing' that lies behind the image is a fiction we impose on the flux of images. What we have is appearance or imaging itself: a world of simulacra without ground.

Image and simulacra

Following the French philosopher Henri Bergson, Deleuze uses the word 'image', not to describe a copy or secondary doubling of the actual world but rather sees the image as actual-virtual: 'There are images, things are themselves images, because images aren't in our brain. The brain's just one image among others. Images are constantly acting and reacting on each other, producing and consuming. There's no difference at all between *images, things,* and motion' (Deleuze 1995, p. 42). Think of the way in which a human brain perceives an object. To begin with, experience reaches the thing itself; we do not experience pictures or representations. I see a chair, not the picture or mental representation of a chair. I do not have a perception and then conclude or infer that there must be some thing behind the perception. Perception reaches the thing itself. This is especially clear in molecular or inhuman perceptions; the plant 'perceiving' the sun does not have a representation of the sun. Perception is the direct relation of the different beings of the world, but the being or thing itself is an image. The chair that I see is the contraction of a temporal series into a thing that remains the same through time, disregarding all the fluctuations in light and perspective that constitute duration.

It makes no sense to say that there is a real world which we then perceive through representations. It is not as though there is a world in itself which we then grasp and synthesise through time. The world is a temporal flow or duration, never identical to itself; but there are points of imaging where one flow intersects with another. A human being perceives an object; the flow of human life is slowed down in order for us to image ourselves as subjects, while the flow of things we perceive is slowed down so that we can think of extended matter. Deleuze's idea of the image changes the standard notion of a real world that is doubled by a human viewer's representations. When a human being (or any perceiver) experiences an object, there is an event of imaging or perception. One flow on the univocal plane of being is affected by another. When we think about this event of perception we tend to imagine two points: the perceiving brain and the thing perceived. But both these points—the viewer and the viewed—are images abstracted from the event of perception. According to one of Deleuze's main commentators, it is the cinematic time-image that frees life from any ordered or actualised sequence to its power of becoming: 'The plane of consistency of the time-image is best characterized by seriality: the irrational interval assures the incommensurability of interval and whole. Succession gives way to series because the interval is a dissociative force; it "strings" images together only as disconnected spaces' (Rodowick 1997, p. 178).

In his book on Bergson, Deleuze argues that we need to begin with the hypothesis of a 'pure perception', where there is just the image or affect (Deleuze 1988). There is not a brain that perceives or a subject that is affected. Life is just this pure perception, the affection of one event of becoming on another. But this ideal of a pure perception without delay or reflection, a pure flow of life in and for itself, is only half the story. (It is similar to the notion of absolute deterritorialisation, which does not exist in fact but can only be thought; it is a virtual whole.) If there were nothing more than a flow of images without delay or interruption, life would be purely actual; there would simply be the active, productive and undivided continuum of stimulus and response. We could still refer to this single plane as one of images. But these images would not be recorded. One molecule might respond to another, and so we might say that there has been imaging. But there would be no delay or hesitation whereby that molecule might perceive the other in an unexpected or not already given manner. For localised perception to happen there must be a delay and an interruption of the pure flow of perception by the virtual. (This can occur at the molecular level, where not all aspects of code pass from one connection to another, so that not all the flow has been actualised.)

In human perception, however, this virtual or surplus dimension creates a radical stratification or difference in kind. Perception can be slowed down to the point where we no longer respond at the level of the biological organism but produce virtual domains of sense, memory, art and conceptuality.

The brain and freedom

It is the expansion of the virtual, its capacity (in art and philosophy) to turn back and recognise its emergence from the actual, that constitutes the peculiar power of human brain life. The brain allows a delay or 'hiatus' in the flow of life, allowing the creation of a subject within chaos. The brain is not a thing that stores images, but a gap or point of 'survey':

> If the mental objects of philosophy, art, and science (that is to say, vital ideas) have a place, it will be in the deepest of the synaptic fissures, in the hiatuses, intervals, and meantimes of a nonobjectifiable brain, in a place where to go in search of them will be to create ... thought, even in the form it actively assumes in science, does not depend upon a brain made up of organic connections and integrations ... Philosophy, art, and science are not the mental objects of an objectified brain but the three aspects under which the brain becomes subject, Thought-brain. What are the characteristics of this brain, which is no longer defined by connections and secondary integrations? It is not a brain behind the brain but, first of all, a state of survey without distance, at ground level, a self-survey that no chasm, fold or hiatus escapes (Deleuze & Guattari 1994, pp. 209–10).

The perception of a thing as really there or as actual is co-determined by the presence of the virtual; memory and sense (or meaning) are virtual domains that allow the plane of immanent imaging to be thought or perceived as actual. If I perceive a cat then I rely on the virtual presence of memory; I do not just receive and act upon the inflowing data of furriness, greyness and all the other images that confront me. I allow previous perceptions (of other cats) to enter this present perception so that I can recognise this image as an instance of what I perceived in other images. Memory halts the flow of pure perception, giving me not just an influx of chaotic data but a world of ordered objects. Sense also cuts the continuous flow of perception into ordered objects.

Deleuze insists that sense and memory are virtual domains that do not double or copy the actual world that we receive. They are autonomous and co-present. Perception is never pure but is divided at once into actual and virtual. We cannot explain either memory or sense as being actual contents of the brain or mind. How could we act if all our memories were already and always actually there in our minds? How could we speak if all the meaning or sense of language were actually before us, 'in' the very sounds we uttered? Both sense and memory are virtual and alongside the actual. The brain locates itself variously along the planes of actuality and virtuality: I can see in the present, or I can be back in the past. I see a cat, and I don't have to sift through a database of memories in my brain; and I certainly don't have to shuffle through every previous perception I've had of a cat and then subject the present actual perception to all these virtual copies. On the contrary, every perception is actual-virtual. I see this cat here and memory intervenes at once, alongside perception, only because it was there all along. Lying there, virtually, only to be activated or actualised. When we have a conversation and I use the word 'cat', you don't have to take my word and tie it to some picture in your head. You are immediately in the virtual domain of sense which, like memory, exists and is real, even if it is not actualised.

We can, therefore, imagine speaking and perceiving as ramified versions of a plane of being that is already one of images. It is not that we have a real world that we then represent or image in words or mental perceptions. We have to imagine the real plane of being as already imaging, with a molecule imaging or perceiving when it is affected by another molecule. In humans and other organisms the pure flow of imaging splits into actual and virtual. We could say that it slows down. We do not just perceive and respond; we are not flush with the real or at one with the flow of life. We perceive the world *as* this or that; memory and sense intervene to organise the flow of the world into matter. The virtual, then, is not some static storehouse of memories or sense, for it is constantly opening and expanding with each new perception. This means that the flow of time and perception is split in two. The perception I have of this cat is at once here and now (or actual), oriented towards the present perception; at the same time the virtual domain of memory is also expanded with each new perception.

According to Bergson, whom Deleuze was following in his affirmation of the co-presence of the virtual with the actual, this solves many problems with regard to time, free will and the status of reality. We often think of a real world that we grasp through images. But if we ask who this perceiving 'we' is, we are given yet another image, such as the image of the brain. We need to begin not from the two images of brain and world but from a flow of images in general, and then explain how one image (the brain) appears as the origin of all images. This occurs because of the power of the virtual. There is not just the pure flow of images— the flow is delayed by the intervention of the virtual. It is through memory and sense that we can order, judge and be positioned in relation to images. We are not just within time, caught up in its flow; we can distance ourselves from automatic or immediate response because we can perceive that world *as* this or that. It is the virtual that opens the power of human decision or freedom. We have an image of who we are in relation to a being that we are not.

We have tended to think of freedom as something that we have in relation to the beings outside us. But for Deleuze, following Bergson, freedom is not a feature of human beings; freedom is what happens when we do not respond automatically and immediately; it is a question of speed and slowness. There is a delay between stimulus and response because of the intervention of the virtual (memory or sense)—and it is this delay that leads us to believe that 'we' were the authors of this freedom. Really, however, it is more accurate to say that there is a flow of time or imaging which is slowed down or disrupted by the virtual. It is only from this disruption that we then distinguish between the human perceiver and the world perceived, between human freedom and organised matter. We imagine that the free human being was there all along, as some actual point that then perceived the world. Deleuze, however, insists that the virtual is an inhuman power. 'Our' freedom is given to us when memory, sense or the virtual intervene or do violence to the sequence of the present. Freedom or thinking is what happens to us; it disengages us from present perception precisely because the virtual is positive: always transforming, open and as productive of the actual as the actual is of the virtual. Freedom is not, then, a human power set over and against a world. It is not a separate judgement of the world; freedom is the very becoming of the world.

The possible and the virtual

We can think of virtual difference in a number of ways, ranging from art to evolutionary theory. Art is not a simple copy of the world, a virtual double of the actual. Anyone who studies literature knows that novelists do not just deliver pictures of the world; narratives transform the way we see the world, the way we see ourselves and the way we act. The image or supposed copy of the world can produce a reality. But this is not to say that, once created, the virtual domain of images can influence the actual world. Both Deleuze and Bergson go further, with the idea of 'creative evolution'. A limited idea of evolution would argue that the actual world is the outcome of a certain number of possibilities, and the number of possibilities would be limited by the nature of the actual world. Let us say that we have a being—such as human life—and it has x number of possible developments. These developments are selected or decided according to the demands of the already given world. If this were the case, then future would be the playing out of so many given possibilities, some of which would take place while others would not. In this case the possible is what we trace back from the actual; we see humans in their present-day form and assess the possibility and probability of their evolutionary development. On such an understanding, both the past and the future would be explained from the actual present. The past would be all that might have occurred, while the future would be a selection from a static set of already selected possibilities—what might occur. If, however, we were to think of the positive and open character of the virtual, it would neither be based on the actual nor would it be already given. The virtual would be as much open to revision or transformation as the actual, such that each time a possibility passed into actuality, the whole domain of the possible would be re-figured.

To understand this, imagine that a certain possible development takes place, such as the development of vision. One explanation—looking back from the actual—is to say that vision responded to an actual need. We look at the past as leading up to the present; we look at the past mutations in life that formed the eye as possibilities for vision. But as Bergson points out, the developments that lead up to the formation of the eye are so complex and diverse that, for the most part, we cannot just explain them as caused by some external end. Rather, life itself must have the creativity or tendency, not just to respond to the outside, but to respond and become in its own way, from tendencies or positive differences that are virtual and that can be actualised. Evolution is creative not because it is directed towards an end such that some final goal or purpose limits possibilities. The process is truly one of becoming. Vision was the outcome of a series of changes and responses that were possible only because life bears a virtual creativity that allows it to respond to life not mechanically but as a problem. This means that the outcome of these creative responses will also create new problems. Once vision occurred, this transformed the very process of evolution or character of becoming; entirely new responses and developments were possible. The virtual, or what can be actualised, is itself transformed. So instead of a sequence in which a number of possibilities lead up to what actually occurs, we have an array of series. Some would lead to becomings, such as vision, which then created new series and new divergences. What is possible, therefore, is never given once and for all, but expands with each development of potential.

Seriality beyond good and evil

The idea of series is not just the reversal of the relation between original and copy; it undoes the distinction between original and copy. The series is not a sequence (with a proper order); it is a connection with no ground or reason outside itself: '[C]onstructing series on the basis of determinable multiplicities makes it impossible to spread out history in the sequential way' (Deleuze 1988, p. 21). This also means that there can be no privileged or governing series, nor could there be a closed series. One more element could always be added, and new series could always be formed.

If we are to be committed to immanence then we have to abandon the idea that one point of being could provide a point of judgement or foundation for being as a whole. This means that any connection of beings would be serial rather than sequential, a connection rather than an order. It follows also that series are necessarily multiple and divergent. There can be no single or definitive series, and there can be no way in which all these series could be seen to converge into some harmonious unity. The notion of series is inextricably tied to the expansion of perception beyond the human viewer or knower into the universe in general. A linear evolution subordinates becoming to some final end; man can look back and see all changes leading up to his own development. From the point of view of the present the past is only presented as a sequence of ordered conditions or causes. But if we see the whole universe as perceptive, then there are changes, responses, creations and mutations that cannot be explained in terms of the present or in terms of the human point of view.

This is where Deleuze's use of Bergson ties in with Nietzsche's critique of history. We should look at the past not as some process that culminates in the present human being that we take ourselves to be but as a virtual whole of possibilities that can be retrieved and activated. Affirming life means affirming the contingency, divergence and multiplicity of becomings: all those changes, mutations and geneses that exceed intent, purpose, recognition and meaning. Philosophy is not about the justification and elevation of the human point of view; it is, rather, an attempt to think eternally or, one might say, in an *untimely* manner: an attempt to think the becoming of life well beyond the conceptions we have ourselves. This means affirming all those perceptions that create, transform and transfigure life well beyond any meaning or purpose.

This is the true sense of freedom, an embrace of the virtual that is not limited to the possibilities that are contained within our present point of view. Freedom and perception must therefore be freed from their location within the point of view of man, for it is not as though there are human beings who then perceive or who then act freely. The opening of life by the virtual cannot be grounded on an actual being. Rather, there are series of perceptions, ranging from molecular perceptions to the molar formations of 'man'. The error of transcendence has been to order the series of perception, becoming and freedom by establishing some original point from which perception occurs.

We have tended to subordinate both image and perception to some sequence, as though perceptions were the perceptions of some (human) viewer, and as though images were images of some underlying real world. Deleuze's redefinition of the image frees the image from its subjection to some supposed pre-imaged real. All we have are series of images, for the real is itself image, insofar as it is nothing more than continual response, becoming and creation. A sequence places original before copy, ground before effects, presence before representation; the sequence is an act of connection that presents its connections as an immutable order. The series, by contrast, is active and affirming, recognising the ungrounded character of its connections. If this is so there can be no original as opposed to the copy, which is why Deleuze refers to the simulacrum. If we were to say that all we had were copies, this would suggest that there is some real world that lies outside our reach, and that we are condemned to think this world through the images we have of it. The simulacrum is not a copy because there is no original; it is not the mediation of the world, it is the world itself. 'The simulacrum is not just a copy but that which overturns all copies by *also* overturning the models' (Deleuze 1994, p. xx). It is not that we are trapped within a world of representations, such that we are destined always to be separated from presence in itself, for the world is nothing other than simulation. In order to understand this we need to see, finally, how Deleuze creates a positive concept of the virtual.

The positivity of the virtual

We tend to think of the virtual as a pale copy of the real (such that there is an actual world and then its virtual representation in thought, images and signifiers). This would mean that there is only a difference of degree between the virtual and the actual. We would measure art by how true to life it was; we would assess thinking according to how factual or correct it was. At its best the virtual would come close to the actual. We also tend to think of the virtual as coming after the actual, as either an effect or response to the actual. We even tend to think of the actual as real and the virtual as unreal. Deleuze, however, wanted to argue that the virtual is real. Reality includes the actual and the virtual. There is also a difference in kind between actual and virtual; the latter is not a pale copy of the former, but bears its own power of difference.

Anti-Oedipus, for example, charts the remarkable politics of the virtual. Desire creates virtual productions: the notion of the State, of capital, of Oedipus, of 'man'. And these productions have a force that is remarkably real. Bodies behave in certain ways because of desire's virtual productions. Schizoanalysis, as outlined in *Anti-Oedipus*, is in many ways a political theory of virtual life. Schizoanalysis looks at how images such as 'man' have been composed from perceptions of body parts, from sensations, from pains and pleasures: how, for example, events of punishment or marks on bodies produce the 'law'. Politics is as much virtual as actual; it is both the concrete interaction of bodies (scarring, working, punishing, assembling) and the virtual productions of those bodies (regular desires, paths of pleasure, imagined forces). When Deleuze and Guattari write about the ways in which 'investments' organise life they are referring to the production of a virtual, immaterial or anticipated realm of images (such as the imagined threat of the despot or the measure and flow of capital) and our subjection to images.

This brings us to Deleuze's second point about the virtual coexisting with the actual. We usually understand the notion of images by referring to some actual or material thing, such as the brain, and then thinking of the image as a picture within the brain. The image would be a virtual doubling of the actual world, and would be located in some actual thing (such as the mind, the brain or the subject). But if we ask ourselves what the brain is, then we are given another image; the same goes for mind or subjectivity. We are trying to take one image to explain all other images. The brain is itself an image and so it cannot be used as the explanation for all images. Does this mean that Deleuze is rejecting the idea of a real world? No; he is simply getting rid of a dogma about what constitutes the real. We think of the real world or matter as something that lies behind the image or as something that is represented by our perceptions. So we separate the world from the images we have of it. How do we do this? By constructing some image of the brain that acts as a virtual theatre where the actual world is repeated. But reality does not lie behind images or the virtual; reality is image and virtual.

First, let us think of a reality that is nothing but images. There is not a subject who then has a perception or image of the world. The world is perception and imaging. This goes back to Deleuze's reading of Spinoza, who argued that a thing is nothing other than its affective power. A limited being has only a limited affective power—a simple molecule does in some way perceive another molecule. Because life is dynamic each point of being is affected by some other point, and what a thing *is* lies in its power of affection, the degree to which it affirms itself or its own power through the perception or response to life: 'Even when they are nonliving, or rather inorganic, things have a lived experience because they are perceptions and affections' (Deleuze & Guattari 1994, p. 154). A simple being can only respond in a limited way. A more complex animal is capable of a greater range of affect. This means that power, or the force of a being, is the degree of its perception or its capacity to respond actively to what it encounters. Power is not negative: the repression or illusions I impose on you. Power is positive: I have power to the extent to which I am capable of expanding my attention to imagine or perceive the whole of life.

Perception and imaging are directly tied to power. To perceive some thing is to be affected; what a thing *is* is nothing more than its range of affect or response. When I perceive some thing I do not take a mental picture of it, I am prompted to respond or become. This affection is not some mechanical or predetermined response. For each being can only be affected in a becoming that is specific to its own power and capacity for imaging. I am nothing other than this becoming through affection, but there are distinct powers of becoming. We might think of philosophy as just one of these powers of imaging, for the philosopher does not just respond mechanically to present states of affairs but imagines or conceptualises the virtual whole of being. (Philosophy, like art, is not a picture of the world but a becoming in response to a world.) In various ways—such as art, science or philosophy—life responds or becomes through images. But the human brain is not the sole origin of imaging and perception, nor does imaging stop with animal life. Both Deleuze, and Deleuze and Guattari, insisted on the perception and imaging of both organic and non-organic life. Genes, molecules, plants and rocks—all in some way are affected. Whereas a philosopher or artist might be able to imagine a complex world, the image that one cell has of another is of a far more limited affective power. The world is made up of powers of perception or imaging. My 'imaged' world is just that range of life that I have the power to be affected by. But there are all sorts of imagings or becomings that are inhuman.

Eternal return

Perception is also crucial to the ethics of 'eternal return' which Deleuze gathers from Nietzsche. Perception has always been an important concept for readings of Nietzsche, but perception has often been regarded as tied to a point of view or perspective on the world. Deleuze wants to free the notion of perception from point of view. If we are always located within a point of view, then we would never grasp all of what *is*. We would be enclosed within our particular perspectives and the world would be some unknowable 'outside'. Many have read Nietzsche as arguing for this sort of 'perspectivism' or 'subjectivism'. Because we can have no impartial view of the world we must affirm the inherently value-laden or 'perspectival' nature of reality. We do not grasp facts, only interpretations.

Deleuze, however, uses Nietzsche's notion of eternal return to challenge this supposed imprisonment within point of view or perspective. Perception does, indeed, affirm the eternal whole of being. It is just that this eternal whole is never given once and for all; for each perception affirms this eternal whole differently (and also, through perception, contributes to the change and creation of the whole). It is not that there is a pre-given eternity, which our location within time precludes us from perceiving. (If this were so, eternity would be already given, would have an end, and would not be eternal.) The eternal is not actual but virtual, a whole or non-presence opened by each perception. For Deleuze, the ethics of eternal return is an ethics of affirmation and *the* ethic of philosophy. There is no eternal plane within which points of view or time are located. The eternal or single plane of immanence is not perceived from points of view. The eternal or immanent is nothing other than each of its percep-tions. Each perception is a fold creating a now and an eternity: '[T]he whole world is only a virtuality that currently exists only in the folds of the soul which convey it, the soul implementing inner pleats through which it endows itself with a representation of the enclosed world' (Deleuze 1993, p. 23). Each soul or percep-tion opens out onto a whole, which is never given as such but can only be thought as the virtual whole of all monads. The eternal is therefore not some already given ground, but that imagined, virtual or open whole beyond any single soul or point of view.

It is dogmatic morality that assumes that the ground or eternal pre-exists souls and perceptions, so that perceptions or perspec-tives can be seen as perspectives of some whole. Deleuze's ethics, by contrast, follow Nietzsche in arguing that each perception 'ungrounds' any stable point of view. Ethics, therefore, cannot be the judgement of the world from some point of view. It can only be the affirmation of the eternal perception of the world, affirming and perceiving the world infinitely. From a limited or finite perception I regard those forces and perceptions that are other than my own as negative, evil or malevolent. But if I expand my powers of perception—through art, philosophy or cinema—to embrace other series of perceptions, then I am given an ethic 'beyond good and evil'.

Deleuze's entire philosophy is directed towards finding this immanent ethics. Rather than assume some good or law from which the world might be judged, we need to comprehend the emergence of moral judgement, to assess its forces. This requires an expansion of perception: in *Anti-Oedipus* we step back from the moral unit of the family to see its historical emergence; in *A Thousand Plateaus* all forms of life and language are traced back to their molecular emergence. In his books on literature and cinema Deleuze also shows how art leads perception beyond closed and extended forms to intensities and singularities. Whereas philosophers create concepts that lead thought to the plane of pure difference from which intensities emerge, artists present us with those intensities. In both cases—philosophy and art—we are involved with the virtual. Pure difference as such is never actually presented, perceived or given, but concepts allow us to think of pure difference as the virtual plane from which different forms of difference are differentiated. (Bergson, for example, used the ideal of pure perception—a perception not enclosed within any actual point of view—to create the concept of 'duration': a flow of images from which actual perceived and punctuated images are drawn.) In the case of art we step back from actual perceptions, not to a concept but to the singular essence of those perceptions. In philosophy and art, and to a lesser extent science, we enhance or affirm life by moving beyond the finite present of our perceptions to an imagined eternal whole of difference: eternal because it is freed from any located narrative order. Philosophy can give us concepts of difference itself, not just the difference between this and that thing. Science can create functions, such as those of physics, that will be true for any point of view whatever, regardless of historical or cultural context. Art presents us with percepts and affects, not just what I see here and now, but what is there to be seen for all time. The affirmation of the eternal, or eternal return, is just this ceaseless striving by thought to move beyond its located perspective or point of view in order to think of all the perceptions which make up the whole of life: not just the perceptions of beings other than ourselves, but past and future perceptions.

Art and ethics

We have already looked at Deleuze's notion of art as the creation of impersonal affects (as it is defined in *What is Philosophy?*). It might seem that Deleuze's emphasis on affect in art, as opposed to concept, elevates and privileges a certain mode of art, such as abstract modernism (those forms of art not tied to narrative and meaning). He does offer examples that would appear to support such a conclusion. The literature of Lewis Carroll and the poetry of e.e. cummings tend to present words not as meanings but as sounds, rhythms or 'surface effects'. But Deleuze is not insisting that all art needs to be meaningless, or pure affect and sensibility devoid of sense. It is just that if we really want to think about art, about what is essential to art, we need to see the way in which meaning resonates with its non-meaningful and real conditions of emergence. If we simply look for a work's meaning, Deleuze insists, we merely replace one set of signs with another. By asking what it means we do not consider how art works; how meaning is produced and how what is in excess of meaning also transforms the sense of art. We need to consider how art works. In some cases, such as the poetry of cummings, we are given the sounds, script and sensible affects from which meaning is assembled. But there are other ways in which Deleuze approaches what he refers to as 'literary machines'. In the case of the novelist Proust, art takes meaningful signs and connects them in such a way that we are ultimately presented with a virtual perception. (Proust describes memories that begin as memories of a specific childhood event, but then allow us to think of the past as such, as that virtual or non-present potential that any perception can recall.) Even the non-visual arts, for Deleuze, allow the creation of percepts— perceptions no longer tied to characters or located viewpoints.

In his childhood the narrator of Proust's *Remembrance of Things Past* tastes a madeleine. Later in life he repeats the experience; it is this second experience, which brings back the memory of the first, that is recounted in the novel. The first thing to note is the type of memory described or narrated. For the most part our habitual and everyday memory is attached to general forms; if I perceive this biscuit as a madeleine it is because I eliminate all the tiny differences between one experience and another and call all these instances a 'madeleine'. The form of memory here is habitual, generalising and voluntary—tied to the actions, projects and purposes of life. If, however, while tasting this madeleine I recall a specific and singular memory—that moment in Combray when, as a child, I tasted a madeleine with tea—the memory is involuntary and different in kind from habit-memory. 'I' am not recalling a general and repeatable external form. One moment in time resonates with another to produce a singularity, the taste of madeleine in all its specificity and essential singularity. This recollection is something that happens to 'me', such that the 'me' or 'I' dissolves and there is just the resonance of the past. When the past floods back in this way, not tied to the narrative of everyday events and meanings, then the very essence of the past is disclosed. I experience that past moment in its true pastness, not as some vague and generalisable form but as it is in itself. It is no longer my personal past or time, but pastness in general. The moment recalled is freed from any particular point of view.

For Deleuze, time discloses itself in true repetition. This is not a repetition of external forms. You do not get a sense of time by mechanically repeating what you did as a child. Time is truly sensed when memories rather than habits are repeated; for a habit is pretty much the same from moment to moment, while a memory recalls the specificity of a distinct moment of the past. When a singular and involuntary memory invades the present, then what is repeated is the force of time itself, for time is nothing other than this radical and singular difference. Habit and generalisations are the reduction of time; in seeing events as generally the same we fail to embrace the real repetition of time.

Time is repeated and affirmed only in difference; we experience the disruptive power of time when we remember an event as really different, as radically other than the present. This sort of memory can only occur when the past is truly repeated, when we seem to be tasting the madeleine again with all the freshness and firstness of childhood. The repetition of the singularity of the past displays the difference of the past. And for Deleuze there is an ethics and politics to the difference and repetition of time, an ethics tied to art and philosophy. If we really want to repeat philosophy we do not recite old arguments. We create concepts by taking up over and over again the forces of philosophy, which should not be confused with already existing philosophies. If we really want to repeat art then we create affects and percepts with a force that would render all existing art new again. Repeating Plato means producing philosophy as disruptive of our present as Plato's dialogues were of his; repeating Picasso means transforming perception with the same force as Picasso's original canvases.

And why is this an ethics? It is an ethics precisely because it is not a morality. Thinking and perceiving are freed from a slavishness to already given terms and the dogmas of common sense. The project of immanence is one of *not* assuming that there is an already given and determinable outside to thinking; whatever is 'unthought' or 'outside' will constantly transform thinking and perception. Immanence aims to affirm the freedom of thought and perception and to become towards what is not already given.

In order to understand how an ethics of immanence might transform the politics of perception we can take a fairly unremarkable instance of narrative cinema. *Philadelphia*, 'about' sexuality, in particular homosexuality and AIDS, combines the classic narrative cinema genres of 'buddy' movie and courtroom drama. It traces the personal relationship between the two male protagonists (played by Tom Hanks and Denzel Washington) alongside a political confrontation of a legal discrimination case. The main character (Hanks) is a white, gay, high-earning lawyer who finds himself dismissed from his law firm once his positive HIV status becomes known. He engages the services of a black lawyer (Washington), who appears to have his own prejudices regarding homosexuality and AIDS. The narrative plays upon these tensions of politics and oppression: all the ways in which race and sexuality produce differences in class, and the way all these differences are excluded and marginalised in analogous but complex forms. Who has more power or inclusion, the straight black or the middle-class homosexual white? The narrative is driven by the demand for inclusion and recognition: not just the white lawyer's attempt to gain justice in the court, but also the recognition of the two lawyers of each other, across race and sex divides. Such a film prompts, and has prompted, questions of competing ideological interpretations. On the one hand, we can see the film as a critique of prejudice and power. On the other hand, we can read it as a way of rendering a prejudiced society more palatable; in the end the rights of the black and the homosexual win out over white heterosexual dogma, thereby affirming the supposed real justice of the world.

This is a typical interpretive problem in any political form of cultural studies or literary criticism. We can ask: is this film progressive in its presentation and critique of racial and sexual differences, or does it provide some sort of aesthetic pasting-over of power and politics by reducing political issues to the relations between compassionate individuals? A lot of film and literary criticism tends to operate around questions of this sort. We ask whether a work of art challenges or transgresses dominant powers, or whether it provides a safety valve for releasing political tensions by representing a resolution that will never take place.

The value of Deleuze and Guattari's approach lies in its strict formalism. Rather than being concerned with the narrative meaning of a work, we need to look at what makes up a work's style and components. Hollywood continually produces politically affirmative films—the fight for gay rights in *Philadelphia*, the feminism of *Boys Don't Cry* or *Thelma and Louise*, even the anti-colonialism of Disney's *Pocohontas*—but it always does so using the extensive investments of humanism. The political issues—however they are resolved in the narrative—are always composed from human interactions, and the narratives all work to compose an image of the moral individual. Deleuze and Guattari, however, insist that racism and colonialism operate not by exclusion but by inclusion; deep down we are all human. Sexual, racial and political differences are all reducible to the substrate of humanity which normalises us all. The conclusion of *Philadelphia*, for example, returns to an American home movie of the gay central protagonist, affirming his innocence and humanity. You see, it seems to say, even the homosexual was a child once, prior to the mark of sexual preferences. (And we might also consider all the ways in which 'America' as a molar formation is produced from an investment in the image of the innocent child, for 'America' is just this pre-sexual, infant and timeless human origin prior to the corruption of political life.) Against this, Deleuze and Guattari's political theory aims to trace the human from its various intensities. The general notion of 'man' is always the conjunction of far more complex political intensities. 'Humanness' is never a general form or substance, for all we have are intensities; 'man' is always a coding of intensities. The homosexual, the black and the AIDS sufferer can be seen as human only if they, too, partake in all those investments that organise bourgeois man. In the case of *Philadelphia* the homosexual is humanised by being presented as all-American: not only in the family scenes and the final home movie, but in his buddy relationship, his position as a lawyer, and even in a scene of romantic love where he enjoys a high school 'prom' style dance with his lover (Antonio Banderas). Far from deciding whether the film's narrative meaning is revolutionary or reactionary, Deleuze and Guattari's approach suggests that we focus on the pre-political investments that produce persons. In *Philadelphia* all the visual and sexual intensities are reduced to a human drama, while the human is organised from various images of American family life, which then code the black, the gay and the activist. A positive reading of this film would therefore look at the intensities that have been composed into human wholes: the contrasts between black and white skin, the sounds of different class and race accents, the subtly lit interiors of the prestigious law firms, the never-seen but mentioned homosexual actions as opposed to the 'heterosexualised' representation of the gay couple.

Politics is made up of these intensities; politics occurs when intensities—such as whiteness, Americanness or maleness—are coded into an image of the human. It is this intensive nature of the political that is explored with great force in Spike Lee's film *Summer of Sam*. Here, two bands of characters are marked out by different styles and investments. The film presents a group of 1970s Italian Americans composed of polyester, disco, big hair and rigid dating codes. A character returns to the group as a punk, having spent time away. He wears a Union Jack T-shirt, speaks in a feigned London accent and has a Mohawk hairdo. Punk, here, is not a political position of ideas; it has nothing to do with anarchism or fascism, but it is shown as no less political for all that. Groups are formed, not through ideas, but through investments in styles: gathering around a certain haircut in the way tribes gather or assemble around a body part or animal. Lee's film shows the ways in which political groupings and tribal street warfare are produced from an investment in intensities. The lived political landscape is produced from an opposition in affects: the punk desire for a music of distortion versus the clean beat of disco; the investment in torn clothing and marked bodies versus clean outlines and smooth surfaces. The film shows different and divergent compositions of the human; this is not a film about the conflict of ideas across a human space of consensus. It is not a film about a conflict within society. It is an event of schizoanalysis that takes a certain slice of the social whole and shows the meaningless investments that then become ordered into classes and groups. The conflicts (and human groupings) are opened through styles: one becomes a person through manners, colours, rhythms and sexual gestures. There is no shared humanity in this film, only localised productions of incommensurable selves.

Deleuze's visual theory would add to this political theory by showing the ways in which cinema can compose and 'schizophrenise' such political investments. Cinema has a radical potential that disrupts narrative logic. For the most part we view cinema in terms of actions of human characters, but such characters are only possible through the production and coding of intensities. The luminosity of white flesh in close-ups and up-lighted shots, the violent and jerky camera movements that construct cityscapes as opposed to languid panning shots of countryside, and the confronting light of certain horror scenes as opposed to the darkness of certain suspense films: all these non-narrative intensities produce a politics well before the meaning of a film. The extended units of cinema are built up from more dynamic intensities. But Deleuze also argued for a specific power of cinema, which takes the form of the movement-image and the time-image. If western thought and ethics has tended to be subjected to transcendence—the idea that there is some outside world, there to be viewed and judged—cinema frees viewing from the fixed position of the subject. In the movement-image the mobility of the camera encounters the mobility of various components. Instead of viewing a static and already present world, the cinema-goer is inserted into a series of different mobile sections where time is presented indirectly, as the sum of a series of movements which is never given, and can never be given, all at once. On the other hand, in the time-image time is presented directly. If thinking tends to immobilise life in order to act, cinema releases perception from this imperative to cut flowing life up into ordered sections: 'This is a cinema of the seer and no longer of the agent' (Deleuze 1989, p. 2). Modern cinema presents the impersonal flows or durations of life released from action and extended units.

It would be a mistake, I think, to see cinema as the only or complete fulfilment of this project of re-encountering the intensive flow of existence. Not only are there many forms of cinema which tend to organise visual intensities into narrative units, many forms of contemporary art practice are also trying to free vision from a fixed point of view. There are forms of architecture that multiply walls and facades to create disorientation, forms of installation art that construct a series of cameras incapable of being viewed as a whole, novels that multiply possible worlds and viewpoints, and musical compositions that create soundscapes or sheets of sound that are neither ordered by tonality, nor directed against tonality. What we ought to strive for in art (and life) is the expansion of perception, which does not mean that we need to see more or include more. It means seeing *differently*—allowing what we see to confront and transform thinking and point of view, rather than having a moral image of what art *ought* to be.

While Deleuze frequently used examples from high modernism or modern cinema, we should be careful of mistaking the example for the transcendental principle. What Deleuze was affirming was the way in which thought was confronted or mobilised—by the writing of Virginia Woolf, the music of Pierre Boulez or the art of Paul Klee. Far from repeating these examples as models, Deleuze's work suggests that we need to produce and affirm new confrontations. Deleuze and Guattari acknowledge that there can never be an absolute deterritorialisation or freedom from the subjective location of point of view. Transcendental immanence, the challenge to think *the* plane of immanence is less, therefore, a philosophical theory than it is a challenge to think the return of the new, over and over again. Only this can be an ethics, a freedom from all moralism:

> A thought that would *affirm* life instead of a knowledge that is opposed to life. Life would be the active force of thought, but thought would be the affirmative power of life. Both would go in the same direction, carrying each other along, smashing restrictions, matching each other step for step, in a burst of unparalleled creativity. Thinking would then mean *discovering, inventing, new possibilities of life* (Deleuze 1983, p. 101).

Bibliography

Works by Deleuze and Deleuze & Guattari

Note: Quotations within the text are referenced by the publication date of the English edition

——1953, *Empirisme et subjectivité*, English edn 1991 *Empiricism and Subjectivity: An Essay on Hume's Theory of Human Nature*, trans. Constantin V. Boundas, Columbia University Press, New York

——1956, 'La conception de la différence chez Bergson', English edn 1999 'Bergson's concept of difference' trans. Melissa McMahon, in John Mullarkey (ed.), *The New Bergson*, Manchester University Press, Manchester, pp. 42–65

——1962, *Nietzsche et la philosophie*, English edn 1983 *Nietzsche and Philosophy*, trans. Hugh Tomlinson, Athlone, London

——1963, *La philosophie critique de Kant*, English edn 1984 *Kant's Critical Philosophy: the Doctrine of the Faculties*, trans. Hugh Tomlinson and Barbara Habberjam, Athlone, London

——1964, *Proust et les signes*, English edn 2000 *Proust and Signs*, trans. Richard Howard, Athlone, London

——1966, *Le bergsonisme*, English edn 1988 *Bergsonism*, trans. Hugh Tomlinson and Barbara Habberjam, Zone Books, New York

——1967, Sacher-Masoch: Presentation de Sacher-Masoch: English edn 1971 *Sacher-Masoch: An Interpretation*, trans. Jean McNeil, Faber, London

——1967a, *Presentation de Sacher-Masoch, le froide et le cruel*, English edn 1989 *Masochism: Coldness and Cruelty*, trans. J. McNeil, Zone books, New York

——1968, *Spinoza et la problème de l'expression*, English edn 1992 *Expressionism in Philosophy*, trans. Martin Joughin, Zone Books, New York

——1968a, *Différence et repetition*, English edn 1994 *Difference and Repetition*, trans. Paul Patton, Columbia University Press, New York

——1969, *Logique du sens*, English edn 1990 *The Logic of Sense*, trans. M. Lester, ed. C.V. Boundas, Columbia University Press, New York

——and Claire Parnet 1977, *Dialogues*, English edn 1987 *Dialogues with Claire Parnet*, trans. Hugh Tomlinson and Barbara Habberjam, Columbia University Press, New York

——and F. Guattari 1972, *Capitalisme et schizophrénie 1. L'anti-Oedipe*, English edn 1983 [1977] *Anti-Oedipus: Capitalism and Schizophrenia*, trans. Robert Hurley, Mark Seem and Helen R. Lane, University of Minnesota Press, Minneapolis

——1975, *Kafka: Pour une littérature mineure*, English edn 1986 *Kafka: Toward a Minor Literature*, trans. Dana Polan, University of Minnesota Press, Minneapolis

——1980, *Capitalisme et schizophrénie 2: mille plateaux*, English edn 1987 *A Thousand Plateaus: Capitalism and Schizophrenia*, trans. Brian Massumi, University of Minnesota Press, Minneapolis

——1991, *Qu'est-ce que la philosophie?*, English edn 1994 *What is Philosophy?*, trans. Hugh Tomlinson and G. Burchill, Verso, London

——1981 *Francis Bacon: Logique de la sensation*, Editions de la Différence, Paris

——1981a *Spinoza: philosophie pratique*, English edn 1988 *Spinoza: Practical Philosophy*, trans. Robert Hurley, City Light Books, San Francisco

——1983, *Cinéma 1: L'image-mouvement*, English edn 1986 *Cinema 1: The Movement-Image*, trans. Hugh Tomlinson and Barbara Habberjam, University of Minnesota Press, Minneapolis

——1983, *Nietzsche and Philosophy*, trans. Hugh Tomlinson, Athlone, London

——1984, *Kant's Critical Philosophy: The Doctrine of the Faculties*, trans. Hugh Tomlinson and Barbara Habberjam, Athlone, London

——1985 *Cinéma 2: L'image-temps*, English edn 1989 *Cinema 2: The Time-Image*, trans. Hugh Tomlinson and Robert Galeta, University of Minnesota Press, Minneapolis

——1986, *Cinema 1: The Movement-Image*, trans. Hugh Tomlinson and Barbara Habberjam, University of Minnesota Press, Minneapolis

——1986, *Foucault*, English edn 1988 *Foucault*, trans. Séan Hand, Athlone, London

——and F. Guattari 1986, *Kafka: Toward a Minor Literature*, trans. Dana Polan, University of Minnesota Press, Minneapolis

——and F. Guattari 1987, *A Thousand Plateaus: Capitalism and Schizophrenia*, trans. Brian Massumi, University of Minnesota Press, Minneapolis

——1988, *Bergsonism*, trans. Hugh Tomlinson and Barbara Habberjam, Zone Books, New York

——1988, *Le pli: Leibniz et le baroque*, English edn 1993 *The Fold: Leibniz and the Baroque*, trans. Tom Conley, Athlone, London

——1989, *Cinema 2: The Time-Image*, trans. Hugh Tomlinson and Robert Galeta, University of Minnesota Press, Minneapolis

——1990, *Pourparlers 1972–1990*, English edn 1995 *Negotiations 1972–1990*, trans. Martin Joughin, Columbia University Press, New York

——1990, *The Logic of Sense*, trans. M. Lester, ed. C.V. Boundas, Columbia University Press, New York

——1991, *Empiricism and Subjectivity: An Essay on Hume's Theory of Human Nature*, trans. Constantin V. Boundas, New York, Columbia

——1992, *Expressionism in Philosophy*, trans. M. Joughin, Zone Books, New York

——1993, *Critique et clinique*, English edn 1997 *Essays Critical and Clinical*, trans. Daniel W. Smith and Michael A. Greco, University of Minnesota Press, Minneapolis

——1993, *The Fold: Leibniz and the Baroque*, trans. Tom Conley, Athlone Press, London

——1994 [French 1968] *Difference and Repetition*, trans. Paul Patton, Columbia University Press, New York

——and F. Guattari 1994, *What is Philosophy?*, trans. Hugh Tomlinson and G. Burchill, Verso, London

—1995, *Negotiations 1972–1990*, trans. Martin Joughin, Columbia University Press, New York

—1997, *Essays Critical and Clinical*, trans. Daniel W. Smith and Michael A. Greco, University of Minnesota Press, Minneapolis

—1999, 'Bergson's Concept of Difference', trans. Melissa MacMahon, in John Mullarkey (ed.) *The New Bergson*, Manchester University Press, Manchester, pp. 42–65

—2000, *Proust and Signs*, trans. Richard Howard, Athlone, London and F. Guattari 1983, *Anti-Oedipus: Capitalism and Schizophrenia*, trans. Robert Hurley, Mark Seem and Helen R. Lane, University of Minnesota Press, Minneapolis

—2001, (No French title; English collection), *Pure Immanence: Essays on a Life*, ed. John Rajchman, trans, Anne Boyman, Zone Books, New York

Other references

Althusser, Louis 1971, *Lenin and Philosophy, and Other Essays*, trans. Ben Brewster, New Left Books, London

Ansell-Pearson, Keith (ed.) 1997, *Deleuze and Philosophy: The Difference Engineer*, Routledge, London

Ansell-Pearson, Keith 1999, *Germinal Life: The Difference and Repetition of Deleuze*, Routledge, London

Badiou, Alain 2000, *Deleuze: The Clamor of Being*, trans. Louise Burchill, University of Minnesota Press, Minneapolis

Barthes, Roland 1982, 'The Death of the Author' in Susan Sontag (ed.) *A Barthes Reader*, Cape, London

Beauvoir, Simone de 1969 [French 1949] *The Second Sex*, trans. H.M. Parshley, New English Library, London

Bogue, Ronald 1989, *Deleuze and Guattari*, Routledge, London

Boundas, Constantin V. (ed.) 1993, *The Deleuze Reader*, Columbia University Press, New York

Boundas, Constantin V. and Olkowski, Dorothea (eds) 1994, *Gilles Deleuze and the Theater of Philosophy*, Routledge, New York

Braidotti, Rosi 1994, *Nomadic Subjects: Embodiment and Sexual Difference in Contemporary Feminist Theory*, Columbia University Press, New York

Bricmont, Jean and Sokal, Alan D. 1999, *Fashionable Nonsense: Postmodern Intellectuals' Abuse of Science*, Picador, New York

Brusseau, James 1998, *Isolated Experiences: Gilles Deleuze and the Solitudes of Reversed Platonism*, State University of New York Press, Albany

Bryden, Mary 2000, *Deleuze and Religion*, Routledge, London

Buchanan, Ian (ed.) 1999, *A Deleuzian Century?*, Duke University Press, Durham

——2000, *Deleuzism: A Metacommentary*, Edinburgh University Press, Edinburgh

Buchanan, Ian and Colebrook, Claire (eds) 2000, *Deleuze and Feminist Theory*, Edinburgh University Press, Edinburgh

Buchanan, Ian and Marks, John (eds) 2000, *Deleuze and Literature*, Edinburgh University Press, Edinburgh

Butler, Judith 1993, *Bodies that Matter: On the Discursive Limits of 'Sex'*, Routledge, New York

——1997, *The Psychic Life of Power: Theories in Subjection*, Stanford University Press, Stanford

Descartes, René 1968 [1641], *Discourse on Method and the Meditations*, trans. F.E. Sutcliffe, Penguin, Harmondsworth

Descombes, Vincent 1980, *Modern French Philosophy*, Cambridge University Press, Cambridge

Foucault, Michel 1979 [French 1975], *Discipline and Punish: The Birth of the Prison*, trans. Alan Sheridan, Penguin, Harmondsworth

——1981 [French 1976], *The History of Sexuality, Volume 1: An Introduction*, trans. Robert Hurley, Penguin, Harmondsworth

——1984, 'What is an Author?' in Paul Rabinow (ed.) *The Foucault Reader*, Penguin, Harmondsworth

Genosko, Gary (ed.) 2000, *Deleuze and Guattari: Critical Assessments of Leading Philosophers*, Routledge, London & New York

Goodchild, Philip 1996a, *Gilles Deleuze and the Question of Philosophy*, Associated University Presses, London and Cranbury, NJ

——1996b, *Deleuze and Guattari: An Introduction to the Politics of Desire*, Sage, London

Grosz, Elizabeth 1994a, 'A Thousand Tiny Sexes: Feminism and Rhizomatics' in Constantin V. Boundas & Dorothea Olkowski (eds) *Gilles Deleuze and the Theater of Philosophy*, Routledge, New York, pp. 187–210

——1994b, *Volatile Bodies: Toward a Corporeal Feminism*, Allen & Unwin, Sydney

——1995, *Space, Time and Perversion: Essays on the Politics of Bodies*, Routledge, London & New York

Hardt, Michael 1993, *Gilles Deleuze: An Apprenticeship in Philosophy*, University of Minnesota Press, Minneapolis

Hardt, Michael and Antonio Negri 1994, *Labor of Dionysus: A Critique of the State-Form*, University of Minnesota Press, Minneapolis

Hayden, Patrick 1998, *Multiplicity and Becoming: The Pluralist Empiricism of Gilles Deleuze*, Peter Lang, New York

Hegel, G.W.F. 1977a [German 1801], *The Difference Between Fichte's and Schelling's System of Philosophy*, trans. W. Cerf and H.S. Harris, State University of New York Press, Albany

——1977b [German 1807], *The Phenomenology of Spirit*, trans. A.V. Miller, Oxford University Press, Oxford

Holland, Eugene W. 1999, *Deleuze and Guattari's Anti-Oedipus: Introduction to Schizoanalysis*, Routledge, London

Husserl, Edmund 1970 [German 1954], *The Crisis of European Sciences and Transcendental Phenomenology: An Introduction to Phenomenological Philosophy*, trans. David Carr, Northwestern University Press, Evanston

Jameson, Fredric 1997, 'Marxism and Dualism in Deleuze', *South Atlantic Quarterly*, 96:3, pp. 393–416

Jardine, Alice 1985, *Gynesis: Configurations of Woman and Modernity*, Cornell University Press, Ithaca

Kant, Immanuel 1986 [German 1787], *Critique of Pure Reason,* trans. Norman Kemp Smith, Macmillan, London

Kaufman, Eleanor and Heller, Kevin J. (eds) 1998, *Deleuze and Guattari: New Mappings in Politics, Philosophy and Culture,* University of Minnesota Press, Minneapolis

Kennedy, Barbara M. 2000, *Deleuze and Cinema: The Aesthetics of Sensation*, Edinburgh University Press, Edinburgh

Kojève, Alexandre 1969 [French 1947], *Introduction to the Reading of Hegel*, ed. Allan Bloom, trans. James H. Nichols, Basic Books, New York

Lacan, Jacques 1977 [French 1966], *Écrits: A Selection*, trans. Alan Sheridan, W.W. Norton, London

——1982, *Feminine Sexuality*, trans. and ed. Jacqueline Rose, Juliet Mitchell and Jacqueline Rose, Macmillan, London

Lambert, Greg 2002, *The Non-Philosophy of Gilles Deleuze*, Continuum, New York and London

Landa, Manuel de 1991, *War in the Age of Intelligent Machines*, Zone Books, New York

——1997, *A Thousand Years of Nonlinear History*, Zone Books, New York

Lévi-Strauss, Claude 1968 [French 1958], *Structural Anthropology*, trans. Claire Jacobson and Brooke Grundfest Schoepf, Allen Lane, London

Lorraine, Tamsin 1999, *Irigaray & Deleuze: Experiments in Visceral Philosophy*, Cornell University Press, Ithaca

Lucy, Niall 1999, *Postmodern Literary Theory*, Blackwell, Oxford

Malpas, J.E. 1999, *Place and Experience: A Philosophical Topography*, Cambridge University Press, Cambridge

Marks, John 1998, *Gilles Deleuze: Vitalism and Multiplicity*, Pluto Press, London

Massumi, Brian 1992, *A User's Guide to Capitalism and Schizophrenia: Deviations from Deleuze and Guattari*, MIT Press, Cambridge, MA and London

Massumi, Brian 1996, 'The Autonomy of Affect' in Paul Patton (ed.) *Deleuze: A Critical Reader*, Basil Blackwell, Oxford

May, Todd G. 1991, 'The Politics of Life in the Thought of Gilles Deleuze', *Substance* 20:3, pp. 24–35

——1994, *The Political Philosophy of Poststructuralist Anarchism*, Pennsylvania State University Press, University Park, PA

May, Todd 1997, *Reconsidering Difference: Nancy, Derrida, Levinas, and Deleuze*, Pennsylvania State University Press, University Park

Nietzsche, Friedrich 1967 [German 1887], *On the Genealogy of Morals and Ecce Homo*, trans. Walter Kaufmann and R.J. Hollingdale, ed. Walter Kaufmann, Vintage, New York

Olkowski, Dorothea 1999, *Gilles Deleuze and the Ruin of Representation*, University of California Press, Berkeley, CA

Patton, Paul (ed.) 1996, 'Concept and Event', *Man and World* 29:3, pp. 315–26

——1996, *Deleuze: A Critical Reader*, Basil Blackwell, Oxford

——1997, 'The World Seen from Within: Deleuze and the Philosophy of Events', *Theory and Event* 1:1 [http://muse.jhu.edu/journals/theory_and_event/toc/]

——2000, *Deleuze and the Political*, Routledge, London

Plath, Sylvia 1981, *Collected Poems*, ed. Ted Hughes, Faber, London

Plato 1963, *Collected Dialogues*, ed. Edith Hamilton and Huntingdon Cairns, Princeton University Press, Princeton, NJ

Protevi, John 2001, *Political Physics: Deleuze, Derrida, and the Body Politic*, Athlone, NJ

Rajchman, John 2000, *The Deleuze Connections*, MIT Press, Cambridge, MA

Rodowick, D.N. 1997, *Gilles Deleuze's Time Machine*, Duke University Press, Durham

Sartre, Jean-Paul 1957 [French 1943], *Being and Nothingness: An Essay of Phenomenological Ontology*, trans. Hazel Barnes, Methuen, London

——1973 [French 1946], *Existentialism and Humanism*, trans. Philip Mairet, Methuen, London

——1976 [French 1960], *Critique of Dialectical Reason, Volume One*, 2nd edn, trans. Alan Sheridan Smith, New Left Books, London

Saussure, Ferdinand de, 1960, *Course in General Linguistics*, P. Owen, London

Stivale, Charles S. 1998, *The Two-Fold Thought Of Deleuze And Guattari*, Routledge, 1998

Sturrock, John. 1979, *Structuralism and Since: From Lévi-Strauss to Derrida*, Oxford University Press, Oxford

Woolf, Virginia 1989, *The Complete Shorter Fiction of Virginia Woolf*, ed. Susan Dick, The Hogarth Press, London

Wright, Elizabeth 1984, *Psychoanalytic Criticism: Theory in Practice*, Methuen, London

Zizek, Slavoj 1991, *For They Know Not What They Do: Enjoyment as a Political Factor*, Verso, London

——1992, *Enjoy your Symptom: Jacques Lacan in Hollywood and Out*, Routledge, London

Index

Index

Related titles

Understanding Foucault
Geoff Danaher, Tony Schirato and Jen Webb

'Do not ask who I am and do not ask me to remain the same . . .' Michel Foucault.

Derided and disregarded by many of his contemporaries, Michel Foucault is now regarded as probably the most influential thinker of the twentieth century—his work is studied across the humanities and social sciences, among other disciplines.

Understanding Foucault offers an entertaining and informative introduction to his thinking. It covers all the issues Foucault dealt with, including power, knowledge, subjectivity and sexuality and discusses the development of his analysis throughout his work. Each topic is illustrated with topical examples from popular culture so that readers can see how to use Foucault's theories in their own writing. *Understanding Foucault* is a 'must read' for anyone tackling him for the first time.
ISBN: 1864489677

Understanding Bourdieu
Jen Webb, Tony Schirato and Geoff Danaher

You name it, Pierre Bourdieu has written about it. Now considered one of the most influential thinkers of the 20th century, he has left his mark on most of the 'big' theoretical issues in the world of contemporary theory: gender, subjectivity, the body, culture, citizenship, and globalisation. His terms are now commonplace: 'social capital', 'cultural capital', 'field', and 'habitus'.

Bourdieu examines how people conduct their lives in relation to one another and to major social institutions. He argues that culture and education aren't simply minor influences, but are as important as economics in determining differences between groups of people. '*Understanding Bourdieu* is a comprehensive and lucid introduction to his work. Measured and judicious, it's the best road map of this significant body of work currently available.' (John Frow, Regius Professor of Rhetoric and English Literature, University of Edinburgh.)
ISBN: 1865083631

Jen Webb is Program Director of Writing in the School of Creative Communication and Culture Studies at the University of Canberra. **Tony Schirato** is co-author of *Communication and Cultural Literacy* and *Asia: Cultural politics in the global age*. **Geoff Danaher** teaches in the School of Contemporary Communication at Central Queensland University.

Made in the USA
Lexington, KY
13 August 2010